Edward Vernon

Practice makes perfect

Pan Books in association with
Macmillan London

to my mother and father

First published 1977 by Macmillan London Limited
This edition published 1979 by Pan Books Ltd,
Cavaye Place, London SW10 9PG
in association with Macmillan London Limited
© Edward Vernon 1977
ISBN 0 330 25708 0
Printed and bound in Great Britain by
C. Nicholls & Company Ltd, Philips Park Press, Manchester

Practice makes perfect

Born in Walsall, Staffordshire, Edward Vernon is married with two young children. His hobbies include collecting books, cricket, and sitting in Parisian cafés.

one

I slid into Rosewater Avenue with a rubber-wasting squeal and peered through the windscreen anxiously. I'd asked Mr Jenkins to leave the porch light on so that I could spot the house easily, without having to examine each gatepost and front door to find No 54. In my innocence I'd hoped that I could home in on the lamp like a moth fluttering towards a candle. Being new to general practice, I wasn't yet aware of the extraordinary fact that even at three or four o'clock in the morning there will be lights burning in a good proportion of the houses in any part of town.

Eventually, with the aid of my car headlights and a rubber-covered torch in which I'd invested a good percentage of my savings, I picked out the house.

'Hello, Doctor,' whispered Mr Jenkins, opening the front door and taking me in out of the rain. I followed him upstairs and into the bedroom. His wife was lying flat on her back, coughing. 'She's been like this all night,' explained Mr Jenkins, hovering behind me.

I put my black bag down, sat down and felt for her pulse. I placed my stethoscope down on the bed in a prominent position, took out my pocket torch, aimed it down Mrs Jenkins' throat and asked her to say 'Aaaah'.

She looked puzzled, but obeyed. I could see nothing, and I fiddled with the clip on my torch. Still nothing happened. Then I realized that I was aiming my fountain pen at Mrs Jenkins' tonsils.

Whenever a doctor is confused or embarrassed he uses his stethoscope. With that firmly planted in his ears, and his eyes closed in concentration, he is untouchable. So I got Mrs Jenkins to sit up, and I put my stethoscope in position. To my surprise she seemed to get better almost immediately. I was told in medical school that the mere sight of a stethoscope will cure a quarter of all the patients a doctor meets.

I could tell within a few seconds that there wasn't anything very much to worry about, but I decided that an injection was the order of the night. I couldn't leave without doing something, and the right drug would ensure that we all had a good night's sleep. So I opened my bag and rummaged around inside, looking for something suitable. Finally I picked out a syringe, a needle and two glass ampoules full of pharmaeutical goodness. With difficulty I took the syringe out of its sterile pack, took the needle from its plastic container and joined them together. Then I tried to break the top off one of the glass ampoules.

Encouraged no doubt by their colleagues in the shirt-packing industry, the moguls of the drug business have chosen to pack their wares in wrappers and containers which are, to all practical intents and purposes, inviolable.

The next thing I knew, I had a handful of broken glass and a tranquillizer which, despite its efficiency, is not known for its effectiveness when allowed to dribble on to a bedroom carpet. I reached into my bag to find another edition of the now thoroughly useless ampoule, hoping – vainly, I'm sure – that Mr and Mrs Jenkins would imagine that breaking the first was a necessary part of the treatment.

It was as I lifted out the new one that I noticed the blood, which was mixing well with the tranquillizer. The mixture was sticky and messy and, like all blood cocktails, it went a long way very quickly. Within seconds it was on my coat, my shirt, my trousers, the carpet, the bedclothes and my bag. I knew that if I didn't do something quickly it would soon have spread on to my stethoscope, the wallpaper, Mr and Mrs Jenkins, the dressing-table and my car outside.

I swabbed at the wound with a piece of dirty tissue that I found in my pocket, plucked a small piece of glass out and tossed it into a waste-bin. Then I watched with interest as blood welled up out of the dark hidden recesses of my hand.

'Oh dear,' said Mrs Jenkins solicitously, 'have you cut yourself?'

'I think so,' I said, hoping that my lack of panic would spread. With my free and as yet unstained hand I hunted in my bag for something with which to restrain the flow. Needless to say, though I had powerful drugs with which to combat the most dangerous diseases, and equipment to enable me to peer into all the nooks and crannies of the human body, I didn't have any sticking-plaster. Somehow it was something that had never crossed my mind.

'Excuse me,' I said to Mr Jenkins, 'but I don't suppose you have such a thing as a small piece of sticking-plaster, do you?'

Mrs Jenkins, now looking a great deal better and taking an unhealthy interest in my misfortune, leant forward to get a better look. 'There's some in the bathroom,' she said to her husband. 'In the cabinet.'

Her husband obdiently hurried off to the bathroom, returning a few minutes later with a small tin.

'Hold it up, love,' said Mrs Jenkins. 'It'll help stop the bleeding.'

I took the tin from her husband and held it up. I couldn't see why it should help, but I was willing to try anything.

'The hand you've cut,' said Mrs Jenkins. 'Hold it up in the air. The blood won't come out so easily then.'

I did as she advised, and then Mr Jenkins helped me to fit a plaster over the cut.

'That's fine,' said I gratefully. 'Thank you very much.'

'Now, are you sure you'll be all right to drive yourself home?' asked Mrs Jenkins.

'No, it's all right, thank you,' I said. 'I'll be able to manage.'

I picked up my bag, fastened it and started off down the stairs.

'Mind how you go, Doctor,' said Mr Jenkins, seeing me out.

'Thank you,' I said, hurrying off. I clambered into the car and drove carefully home. I was back in bed before I realized that I'd left my stethoscope on Mrs Jenkins' bedside table.

two

I'd taken a job as assistant to an elderly general practitioner working in a small Midland town. It was my first job in general practice; my first brave excursion into the dangerous world where patients walk around in their clothes, and where the doctor must often meet them on their own ground. It was the first time I'd practised medicine outside the comforting confines of a hospital, without a white coat, without the authority which a plastic name-badge gives, and without the knowledge that all the patients I saw were actually ill, diagnosed by someone else.

Dr Oaks, my employer, worked alone in a single-handed practice and lived in a town which was, like the surgery, beginning to show signs of looking tired of the twentieth century. The surgery and waiting-room were in his large Victorian house. Until 1966 Dr Oaks had hardly had a day's holiday. So he had an understanding with one of his colleagues in the area, and they would look after each other's patients for one night a week one weekend a month.

Then the town had been changed by the building of two factories near the surgery. A new housing-estate had sprung up almost overnight, and parking-meters had been installed. Three new doctors came to the town to help look after the influx of patients and they also took over the practice which had been managed by Dr Oaks' colleague. They invited Dr Oaks to join with them. He thought about it for a long time and eventually agreed to participate in a rota system with them, although he insisted on preserving his independence in all else.

Now in his sixties, round, balding and decidedly worn, Dr Oaks had decided that the time had come for him to take things a little easier. Hence his advertisement, my application and my presence as his assistant.

Before I arrived I had no idea where I'd be staying. In the end I found myself in a small flat at the top of the house. I discovered afterwards that Dr Oaks had had the flat equipped for a housekeeper, but after his housekeeper had died he'd never bothered to employ anyone else. It suited me fine; there was a small bedroom, a living-room, a bathroom and a kitchen. None of it was spectacularly furnished, but it was better than living in a hospital room, six feet square and equipped with standard hospital furniture.

There was a telephone on a small bedside table, an extension from the surgery. A back stairway led up to the flat from the hall at the rear of the house and provided a virtually private entrance which would enable me to get down to the surgery or back to the flat without having to go through Dr Oaks' rooms. A small cooker in the kitchen ensured that I could make my own coffee, and a fridge provided somewhere for me to store milk and beer, the only two foodstuffs likely to need storing.

The surgery below looked as if it had been built and equipped between the two world wars; since then little, if anything, had been replaced and nothing much of value had been added. The couch was worn, low and sagging dangerously. Horsehair escaped through the leather in uncomfortable clumps, and the carpet had long since lost any pretence of having a pile left. Now wafer-thin, it served only to dull the click-clack of heels on the linoleum underneath.

It was late one Sunday evening when I first arrived. I found a message for me lying on the dining-room table. It was a simple one: Dr Oaks had decided to take a few days' holiday and would see me on his return.

So, the following morning, I found myself settled in Dr Oaks' swivel chair, an ancient and wonderful piece of furniture which was suffering from a weird, noisy form of arthritis. It creaked and groaned in protest whenever I moved, and often shuddered violently, obviously regarding me as a usurper. I had not been in a doctor's surgery since I'd damaged my knee some fifteen years before, and it felt strange to be sitting on the other side of the desk, with only a few short years in medical school behind me, and a pen, a stethoscope and prescription pad in front of me.

I couldn't remember ever having seen a case of measles; the only person I'd ever seen with chicken-pox was me. I knew nothing of such minutiae as the menarche and the menopause – minutiae to me and my far-away mentors who had described them only in physiological terms, but important, urgent and here-and-now to the patients in the waiting-room. What did I know about earache and tummy upsets? I anxiously thumbed through a pharmacology textbook looking for clues, and looking for the names of some useful compounds with which to cure the world of all its ills. I suddenly realized that, however much

I might know about renal transplant surgery, hypercholestero-laemia and Von Willebrand's Disease, most of my patients probably knew more than I did about rashes on pink tummies, gurglings in elderly ones, and the vagaries of the social services.

Why, I wondered, could we not have had courses in triviology, in which experts could have given their advice on such vital matters as catarrh, cystitis, corns and hay fever? Why couldn't my professor of medicine have recommended a few good tonics?

And why didn't they tell me what to say when I saw my first patient?

As I slowly wandered around the surgery getting my bearings I noticed that, though there was no electrocardiograph or ophthalmoscope in the room, enough pharmaceutical goodies were packed into the cupboards to keeep the National Health Service going for a year. Clearly Dr Oaks was something of a hoarder. All general practitioners are visited regularly by the smooth-tongued representatives of the pharmaceutical companies, who hand out free samples from their bulging briefcases like so many Father Christmases visiting children's parties. Just as patients, when they visit the doctors, expect to be given a prescription to take away with them, so doctors, when visited by representatives, expect to have something to show for their trouble. And Dr Oaks, instead of handing on his samples to his patients, had kept them all.

There were enough bottles full of iron capsules to build a mini-car, enough antibiotics to sterilize Scotland and enough sleeping-tablets to keep Rip Van Winkle very content. The collection was magnificent. There were tablets in one colour, tablets in two colours, multicoloured capsules and variegated powders. There were bottles and pots, boxes and foil containers, tins and jars, plastic display-packs and cardboard wallets.

Around the rest of the surgery there were the other remnants of a thousand visits from a hundred representatives. There were five-year-old calendars, plastic handouts, little models of the human brain, big books containing details of a new wonder-drug guaranteed to revolutionize something, free pens and free pencils. Free blotting-paper, appointment books, diaries for 1958 and visiting-cards left by colleagues and representatives filled in the empty spaces.

Incongruously, in a corner, there stood a lonely pepper-pot. On a drug-trolley, loaded high with disposable spatulas advertising antibiotics, there was a small bottle full of plant-fertilizer. There was a roll of sticking-plaster that had stuck to itself, a pile of out-of-date X-ray forms and a pair of seedy-looking scissors that I suspected had been used for pruning the collection of plants on the window-sill. Despite the fact that there was a hoard of virgin notebooks in the surgery, the desk was littered with scraps of paper, old letters, envelopes and so on, all covered in notes. There was a small basket packed tightly with returned tablets, and a notice reminded patients to bring in to the surgery any tablets they had not used.

I looked at my watch. It was nine o'clock. Time to start the surgery. I pressed the little button hidden under the desk and a bell rang in the waiting-room next door. Within seconds the first patient was with me. I smiled; he sat down. A boy of fifteen with a plaster on his hand.

'I've come to have my stitches taken out,' he said nervously.

I scrabbled round in the top drawer of the desk, found a clean pair of scissors, washed them under the hot tap and snipped at the short row of neat stitches which had for a week been holding the boy's hand together. The boy rubbed his young scar nervously, smiled at me again and left, leaving me with a handful of old stitches. I hesitated for a moment, then pushed the bits of cotton into an empty pill-bottle and left it on a far corner of the desk. I wanted to run the practice just as Dr Oaks had run it. It was, after all, his practice.

The normal routine was to do a morning and an evening surgery and, in between, to visit those patients unable to get to surgery, deal with the paperwork which is today an inescapable part of general practice and somehow find time to get something to eat. As the evening surgery came towards its end I began to feel in need of a doctor myself. There had been many, many faces, many, many names and a lot of problems to solve.

Thirty or forty times I had had to explain that I was Dr Oaks' new assistant – although, towards the end of the day, word had got around, and people would come in, introduce themselves and say, 'You're Dr Oaks' new assistant, aren't you?'

There were only two or three patients left in the waiting-room when the telephone rang. The caller introduced himself as a Dr Edwards from a practice nearby – the practice with which Dr Oaks had his on-call arrangement. He informed me that it was my lucky night. I was on duty for a total of approximately 12,000 patients.

And the call to visit Mrs Jenkins of Rosewater Avenue was the first night-time emergency of my general-practice career.

three

Most of Dr Oaks' patients lived in the town, but a few of them lived on farms in outlying villages. They had been on his list since he'd first come to put up his plate and they had been faithful through the years. I had a telephone call asking me to visit one of them on the first Thursday afternoon. The caller sounded genuinely worried, and I had difficulty in obtaining even the simplest information from her. Eventually I set off with only the vaguest idea of where I was going. I had the name of the village and the name of the caller, but little else. I stopped at a public house in the village of Berrowham and asked for directions. They sent me on to the local shop where, they told me, I'd be able to obtain the final directions. It was all rather like a motor-club treasure-hunt.

The farmhouse I was looking for was at the end of an unmade road about two and a half miles long. It was a large square red-brick building, surrounded by a wide variety of ramshackle outhouses which mostly seemed to have been built with the aid of old fence-posts and pieces of corrugated iron. A huge barn, half-filled with hay, dominated the yard. Parked carelessly in the shelter of a surprisingly sturdy-looking stable were two ancient tractors and various other rusting pieces of machinery, including an old Ford van with three wheels and no doors. Prowling around amidst all this evidence of unfulfilled ambition there were several hungry-looking dogs. Apart from saying that none of them was a poodle but that one or two of them could have been Alsatians, I had no idea what breed they were.

Since I was a small boy I've been terrified of any dog which is too big to sit on the back window-ledge of a motor-car. So, when I stopped my car and was immediately surrounded by a pack of wolfish animals barking furiously, I felt distinctly uncomfortable. I sounded my horn, but that simply made the dogs bark louder. I was worried about my patient but I imagined I wouldn't be much good to him after I'd been savaged by a bunch of rabid dogs.

The front door of the farmhouse was guarded by a small garden and a once-white picket-fence, but I could see that there was a back door which opened straight on to the farmyard.

I backed my car, a rarely washed Mini-Traveller, until it was parked directly outside the back door, with the front and rear wings only an inch or two away from the house wall. I opened my window, reached through and opened the house door, and then opened the car door so that I could squeeze out of the car into the house without ever having to set foot in the yard. The dogs barked and howled with frustration a few feet away.

'Doctor?' asked a plump middle-aged woman as I peered out of the kitchen into the hall. She was slowly making her way down the stairs as she spoke.

I nodded.

She looked past me at my car, the door of which was still sticking into the kitchen.

'I didn't want to waste any time,' I explained. 'It sounded urgent.'

'They don't bite much,' the woman promised, ignoring my explanation. 'You'll be wanting to see my husband.'

'Thank you,' I said, following her back up the stairs.

'It was Mildred who phoned you,' explained the woman. 'She helps with the cleaning. I sent her down to the village to telephone.'

'Ah,' I said. I couldn't think of a more suitable reply since

13

the house didn't look as if it had been cleaned for many years. It was the sort of house where you wipe your feet when you go outside.

The farmer himself, Mr Thomas, was in bed, surrounded by an extraordinary collection of bedroom impedimenta. There were two full bags of cement, a crate of empty beer-bottles, part of a car engine, a pile of old newspapers and farming magazines and a sackful of rotting apples. The walls were decorated with trade calendars and patches of damp.

'Sorry to bring you out, Doctor,' moaned the farmer. 'It's a long time since I saw a doctor. Dr Oaks retired, has he?'

I explained the situation.

'I've got this pain,' said Mr Thomas. 'It's been with me since last night. I thought it would go away, but it seems to be getting worse again now.'

'You lie still,' I told him. 'Let me have a look at you first.'

I knelt on the bed to get closer so that I could listen to Mr Thomas's chest and take his blood pressure. The screech that my knees elicited from the bedclothes would have done credit to the soundtrack of a horror film. As I sat on the edge of the bed, rubbing my head where it had collided with the ceiling, a large black cat emerged from underneath the bedclothes and glared at me angrily. I apologized to it and tentatively felt my way back towards my patient.

Mr Thomas was cold and sweaty. His blood pressure was low, his pulse slightly erratic and his heart faint. He told me that the pains had started in the centre of his chest, gone straight down his left arm and ended up as a dull ache.

'Have you ever had any heart trouble?' I asked.

Mr Thomas shook his head. 'Healthy as a rock,' he muttered.

'What were you doing yesterday?' I asked him. 'Anything heavy?'

I suspected that he might have been doing something requiring exceptional effort. Repairing fences or something similar. He thought for a moment, however, and shook his head.

'You haven't been baling, have you?' I asked, remembering hot summer days spent helping on a friend's farm. It had amazed me to discover the effort needed to lift a bale of straw. They look so light on television.

14

Mr Thomas looked at me with curiosity. 'In June?' he asked.

'Ah, no,' I agreed. 'Rather early, isn't it?'

He nodded.

'I wasn't doing anything energetic,' he replied. 'Just watching the telly.'

'What was on?' I asked, as much to keep the conversation going as for any other purpose.

'Soccer,' said Mr Thomas. 'England versus Poland.' He scowled. 'Shocking load of rubbish,' he moaned. 'Bloody terrible rubbish.' He started to turn a rather ruddier colour as he proceeded to explain why the team should find themselves the victims of some unusual and imaginative experiments. His voice moved upwards an octave or two, and then he fell back clutching his chest. Sweat stood out on his forehead, and it was obvious even to me that he was having another heart attack.

'Ah,' I cried, pleased with my own diagnostic acumen. 'It was the football match which brought it on. It can, you know! During the last World Cup dozens of men all over the world had heart attacks. It was written up in the medical journals.'

Mr Thomas nodded gratefully, and slid down the pillow another inch or two. His wife stumped round the room. 'He's off again,' she complained, giving the bag of apples an angry kick.

I opened my black bag and took out a syringe, needle and ampoule of morphine, and this time, I'm pleased to say, the ampoule broke more or less as it was supposed to do. I slipped it inside my tie, and the protection the cloth gave provided me with the extra confidence to give it a sharp snap. I still wore a sticking-plaster on my finger in memory of my accident in Rosewater Avenue.

I injected the morphine straight into the farmer's venous system, putting it into one of the veins on the inside of his left elbow, a favourite hunting-ground for injection-giving doctors. Then I instructed Mrs Thomas to telephone for an ambulance since it didn't seem likely to me that the farmer would receive the best of nursing attention among his bits and pieces of farming equipment.

'We haven't got a telephone, Doctor,' said Mrs Thomas.

That rather stumped me.

'I could go down to the village and telephone from there,' she said. 'I'll go down on the tractor.'

The ambulance turned up less than half an hour later, bumping into the farmyard at tremendous speed. The ambulancemen loaded Mr Thomas into the back of their impressively equipped motor, fitting him with an oxygen mask and settling him down lodged comfortably against the side of the vehicle. The driver, a good-natured fellow with a beaming smile, made little complaint when one of Mrs Thomas's ferocious hounds took a sample bite out of his left leg and aerated his uniform-trousers.

I waited until the ambulance had bumped off down the farm track and then I slipped quietly out through the back door of the house into my small car. As I settled down behind the wheel, preparing to drive back to do evening surgery, I scratched idly at my left calf. I put the key in the ignition, but the itch didn't disappear, so I pulled my trouser leg up in order to be able to scratch more effectively. It was that action which exposed the neat round swelling created by the bite of an annoying little creature known to scientists as *Pulex irritans*, and to ordinary folk and doctors as the common flea.

I might have avoided the dogs, but I'd been bitten.

four

Ten days after my arrival Dr Oaks returned from his holiday. In those ten days I had learnt a great deal about his practice. I had, for example, learnt that, although the waiting-room resembled a public lending library for germs when stuffed full with patients, any attempt to freshen the air by opening a window would be met with moans, groans and strange stares. I also learnt that Dr Oaks had trained his patients to queue outside the waiting-room and to regard a half-hour wait in the pouring rain as a potentially beneficial treatment, a sort of pre-surgery hydrotherapy session.

Patients were let into the surgery directly from the waiting-room and were then allowed out into the street through the french windows on the opposite side of the surgery. This made it possible to deal with up to twenty patients an hour, and on busy days it made twenty-five or even thirty an hour quite possible.

The waiting-room was sparsely furnished, being provided with two dozen hard and extremely uncomfortable chairs, which were bolted to one another and to the floor so that cleaning beneath them was an impossibility, a large old dining-table upon which were spread a good variety of old medical magazines, newspapers and *Reader's Digests* with the pages of medical information torn out to keep the patients comfortable in their ignorance, and two large cabinets which contained the patients' notes.

The notes were supervised by a large spinster whose word was law in the surgery and in the waiting-room. Aged about forty and built like a Centurion tank, Miss Williams made it part of her duty to announce to newcomers their precise position in the league of patients.

The surgery was to many members of the local community a meeting-place where confidences and pieces of gossip could be profitably exchanged and messages left for distant friends and neighbours. Miss Williams was a safe trustee for many of these titbits. She would pass on information about meetings, parties, dinners, trysts and expectations. The guardian of many secrets, she could be relied upon to share the most confidential matters only with her twin sister with whom she shared a house.

Dr Oaks had never had an appointments system at his surgery. His patients simply turned up and took their place in the queue. In order to ensure an early consultation some would arrive half or even three-quarters of an hour before the surgery was due to start. Others would turn up at the last possible moment and join the diminishing crowd in the waiting-room, believing that this cut down their waiting time. These patients, arriving last in the surgery, did, however, have to put up with a doctor who'd already been listening to tales of woe for a couple of hours or so and who would consequently be in a rather tired

17

state of mind. Experienced patients, those who visited the doctor as regularly as they visited their own relatives, would peep into the waiting-room, count the heads and then either sit down or slip out again promising to call back later or on another day. The official surgery hours were from nine until ten every morning from Monday to Friday and from five until six every evening except Wednesday. People would queue in the mornings from eight-thirty and in the afternoons from four-thirty. The surgery doors would be shut at ten and six sharp and surgery would draw to a close an hour or so later.

From time to time, of course, a patient requiring urgent treatment would arrive in the surgery and would have to be seen without waiting. A baby brought in screaming or an old person in a faint would be allowed through without having to sit in line. Even those exceptions drew some condemnation from other patients, who would moan and complain loudly about favouritism. It did no good at all to argue with them or to point out that they too would be awarded similar privileges if they ever arrived at the surgery in desperate need.

As each new patient arrived he would give Miss Williams his medical card and, in return, Miss Williams would tell him how many patients were before him in the queue, point out the patient directly in front of him and even give him a rough estimate of the time he would have to wait. Miss Williams would even tell patients of the magazines she felt most likely to interest them while they waited.

'There's a new issue of *The Field* in,' she would tell Mrs Parkin. 'I think Mr Barrow has it at the moment.' 'There's a couple of recent *Woman's Owns* in there somewhere,' she would tell Mrs Partridge, 'and there's a new *Dandy* for young Willy.'

The magazines on the waiting-room table were always changing. One patient would take a magazine home to finish an interesting story or useful article and another would bring along a pile of unwanted journals. I don't think Dr Oaks ever needed actually to buy magazines for the waiting-room. The patients seemed to regard it as a sort of informally run soft-cover lending library.

Occasionally an awkward patient would consider himself unfairly treated by Miss Williams. 'I'm before him!' the unhappy person would moan. Miss Williams never acknowledged such rebellious behaviour and, as far as I know, no patient ever did more than make a mild vocal protest.

From beginning to end of each surgery Miss Williams sat in front of the cabinets full of notes; sometimes, when work was slack, busying herself with her knitting. She would remove each patient's notes from the file in turn, bringing them into the surgery in small groups of five or six. She knew all the patients by sight and rarely needed to ask a name or address. I hardly spoke to her in those early days or, rather, she hardly spoke to me except to help keep me on the straight and narrow. That meant telling me when I had used the wrong form or the wrong type of rubber stamp, and ensuring that at the end of the surgery the electric fire was switched off and the french windows securely bolted.

Apart from this, however, the administration of the practice remained a mystery to me. I saw the patients as they were ushered into my presence and did my best to solve their many and varied problems. I had little idea about whether or not my attempts were successful.

Dr Oaks, when he returned, asked nothing about the practice. He spoke to Miss Williams for a few moments and then followed the last patient into the surgery, settling himself down in the patient's chair. 'Like cricket?' he asked.

I nodded. I like cricket as much as I detest dogs.

'I'll take you to the Test Match a week on Saturday,' he offered. 'I've fixed up someone to take the calls.' Then he scratched his teeth with his pipe, pulled at his bushy moustache, levered himself up out of the chair and was gone.

five

The following week was hectic – mainly due to the attendances of a young lady called Susan Whitby. She first came in to see me on Monday morning when she complained of a pain in her leg.

I told her to remove her tights and to climb up on to the couch so that I could examine her properly. While she undressed, the telephone on the desk rang and I spoke for a few moments with Miss Williams, who wanted to pass on a message. When I had finished I turned back to Miss Whitby and found she was waiting on the couch.

I examined her leg carefully from toe to thigh but could find nothing of any significance. It seemed a perfectly healthy and shapely leg, and I told her so. This was the first time I had actually looked at her above the waist, and it was only then that I noticed she was really most attractive. It was her eyes which caught my attention; they were sparkling blue and outlined with carefully applied eye make-up. Her hair was golden brown and hanging free around her face. She wore a clinging rust-coloured sweater and simple white necklace.

'There's nothing to worry about?' she asked, her eyes open wide and her hand clasping my arm.

'Nothing at all,' I told her.

'It must have been just a slight strain,' she suggested.

'Probably,' I agreed. 'If you don't feel better tomorrow, come and see me again.' I felt confident that now that she'd been reassured she'd be perfectly healthy again in half an hour.

But she was back again the next morning.

'I've got a pain in my neck now, Doctor,' she said. 'It came on during the night.'

I stood up and walked around the desk. 'Stand up, please,' I said to her. 'Let me have a look at you.'

This time she wore a flimsy cotton blouse, which surprised me since it was raining pretty heavily and desperately cold outside. The blouse was low-necked, so I was able to examine her carefully without asking her to remove it.

'Does this hurt?' I asked, moving her head gently to the left.

'No,' she answered.

'This?' I asked, moving it to the right.

'No,' she said. Her eyes fluttered, and she wet her lips carefully with her tongue. I could feel my heart complaining. It never likes working overtime early in the morning. 'It's just around the back,' she continued. I moved round behind her, and for the first time I noticed that she wasn't wearing a brassière. At least, if she was, it was one which didn't have a strap at the back. The cockles and muscles of my heart were taking a heavy beating.

'I can't find anything,' I said.

'Are you sure?' she asked.

'Positive,' I said. I was puzzled. It seemed a very odd combination, and I was desperately trying to convince myself that there couldn't be a syndrome I'd missed which involved pains in the legs and the neck.

'I'll just check to make sure you haven't got any enlarged glands,' I suggested.

'Good,' said Miss Whitby. 'Would you like me to take my blouse off?'

'Er, no, that's all right, thank you,' I said. 'I can manage.'

I examined her neck and felt underneath her arms for enlarged lymph-nodes. I couldn't find anything.

I reassured her again, gave her a prescription for some vitamin tablets and bade her goodbye.

She didn't come back the next morning, but she was at evening surgery.

'It's my tummy now, Doctor,' she said. 'The pain is in my tummy.'

'And your neck?' I asked.

'My neck is fine,' she said with a smile. 'I think the massage you gave me helped that.'

'The massage?' I asked.

'When you examined me,' she said. She smiled again. She had lovely teeth.

'Of course,' I murmured. 'Well, let's have a look at your tummy, shall we?'

'Certainly,' said Miss Whitby. 'Would you like to have me on the couch?'

'I beg your pardon?' I said quickly.

'On the couch?' the girl asked. 'Would you like me on the couch?'

'Oh, er, yes, please,' I managed to stutter.

She clambered on to the couch. 'Do you want me to take anything off?' she asked.

'Just loosen your skirt, please,' I suggested, 'so that I can see your tummy.'

She loosened her skirt and pushed it down over her hips. She was wearing lace panties which carried some writing on the front.

'What's this?' I asked innocently, puliIng her skirt down a little further so that I could read the message. She said nothing, but simply smiled at me as I read the instruction. It read, 'This way up.'

I smiled and tried hard not to blush. It wasn't easy.

'It's just in the middle,' said Miss Whitby, placing one hand over her navel. I moved her hand away gently and placed my own hand over the same spot. She put her hand on top of mine and pressed it down. Then she moved her hand with mine in it a little further southwards. 'It hurts all the way down here,' she said.

'It doesn't seem to be tender,' I pointed out.

'Oh, it's not tender,' she agreed. 'Just slightly sore.'

'Ah,' I said.

'In fact, it seems to be getting better now,' she confessed. 'You do have very soothing hands.'

'Er . . . yes,' I agreed, quickly moving my hands away and placing them in my pockets where I hoped they would keep out of mischief. 'Well, I think you'd better get dressed now.'

'Have you finished?' asked Miss Whitby.

'Yes, thank you,' I told her. 'I think so.'

She was back again on Thursday morning.

'You'll be getting tired of the sight of me,' she said. 'You must dread my coming in now.'

'Not at all,' I insisted politely.

'Oh, good,' she smiled.

'Pain in the tummy?' I asked.

'No, it's in my chest,' she said. 'It seems to have moved up a little.' She placed a hand over her left breast. 'It hurts just here,' she said. 'Shall I take my blouse off?'

'Er . . . well . . . ,' I murmured uncertainly.

'It does hurt dreadfully,' said Miss Whitby, 'and I wouldn't worry so much, but I live alone and there's no one with me at night.' She began to unbutton her blouse. This one was diaphanous and I could see that she was wearing a brassière. She took that off straightaway and then lay down on the couch.

'Right,' I said, trying hard to regain control of the situation. 'Take off your things and lie down on the couch.'

Her breasts were firm and round, her skin well tanned to within a couple of millimetres of her nipples. They were erect and pink.

'It's warm in here, isn't it?' said Miss Whitby. I'd been about to ask her if she was cold.

'Is it?' I asked.

'This couch is very comfortable,' said Miss Whitby.

'Good,' I said, idly examining a breast while I waited for a chance to ask her what was the matter.

'There isn't much left of me for you to have to imagine,' said Miss Whitby.

'Tell me where the pain is,' I asked her.

'Just there,' said Miss Whitby, pointing to the breast I was examining.

'It seems perfectly normal,' I told her.

'They both seem a little uncomfortable. I can't really explain it. You must get tired of looking at naked women,' said Miss Whitby, sitting up suddenly and bouncing her breast out of my hand. I felt her right arm leaning against my shirt front. 'When you've seen two I suppose you've seen them all,' she said with a giggle.

'Have you had a cough?' I asked.

'Though, of course, there is plenty of variety around, isn't there?'

'There really doesn't seem much wrong here,' I told her.

'Oh, good,' said Miss Whitby. 'I am pleased.' She swung her legs over the side of the couch, leaving her hand on my arm. The manoeuvre left her right thigh straining against my left thigh and her naked breasts pressed against my chest.

'You're right,' I said, 'it is warm, isn't it?' Two beads of sweat dripped off my forehead on to my coat-sleeve, and the stains spread outwards.

Somehow I managed to get back behind my desk and busy

myself writing out a prescription. This time I gave her a prescription for a powerful laxative. I thought it might help keep her occupied elsewhere. Either the laxative didn't work, or she didn't bother to take it, for she was back again next morning.

'You'll think I'm awful,' she said, 'but it makes me feel so much better just to see you that I had to come.'

'Any pains?' I asked.

'Well, not exactly,' said Miss Whitby, 'but I think I've got a gland getting bigger in my groin.'

'Excuse me just a moment,' I said, standing up in desperation. 'Your case is getting too much for me. I think I'll have to see if I can find Dr Oaks to give me a hand.' I rushed past her and out into the corridor. I found Dr Oaks eating his morning egg and reading the newspaper. Quickly I explained the situation to him.

'She's in there now,' I told him. 'Itching to take her clothes off again.'

'Lead on,' said Dr Oaks. 'The cavalry is here.' He followed me back down the corridor and into the surgery.

'Hello, Susan,' he said.

'Oh, hello, Dr Oaks,' said Miss Whitby.

'Take all your clothes off,' said Dr Oaks.

'Pardon?' said Miss Whitby.

'Strip!' said Dr Oaks brusquely. 'We want to find out what's the trouble.'

'Well, it really isn't anything all that much,' said Miss Whitby.

'We need to examine you thoroughly,' said Dr Oaks. He turned to me. 'Get the proctoscope and the vaginal speculum out, will you?' he asked. 'We'll have a look at her from every angle.'

'It's really all right,' said Miss Whitby, backing towards the door. 'It was just a little pain. It seems to have gone now. I feel much better.'

'Well, if it comes back, you come and see us straightaway,' said Dr Oaks, 'and we'll both give you a thorough examination and order some tests at the hospital if we can't find anything wrong with you.'

'Thank you,' said Miss Whitby, and then she was gone.

'My egg will be hard' was all that Dr Oaks said as he disappeared.

six

The Test match was becoming exciting. The Australians were several wickets down. The English bowlers looked like getting on top, and even the bookmakers admitted that, with a little help from the weather, England might be able to force a fighting draw. The sun was shining from a cloudless sky, and I had a pint of refreshment nestling in the shade under my seat and a rather delicious piece of pie nestling in the shade under my diaphragm. Then came the appeal over the loudspeakers. 'If there is a doctor on the ground, would he please go to the first-aid point behind the pavilion.'

'Off you go,' said Dr Oaks, patting my knee like a benevolent grandfather sending a young boy for an ice cream.

That's the trouble with being a doctor. You're never really off duty. And, if you are a salaried assistant accompanying your employer to a ground at which he is an honoured member, then you have little opportunity to hide your light under a bushel. You can be, as I was, a couple of dozen miles away from the patients supposed to be in your charge, happy in the knowledge that another doctor is looking after all those members of your flock who need care and attention, yet you are still liable to be called upon to assist. You never hear of solicitors, accountants or bank managers being summoned while off duty, do you? When is the last time that you heard a loudspeaker announcement asking for an estate agent to go directly to the ladies' washroom?

I went, of course. I couldn't be sure that the bald-headed fellow three rows in front of me was really rushing off in response to the appeal. He might have just emptied his beer-glass and discovered the need to refill it or to make a trip to the used-beer department.

In fact, my journey wasn't really necessary at all. Someone had fainted and the first-aid officers just needed a little re-assurance. But when I got back to my seat one of the star Australian batsmen had been dismissed, and the chap who'd knocked over my beer told me it had been a spectacular catch.

A few minutes after the dismissal and my adventure behind the pavilion, the field was cleared for the luncheon interval. As the players began to walk off, Dr Oaks stood up and started off towards the end of our row. He signalled to me to follow him. 'Where are we going?' I asked, puzzled. He said nothing but just continued on his clumsy way, treading on vacuum-flasks, sandwich-packs, beer-glasses and a variety of assorted feet.

I followed him to the dining-room, where he turned round with a triumphant smile. 'Surprise for you, lad,' he announced proudly. 'Decent bit of lunch.' The place was packed with hungry spectators anxiously looking at their watches and stuffing chicken salads into their mouths, but the food was good and the service extraordinary. Within seconds of our having sat down food appeared in front of us. As soon as that supply had been dealt with, a fresh one was provided with equal speed. There was no time for such refinements as chewing or digesting. The food was simply removed from the plate and placed in the stomach.

It was undoubtedly this speed of eating that was responsible for the alarming incident which occurred at the table next to ours. A tall balding gentleman with an impressive pair of side-whiskers was loudly describing to his dining colleagues the faults of the English team, and at the same time trying to feed himself. He managed the difficult feat with great skill, until an unfortunate slip of the tongue resulted in a piece of chicken sliding into the trachea, or windpipe, rather than the oesopha-gus, or gullet. The gentleman began to choke. It was not a pretty sight.

Dr Oaks stared at him with some interest. In fact, we both stared at him and watched him change colour. Eventually it became clear that the errant piece of bird was not going to remove itself without outside assistance. Medical help was urgently required. Before I could move Dr Oaks sprang and pulled the now blue-faced spectator to his feet. Then he placed both his arms around his waist, turned the man away from him, allowed the man's head, shoulders and upper trunk to hang forward, and pulled back with all his strength, pressing both his forearms against the man's abdomen.

The result was spectacular. The piece of chicken shot out of the man's trachea with a tremendous force and was skilfully caught by a man in a check jacket standing near the cashier's desk. He and Dr Oaks received a round of applause for their work. Within minutes the balding gentleman with the over-whelming side-whiskers was sitting once again in his place at table, insisting on purchasing Dr Oaks and myself double whiskies.

'That was pretty impressive,' I said.

'Ah ha, we old soldiers know a trick or two,' admitted Dr Oaks without reluctance. 'I got that from an American medical journal the other week. The theory is that, since the piece of food is sucked into the lungs when the patient is breathing in, the lungs must contain air when they are blocked. It follows, therefore, that if the lungs are forcefully compressed and emp-tied the air pressure inside will rise, and any foreign body imp-eding the flow of air will be shot out of the way like a cork from a bottle.'

After lunch we joined the balding and fortunate spectator on the roof of the pavilion, sitting in seats normally reserved for the privileged few. Dr Oaks had chosen his patient well.

The tea interval had just been taken when one of the English batsmen received a nasty-looking blow on the arm from one of the Australian fast bowlers. Minutes later, with the bats-man retired hurt in the pavilion, the ground resounded to an appeal put out over the loudspeaker system: 'If there is a doc-tor on the ground would he please go to the England dressing-room . . .'

Dr Oaks was on his feet within seconds. He tapped me on the shoulder. 'You stay here,' he said. 'I'll go.' Generously he hur-ried off to give advice. After a dull half-hour's play he came

27

back and turned me green with his account of how he'd rubbed shoulders with the current heroes of English cricket. He also told me, incidentally, that his passage into the dressing-room had been somewhat impeded by a small crowd of neurosurgeons, skin specialists, psychiatrists and gynaecologists, not to mention two men whom he swore were bishops. None of them was very sure about what to do with a bruise.

There were, it seemed to me, advantages as well as disadvantages in being a cricket-watching doctor.

seven

I'd just put the telephone down after talking to one of the doctors at the local hospital and arranging for an elderly man with an abdominal pain to be admitted fairly urgently, when the infernal machine rang again.

'Is that the doctor's?' screeched the caller in such a tremendous voice that I had to hold the receiver a foot or so away from my ear.

'Yes,' I shouted back, having to shout to make myself heard, now the receiver was so far away.

'Could I have a bottle of my red medicine?' asked the caller. 'I always have the same.'

'Yes, certainly,' I replied, anxious to please. 'Could you—?'

I was about to ask for the caller's name, address and more precise requirements when the telephone was cut off. I heard the distinctive click as she replaced her receiver on the rest.

I called to Miss Williams and explained that I had received a request for a prescription from a caller who hadn't bothered to leave her name.

'What did she sound like?' asked Miss Williams.

'Loud voice,' I said immediately. 'I'm surprised you didn't hear her.'

'What did she want?'

'Bottle of red medicine,' I answered.

'She was in a call-box?' asked Miss Williams.

I nodded. 'I heard the pips go,' I confirmed.

'Since it's Tuesday that must have been Mrs Benjamin,' said Miss Williams with a wise nod. 'She always rings on Tuesdays for her bottle of medicine.'

Miss Williams had a quite extraordinary knowledge of Dr Oaks' patients – and, indeed, of Dr Oaks himself. She seemed to know every patient by name and disease, and would start to write out prescriptions for signature almost as soon as some of them came into view at the bottom of the street. She had also managed to master the apparently inexhaustible variety of forms which are today an integral part of general practice. At the end of each surgery I would tell Miss Williams how many tetanus injections I had given, how many patients had asked for contraceptive advice, how many had needed injections for overseas trips, and so on and so on. Miss Williams would then fill in the necessary forms and leave them on the desk ready for signing before the next surgery. The forms, signed and folded, would be posted off to the Family Practitioner Committee, the administrative office which acts as mediator between the Government and the general practitioners. The staff of the Family Practitioner Committee would in their turn arrange for Dr Oaks to be paid for all his services he had rendered.

Miss Williams could not have been given any more responsibility without actually being allowed to sit in the surgery and press the buzzer herself. And yet the patients didn't seem to object; on the contrary, many seemed happy to consult her rather than trouble the doctor, relying on her to tell them when they had something wrong which needed qualified medical advice.

Miss Williams lived with her sister in a small terraced house about three hundred yards from the surgery. She arrived at the surgery each morning at about eight and left each evening some eleven or twelve hours later, after evening surgery. In between surgeries she would answer the telephone and the front door, attempt to maintain some sort of order in the surgery's drawers and cupboards, and she would knit. Miss Williams was an inveterate knitter who seemed totally addicted to the clicking of knitting-needles. If she ran out of wool and the shops were shut she would simply unravel what she had done and do it again. Dr Oaks had long since built up a stock of enough gloves, socks and scarves to last him the rest of his life, and my presence seemed to give Miss Williams new zeal. She would present me with a pair of socks or gloves at the end of almost every day, and would accompany the gift with a bill from a local knitting-wool shop. I learnt from Dr Oaks that I was expected to pay for the wool but that the labour was free.

At the end of a month, when I had more socks than a centipede had feet, I tentatively asked Miss Williams if she could make me a sweater. Within another month I had a long-sleeved polo-necked sweater, a short-sleeved V-necked sweater, a long-sleeved V-necked sweater, a short-sleeved polo-necked sweater, a jumper with a zip up the front, a jumper with buttons up the front, and a bobble hat.

Two weeks later I had acquired three more bobble hats, a shawl for my mother, a car-blanket made up of many different colours, and a knitted waistcoat with dancing lambs on the chest. Desperate for relief from the welter of garments threatening to force me out of my room, I persuaded one of Dr Oaks' ante-natal patients, a young woman expecting her first, to ask Miss Williams to make her some baby clothes. It proved to be a master move. Ever afterwards, Miss Williams concerned herself with the manufacture of baby clothes, and she received a steady supply of orders from the ante-natal patients.

I once visited Miss Williams and her sister at home when an attack of food poisoning had laid them both low one Sunday. The whole house seemed like a warehouse for home industries – the furniture was piled high with knitted cushions and the walls were all but covered with tapestry work, paintings and neatly framed marquetry. I peered closely at one of the paintings which I found particularly impressive, and only in the sky could you see the numbers showing through.

The two sisters shared a room which contained a small library of books describing a wide variety of harmless activities ranging from pottery to origami. The window-ledge, the mantelpiece, the dressing-table top and the top of the wardrobe held the evidence that the purchasers of the books had not simply read their volumes with passive interest. There were small figures made out of pipe-cleaners, bunches of red crêpe daffodils and, on a chair behind the door, a raffia basket filled with carefully painted beach-pebbles.

Neither Miss Williams seemed to be in any danger; I gave them a bottle of harmless medicine to share, some advice about their diet for the next twenty-four hours and a warning about consuming meat pies bought at half-price.

'Please, let us give you a little something as a token of our thanks,' said the Miss Williams I hadn't seen before.

'Oh, no, that's not necessary,' I murmured quickly in embarrassment.

'We insist,' said the other Miss Williams, with a smile I'd not seen before.

'I'd rather you didn't,' I said, edging towards the door. I couldn't help wondering what I'd do with a home-made nail-picture, or where I'd put another bobble hat.

'Please, take this,' said one of them. I was no longer quite sure which one was talking. She handed me a bottle wrapped in tissue-paper. 'A friend gave it to us, but we don't drink.'

'Well, that's extremely kind of you,' said I, 'but quite unnecessary. I was only too happy to come.' I idly wondered whether it was potato or elderberry wine.

I talked with them for a minute or two more and then left, clutching my bottle. I very nearly dropped it as I circumnavigated the herd of plaster hedgehogs on the doorstep. I got to my car with it safely, and drove round the corner before unwrapping the tissue-paper. I was astonished – and delighted, of course – to find that I'd been given a bottle of malt whisky.

eight

Twenty-five years ago Mrs Nelson had been a cook in one of the largest hotels in London. Her exquisite scones and her ability to produce an omelette which needed to be held down on the plate had resulted in a number of rival hotel-managers making tempting offers for her services. But she had been faithful to her hotel and had stayed there until her retirement at the early age of forty-five – a retirement brought on by her marriage to a travelling salesman who had eventually found it impossible to resist Mrs Nelson and her scones.

When she retired she continued to cook as a hobby. She loved nothing better than to watch a tray full of recently baked scones disappear inside a hungry and appreciative visitor. She provided Dr Oaks with regular supplies of fruitcake, and no local sale of work was complete without a tray of cakes from her.

After her husband died a year or so before, Mrs Nelson was quite heartbroken. She had shared a quarter of a century with him and he had had a tremendous appetite. Mrs Nelson had shopped carefully, and cooked wisely and economically, and they had eaten as well as any other couple I knew. After her husband's death, however, Mrs Nelson lost all interest in cooking. She lived on a diet of jam and bread and cups of tea, with the occasional can of soup warmed up on cold days. She simply had no desire to cook for herself.

I first saw her when she came along to the surgery complaining that she felt too weak to go out, too miserable to see anyone and too tired even to eat. She was complaining of headaches, and she had badly swollen ankles. She was pale and clearly suffering from anaemia.

I examined her to make sure that there was nothing else the matter, and sent off a sample of blood to the hospital so that the technicians in the pathology laboratory could examine it and tell me precisely how anaemic she was.

The result came back a couple of days later and confirmed my initial diagnosis. Mrs Nelson was simply anaemic because she had not been eating properly. She needed a course of iron tablets. However, I had a feeling that, if I simply gave her iron tablets for a couple of months, her immediate problem might be solved but two months later she'd be back again, as badly anaemic as ever.

I was wondering what to do when I was called to see Mr Berridge, a man of about seven-five who happened to live next door to Mrs Nelson and whom I'd never met before. He opened the door to me himself and I was startled by his appearance. Not since my first few months at medical school had I seen such a florid and unmistakable case of thyroid deficiency. Mr Berridge had thick coarse hair, dry and rough skin, a gruff voice and a rather dull look about him which is hard to describe in detail but which is pretty typical of myxoedema. He didn't have a collar or tie on, and I could see quite easily the thin scar across his neck which suggested that at some time or other he'd had an operation on his thyroid gland. I didn't have his medical records with me, and I'd forgotten to study them before I came out, but that didn't matter much – Mr Berridge told me straightaway that he'd had a thyroidectomy some seven or eight years previously.

He'd called me out because he couldn't hear properly. (I found out later that it was wax in his ears which was responsible; the symptoms of thyroid deficiency hadn't bothered him at all.) But I felt certain that I could do more for him than simply improve his hearing.

As a thyrotoxic patient Mr Berridge had been unable to stand the heat, he'd been losing weight, he'd been for ever on the move, worrying and unable to sleep. The operation on his overactive thyroid gland had been effective – perhaps too effective, for the surgeon had removed the entire gland and left Mr Berridge short of thyroid hormone. The result had been that he had gradually become more and more chairbound, he'd put on weight, he'd become unable to tolerate the cold weather and he'd given up looking after himself properly. Although he was overweight, he was anaemic and short of necessary vitamins.

I gave him a prescription for some replacement thyroid tablets and slipped next door to see Mrs Nelson.

'What do you know of your neighbour, Mr Berridge?' I asked her.

Mrs Nelson didn't say much, but shrugged her shoulders. 'I've hardly seen him,' she confessed. 'He keeps very much to himself.'

'He keeps to himself because he's been ill,' I told her. 'He should be a good deal better now that I've started him on the correct tablets, but he really needs a little looking after.'

Mrs Nelson said nothing but looked interested.

'His main problem,' I told her, 'is that he needs to eat properly. He needs a good and varied diet and he needs to eat nourishing food which won't put weight on him.'

'Plenty of protein?' suggested Mrs Nelson.

'Exactly,' I said. 'You know exactly what he should be eating, being an expert cook yourself.'

'Oh, I wouldn't say that . . .' murmured Mrs Nelson modestly.

'If you could perhaps give him some advice . . .' I suggested.

'Oh, I couldn't do that!' said Mrs Nelson. 'He'll not be able to cook properly if he's been ill. I'll cook for him.'

'Good heavens!' I cried. 'That's really too kind of you. Are you sure?'

'It'll be a pleasure,' Mrs Nelson assured me.

A minute or two later I was back knocking at Mr Berridge's door again. I explained to him that his next-door neighbour had been very lonely since the death of her husband, that she wanted company and that I'd arranged for him to take his meals with her. I asked him confidentially to try to make sure that she ate properly. I explained that she would do the cooking and that they could perhaps share the costs of the food. I left the two houses feeling very pleased with myself.

I didn't see Dr Oaks for a couple of days after that. He had taken a little time off to attend a postgraduate course in Scotland. I suspected that since he'd taken his golf clubs with him he might be spending some time on a course of a different kind, but I'd resisted the temptation to say anything. After all, I had been hired as an assistant.

He came back on the Friday and did a surgery himself. I met him at lunch after we'd both done a couple of visits. I was about to tell him about my success with Mrs Nelson and Mr Berridge, when he forestalled me.

'I believe you went to see Mrs Nelson the other day?' he asked.

I nodded and sat back, awaiting the praise which I felt sure was forthcoming.

'And Mr Berridge?'

I nodded again.

'I had to send them both into hospital this morning,' said Dr Oaks.

'Into hospital?' I gasped. 'Why?'

'Mr Berridge went mushroom-picking early this morning,' explained Dr Oaks, 'and Mrs Nelson cooked the mushrooms for their joint breakfast.'

'I don't believe it,' I said. 'Don't tell me . . .'

'I'm afraid so,' said Dr Oaks. 'The mushrooms weren't edible, and Mrs Nelson and her next-door beau are now in the casualty department having their stomachs emptied. Now, what were you about to tell me?' he went on.

'Nothing,' I said hurriedly, putting a forkful of steak pie into my mouth quickly. 'Nothing at all.'

nine

Although the village of Long Bridlington was at least six miles away from the surgery, Dr Oaks had a number of patients living there. Most of them had been on his list since he had sat patiently waiting for his first customers to limp through his front door. The village was a tightly knit community, and the villagers tended to regard outsiders with a mixture of contempt and suspicion; though, to be fair, they always treated me with politeness and quiet civility.

The first villager to try out the new doctor's diagnostic and therapeutic skills was a man in his early sixties who came in complaining of a pain in the back of his left leg.

'It comes on when I've been walking,' he said, rubbing the calf muscles to make sure I understood where the pain was.

'How far can you walk?' I asked.

'How long is a road?' countered the man with an innocent grin.

'How far can you walk before you develop a pain in your leg?' I asked with great patience.

'From our house to the corner of Hounds Lane,' replied the patient after a moment's thought.

'How far is that?' I asked.

'About as far as I can walk,' said the man, nodding to give his answer added emphasis. I looked at him carefully, but the grin had completely disappeared and I could not tell whether or not he was being deliberately confusing. Some patients, although they genuinely want help, seem to delight in misleading their physician. I have heard it said they do this to cover up their own fears and worries.

'I'm trying to help you, Mr Elliot,' I said with great deliberation. 'Try to give me an estimate of the distance you can walk before the pain in your leg starts to give you trouble.'

'About two hundred yards,' came the reply without much hesitation.

'Do you get any pains in your other leg?' I asked.

Mr Elliot shook his head.

'Nothing at all?'

Mr Elliot shook his head again.

'Do you get any pains in your chest?' I asked, trying to introduce a little variety into the conversation.

Mr Elliot shook his head again.

'Does the pain go away when you've rested for a while?' I asked.

Mr Elliot nodded, and I felt quite pleased with myself. The diagnosis wasn't going to be difficult.

'How long do you have to wait before the pain goes?' I asked.

'About five minutes or so,' replied the patient.

'And then you can walk on again?'

He nodded.

'And the pain comes back?'

Another nod.

'And then you rest?'

'That's right,' said Mr Elliot.

'And the pain goes away and you can carry on?'

'That's it. You've got it,' said Mr Elliot. 'I have to stop four times on the way to the Dragon.'

'The Dragon?'

'Our pub,' explained Mr Elliot.

'Ah,' said I, understanding.

'Well, what do you think, Doctor?' asked the patient.

'Do you smoke?' I asked.

'Woodbines,' said Mr Elliot. 'I've always smoked them.'

'How many a day?' I asked.

'It depends how far I walk,' said Mr Elliot.

'I don't understand,' said I.

'I have a cigarette every time I have to stop when I'm walking,' said Mr Elliot in explanation. 'I have to do something, don't I?'

'You've got intermittent claudication,' I told him. 'That means simply that the arteries in your legs are not supplying the leg muscles with enough freshly oxygenated blood.'

'And so I get the pain?' said Mr Elliot.

'That's it,' said I.

'Well, what are we going to do about it?' asked the patient.

'You should give up smoking,' I told him. 'Cigarettes are the major cause of intermittent claudication.'

'That's what Dr Oaks said,' Mr Elliot smiled brightly.

'You've been to Dr Oaks about this?' I asked.

Mr Elliot nodded.

'Has it got worse since you saw him?'

Mr Elliot shook his head.

'Do you want me to get you an appointment with a surgeon?' I asked.

'No, thank you,' said Mr Elliot. 'Dr Oaks suggested that I have an operation, but I told him I didn't want one.'

'Well, what can I do for you?' I asked.

'I just wanted to see if you said it was the same thing as Dr. Oaks said it was,' explained Mr Ellit with extraordinary honesty.

'Oh,' said I.

'Thank you for your time, Doctor,' said Mr Elliot, standing.

'Have you got a bicycle?' I asked before he could leave.

'A bicycle?' asked Mr Elliot.

'A bicycle,' I repeated.

'No,' said Mr Elliot.

'Why don't you get a bicycle, if you don't want an operation?' I suggested.

'A bicycle?' asked Mr Elliot again.

'Then you'll be able to around without having to stop and rest,' I explained.

Mr Elliot slowly nodded his understanding, came forward a couple of feet and held out a hand for me to shake. I took it, noting with surprise that it really wasn't the massive, thick-skinned hand I'd expected.

'Thank you, Doctor,' said Mr Elliot. 'I'll do that.' He shook my hand earnestly and nodded again before leaving.

Over the following few days I saw and heard a good deal of the inhabitants of Long Bridlington. I suspect that when they had first heard of mw presence in the sugery they had kept their ailments and complaints in store ready for the day when Dr Oaks would replace the usurper. When the expected return of the principal himself had not occurred they had obviously sent a man with a gammy leg ahead to test out the new ground. My experiences with the villagers all supported the theory expressed by Miss Williams, who was quite convinced that there wasn't a sane person in the village.

For example, I was asked one morning to visit an elderly lady whose relatives were convinced that psychiatric help was needed. The relatives lived in London and visited the village once a month or so. They rang the surgery one morning and we had a bizarre three-way conversation. Mr Johnson, the old lady's nephew, and his wife Martha both had telephone extensions in their hands and I listened to their advice and reports in comparative silence.

'She keeps the budgie food in the washing machine,' said Mr Johnson.

'And puts the hot-water bottle out at night,' added Mrs Johnson.

'She tries to boil water in the teapot.'

'And keeps the coal in the fridge.'

'She wears all her stockings at once so that no one can steal them.'

'And keeps her vegetables in the wardrobe,' said Mrs Johnson.

'We're getting worried about her,' said Mr Johnson rather angrily.

'It's your job to do something about it,' said Mrs Johnson.

'She can't go on like this,' said Mr Johnson.

'She isn't safe,' said Mrs Johnson.

'What about—?' I began.

'I don't know what you're thinking of, leaving an old lady in her condition alone,' interrupted Mr Johnson.

'You're lucky you haven't been reported to the authorities!' said Mrs Johnson.

'Well, I think we ought to give the doctor a chance to do something,' said Mr Johnson.

'But—' I tried again.

'Well, I hope he does something soon,' said Mrs Johnson. 'It isn't fair to leave the poor old thing there alone. She ought to be in a home.'

'It puts an unreasonable burden on us,' complained Mr Johnson.

'Was that the door-bell?' asked Mrs Johnson.

'I think it was,' said Mr Johnson. 'Shal I go and answer it?'

'Well, you're nearest,' snapped his wife.

'I think—' I began once more.

'Well, hurry!' said Mrs Johnson.

'I'll call on her if you'll tell me her name,' I promised. 'Dr Oaks is not at the surgery at the moment. I'm looking after his patients.'

'Well, I hope you will call on her,' said Mrs Johnson.

I heard her shouting something to her husband.

'Would you give me your relative's name?' I asked.

'What?' demanded Mrs Johnson. 'There's someone at the door.'

'Her name,' I repeated.

'Mrs Ullyett,' said Mrs Johnson. 'She lives next door to the post office.'

'Thank you,' I said. I put the telephone receiver back on to its rest and left quickly before the Johnsons could ring back. I visited the old lady the same morning and she certainly did seem rather confused. I asked her if she would like to go into an old people's welfare home, and felt myself blushing involuntarily at her reply.

'Well, if you don't want to go into an old people's home,' I said, 'what are you going to do?'

'I'm going to stay here, young man,' said Mrs Ullyet. 'And what are you going to do about it?'

I could think of nothing much to say, so I left. Later I tele-phoned a psychiatrist at the local hospital and asked him if he would be kind enough to visit her at home and give me his advice.

'She lives next to the post office,' I told him. 'You can't miss it.'

I spent the afternoon dealing with a variety of strange callers. First, there was a representative from a company making drugs who insisted on showing me a short film his firm had produced. He brought with him a miniature projector and a screen, and within ten minutes he had turned the surgery upside down. The plug on his projector didn't fit the aged and slightly unusual sockets in the surgery, so he had to remove the plug from the table-lamp and put that on the projector. Then he found that to hang up his screen he had to remove most of the ornaments, books and photographs which Dr Oaks had stored on the mantelpiece. The film itself was extremely boring, and the drug company representative wasn't at all the sort of person to sit and watch it with.

Secondly, there was a visit from a woman who was doing a survey for another drug company. She brought with her a long and complicated questionnaire, and clearly her intention was to examine closely my prescribing habits. I tried to persuade her that I didn't have time to answer her questions, but I might as well have saved my breath, for she was quite determined to continue with her investigation. Each time I complained about how long it was taking she reached into a capacious black plastic case and brought out a small gift. By the time we'd finished filling in the questionnaire, the desk was covered with blotting-paper and notebooks and my pockets were bulging with small gadgets. There was a device designed to tell me when my parking-meter time had run out, a device for cleaning out pipes, and a ruler which, for some reason best known to its designer, had a magnifying glass set into it. When we had finally finished she gave me an illuminated scroll telling me I was a qualified medical practitioner, and promised to come back and interview me again some other time.

My third visitor was an administrative medical officer from the Government. He told me that it was his job to visit all general practitioners and ensure that they understoood the rules and regulations governing the use of official forms. I listened to him for half an hour or so, during which time I fear that I heard little of what he said, and then before he left I filled in a form to confirm that he had indeed visited me. While I was musing on the possible ultimate destination of the form I had completed, the telephone rang. It was the psychiatrist who had been out to Long Bridlington.

'Well, she certainly is confused,' he confirmed. 'She apparently keeps the cat's food in the bathroom cabinet and I saw her try to plug the electric kettle into the hot-water tap.'

'I didn't know she'd got a cat,' I said. 'I thought she just had the budgie.'

'Budgie?' said the psychiatrist. 'I didn't see a budgie.'

'It's in the living-room,' I said, 'by the fireplace.'

'Fireplace?' said the psychiatrist.

'Fireplace,' I repeated.

'She's had the fireplace bricked up,' said the psychiatrist.

'No, there's a log-fire always burning there,' I insisted. 'That's what she told me.'

'Are we talking about the same person?' asked the psychiatrist.

'Mrs Ullyet,' I said. 'Next to the post office.'

'Mrs Asprey,' said the psychiatrist. 'That's her name.'

'It's a pink cottage with a thatched roof,' I said.

'No, that's the one on the *other* side of the post office,' said the psychiatrist. The implications of what he'd said dawned on us both slowly.

'Which house did you mean?' asked the psychiatrist.

'The one on the right as you look at the post office,' I said.

'That's Mrs Ullyet?' asked the psychiatrist.

'That's right,' I confirmed.

'I've been to see the other woman, Mrs Asprey,' said the psychiatrist.

'She sounds as dotty as Mrs Ullyett,' I said.

'I'm not going out there again,' said the psychiatrist quickly.

We decided to forget about both Mrs Ullyett and Mrs Asprey.

The memory of this unusual and rather unfortunate episode was still clear in my mind when I received another call to go over to Long Bridlington. Oddly enough, the call was to visit Mr Elliot, the man who'd introduced me to the village.

'The old couple live in a cottage up Burberry Lane,' said the caller, an anonymous villager whose name I never discovered. 'Take the first turning on the right after the Dragon and you'll run into it.'

I followed the instructions carefully and reached the cottage without any delay or mishap. I was congratulating myself on my skill as I clambered out of the car into the small yard outside the cottage door. There was no sign of any canine activity, and I walked towards the door with confidence.

'I'm so glad you could come, Doctor,' said the small, slight woman who answered the door in response to my knock.

'It's Mr Elliot, is it?'

'That's right,' said the woman. 'My husband.'

I followed her into her sitting-room, a tiny well-kept room full of ornaments and souvenirs from seaside resorts. There were twenty or thirty ashtrays there, each advertising a well-known seaside town.

'He's in the bedroom,' said Mrs Elliot. I followed her out of the sitting-room and into an even smaller room at the top of a long narrow staircase. To get to the staircase we had to pass through a door at the back of the sitting-room which looked as if it led into a cupboard. It was clear that the cottage had just the sitting-room and a scullery downstairs and a single bedroom upstairs. I assumed that the toilet must be housed in a separate establishment somewhere in the garden.

Mr Elliot was in bed reading a gardening magazine.

'Hello,' I said. 'Have you bought a bicycle yet?'

'I have indeed, Doctor,' said Mr Elliot. 'And I'd like to thank you for the suggestion.' He pulled his wife towards him and put his arm around her. She sat on the bed for a moment and they looked quite idyllically happy together; the very picture of marital bliss. Then, in a single swift movement, Mrs Elliot pecked her husband on the cheek and edged towards the door.

'I'll be downstairs if you want me for anything, Doctor,' she said.

'Thank you,' I said. I waited until she'd closed the door behind her and then settled down on the edge of the bed.

'Well,' I began, 'what's been the trouble?'

'Water, Doctor,' said Mr Elliot. 'I've been having trouble with my water.'

'What sort of trouble?' I asked.

'Well, I seem to have trouble holding it,' said Mr Elliot quietly. 'I have to go quite frequently, and sometimes I've only got a couple of moments to get there.'

'Do you have to get up at night?' I asked.

'Very occasionally,' admitted Mr Elliot.

'Is it ever painful?'

'Not really.'

'Is there ever any blood in it?'

'Not that I've noticed.'

'Do you get any pains in your abdomen?'

Mr Elliot shook his head. I couldn't help noticing that, compared with his attitude at our last meeting, he seemed quite determined to be helpful and not to annoy me. I assumed that he felt grateful for my advice about the bicycle.

'Well, it sounds as if you could have prostrate trouble,' I suggested. 'I'd better have a look.' I opened the black bag which I'd taken with me into the house and took out a pair of disposable rubber gloves.

'Right,' said Mr Elliot. 'How would you like me?'

'On your side,' I said, 'facing the wall.'

'Right,' said Mr Elliot.

I moved up the bed, keeping bent low to avoid banging my head on the sloping roof of the cottage.

Mr Elliot lay on his side, pulled his knees chestwards and his pyjama trousers downwards.

'This shouldn't hurt at all,' I promised, smearing my gloved index finger with a little lubricant. Carefully I inserted the finger into the old man's rectum. I moved it around in every direction but could feel absolutely nothing resembling a prostate gland.

'You haven't had any operations?' I asked, suddenly wondering if I was making a fool of myself looking for a missing item.

'No, Doctor,' said Mr Elliot very quietly.

'Well, that's very odd,' I murmured, 'but you've got absolutely nothing there likely to cause you any problems.' I gently rolled him over on his back to indicate that the examination was over and to enable me to make a routine examination of the usual apparatus to be found where thighs meet.

There was absolutely nothing there.

I felt a cold sweat breaking out on my back as I silently and slowly parted the man's closed legs. Below the usual clump of short curly hair there were none of the usual accoutrements that one would expect to find adorning the master of any house. Instead there was the unmistakable evidence that Mr Elliot and Mrs Elliot had a great deal in common.

With remarkable self-control I removed the rubber glove from my right hand and replaced it with a fresh glove from my bag. I lubricated the index finger again and then gently slid that adventurous digit into Mr Elliot's surprisingly capacious vagina.

'Ah,' I said, feeling my shirt cling tightly to my back. 'I think you have a slight prolapse, Mr Elliot.'

'A prolapse, Doctor?' said Mr Elliot.

'You'll need a ring pessary to keep it under control,' I said. 'I'll get you one and bring it out for you.'

'You're very kind, Doctor,' said Mr Elliot. I removed the second rubber glove from my hand, and Mr Elliot pulled his pyjama trousers back up.

On my way out Mrs Elliot handed me a bunch of freshly picked spring onions and two large beetroots.

ten

The Simpson family had been with Dr Oaks for several years. Mr Simpson worked as a supermarket manager, his wife helped with a number of voluntary organizations and looked after their two children, Michael and Sarah. I met Michael and Sarah first, and had treated them several times for coughs and colds before I met their mother.

Mrs Simpson had been a model for a local department store before the birth of her first child and she had always been proud of her handsome features. The first time she called me to see her was on a Tuesday morning. It had been raining for four days without a break, and when I ran the doorbell at the Simpsons' house I had to shelter in the doorway out of the rain. I stood there for a couple of minutes, and was about to scribble a message on a visiting-card and leave when the front door opened. I couldn't see anyone, so I stepped inside and looked behind the door. There was Mrs Simpson wearing a dressing-gown, and a towel wrapped around her head, covering most of her face.

We went into the sitting-room, where the curtains were still drawn, and slowly she removed the towel from around her head and the dressing-gown from around her body. Her face, neck and upper chest were all badly sun-burned.

'How did you manage that?' I asked in amazement. 'It's been raining for days.'

Mrs Simpson looked down at her feet, clearly embarrassed. 'I've been trying to keep my tan up with a sunlamp I borrowed from a friend,' she confessed.

'And you fell asleep underneath it?' I suggested.

Mrs Simpson nodded. 'I put the alarm clock on to wake me up after five minutes, but when it rang I couldn't see any difference at all, so I thought I'd give it another couple of minutes, and then I fell asleep again. Can't you do anything about it, Doctor?' she asked. 'All my tan is peeling off, I shall look terrible.'

'I'm afraid there's nothing much I can do about that,' I told her. 'You'll probably lose most of your tan.'

'Oh, no!' cried Mrs Simpson in despair. 'It's taken me months to get that tan.'

'You can get some plain cream from the chemist's,' I told her. 'That will soothe it, but there's nothing I can do to save your burnt skin.'

I muttered a few pleasantries about the skin's ability to recover from all sorts of insults and left. As I opened the door to leave, Mrs Simpson hid shamefully in the sitting-room.

Having visited their home and met three-quarters of the family I felt that I knew the Simpsons moderately well. Mother and children seemed pleasant and wel adjusted enough, so when Mrs Simpson came to the surgery and complained that her husband was treating her unfairly and cruelly I oozed sympathy. I'd read many papers and articles in the popular journals dealing with wife-beating and, like all doctors, I fancied myself as a cross between Robin Hood and Charles Dickens, with the mission of exposing all unfairness and cruelty in society and doing what I could to right the wrongs, support the hard-done-by and batter the cruel and thoughtless.

Mrs Simpson told me that her husband was staying away from home at least two nights a week, that he was being unfaithful to her, that he never gave her enough housekeeping money, that he beat the children and that he was, in sort, a wicked and unreasonable man.

I obediently wrote down all that she told me and when, a day or so later, I received a letter from a local solicitor asking me to write to him describing Mrs Simpson's mental and physical condition and adding my own opinion as to the reasons for her unhealthy state I wrote a lengthy and explosive report in which I described Mrs Simpson as a poor distressed damsel and Mr Simpson as a villain whose malicious thoughts and deeds had scarred the life of his lovely wife.

When Mr Simpson came to visit me I didn't recognize him at first. He was not the bullying giant I had expected, but a slight man about five feet five inches tall and about ten stone in weight. He wore National Health Service spectacles, which surprised me since his wife was always so well dressed, a suit which had seen many better years, and a pair of scuffed, down-at-heel shoes. He had a balding patch, hair hanging over his collar, and an unkempt look which under different circumstances would have suggested to me that he was a bachelor clerk eking out a living on a mere pittance from some miserable employer.

He was clearly an inteligent and educated man, obviously capable and probably once ambitious. He talked for some time about his stomach, which was giving him a great deal of trouble, and eventually mentioned the subject of his wife. He talked of her as of a goddess, describing her lovingly and affectionately. He described his own inadequacies and explained that he quite understood that his wife needed to find sexual solace outside the home because of his own incompetence, but admitted that he found this difficult to bear at times.

I listened to him with astonishment as he explained how his wife mistreated him, and spent all their money on fripperies so that there was nothing left with which to pay the household bills. He mentioned, almost in passing, and certainly without malice, that his wife had nearly made him bankrupt twice and that he knew that she had recently taken up with a man who owned a chain of florist shops. His rival, he knew, had far more money and therefore a much greater chance of winning her affection.

When he left, clutching a prescription for some minor tranquillizer which I hoped might provide him with a temporary solution to a lasting problem, I sat quite still and horrified. I fetched Mrs Simpson's record, took out the copy of the letter I had written to the solicitor and read it with cold sweat on my forehead. There and then I wrote another letter explaining that I did not consider myself properly qualified to report on Mrs Simpson's status or to comment on the possible causes for her state of health. I asked the solicitor to ignore my previous comments and pointed out that I would not be prepared to substantiate them in court, should the necessity arise. That seemed to me to put an end to the matter. When I had written the letter and sealed it in its envelope I sighed with relief.

With that done I vowed never to jump to conclusions, and never to believe what one member of a family told me without having the opportunity to check with the other member or members of the family.

Such vows are, of course, easier to make than to keep. Two days after my traumatic meeting with Mr Simpson I was visited in surgery by a huge black woman whom I had never seen before. From her card I could see that, although she had been on Dr Oaks' list of patients for several years, she had never consulted him.

The woman looked terrified and tired and she spoke in a whisper, looking over her shoulder every couple of minutes as if frightened that she was being followed. It was only when I had actually got up from behind the desk, walked over to the door and locked it that she finally settled down to talk to me.

She told me that her husband was trying to kill her. She said that he had been trying to kill her for months with various spells he had found in an old witchcraft book and that, when that hadn't worked, he had tried to poison her. Her story was a long, complicated one, and I was convinced by it for a few minutes.

It was only after ten minutes of her talking that I remembered Mr and Mrs Simpson. It was then that I realized that I was listening to the mad ravings of a paranoid schizophrenic. She was obvious very disturbed and clearly needed specialist advice.

As luck would have it, I was due to meet a local psychiatrist at another patient's house half an hour or so later, so I telephoned his hospital and left a message for him to call in at the surgery first of all. He turned up less than fifteen minutes later, while I was still talking, or rather listening, to the woman. I couldn't help thinking that the service was good when a patient could be seen by a specialist before the consultation with her general practitioner was over!

Dr Jones agreed with me that the woman was obviously a paranoid schizophrenic. We talked about her together for a few minutes and then decided to admit her to hospital. When we broached the subject with her, however, she insisted that she was perfectly sane.

Dr Jones and I were about to start taking the necessary steps to have the poor lady admited as an involuntary patient to the local mental hospital, when the front door was pushed almost off its hinges and knocked back into an old umbrella-stand of which Dr Oaks was inordinately fond. I heard the stand smash and rushed out to protect the rest of the furniture, leaving the door to the surgery open wide. This enabled the visitor to see his wife sitting with Dr Jones, a sight which apparently enraged him even further, for he leapt past me into the surgery in a wild fury.

'Aaaaaaaaarh!' he screamed, waving both fists in the air. 'You will be punished! Vengeance is mine. I will repay, saith the Lord!'

He lunged forward towards my cowering patient, and Dr Jones and I rushed to get between the two of them.

It took the two of us several minutes to subdue the man, and it was not until I managed to inject a considerable amount of chlorpromazine into his left buttock that we succeeded in getting him under control. Then we had the difficult job of finding his unfortunate and now obviously honest wife. She was cowering in the patients' lavatory, and it was there that I apologized profusely to her.

The police came and fetched the man and, after they'd taken him away and I'd sedated his terrified wife, Dr Jones and I sat drinking a cup of coffee together in total silence. I had learnt that you have to believe some of the people some of the time. My only problem was that I still didn't know which people to believe or when to believe them.

eleven

The first patient in Monday morning surgery the following week was a seven-year-old boy. He had two problems, neither of which needed any introduction from his mother. He had an asthmatic wheeze and an angry-looking rash on his hands and forearms. A quick glance at his medical records confirmed that over the years the problems had recurred many times.

I listened to the boy's chest, but there was obsolutely no sign at all of any chest infection. I examined his skin, but could find no reason for the flare-up of eczema.

'Is anything worrying you?' I asked the boy.

There was no answer.

'Are you happy at school?'

He nodded.

I reached for the prescription pad and began to write out prescriptions for medicine to clear up the wheeze and for cream to help deal with the eczema.

'Thank you,' said his mother, as I handed her the prescription. 'By the way, we're moving house,' she added. 'Would you like our new address for the records?'

Something stirred at the back of my mind.

'How far are you moving?'

'Only about three miles,' came the reply. 'We're buying a larger house.'

'Is Martin going to have to change schools?' I asked.

Martin and his mother both nodded.

'How long have you known about this?'

'It was settled three weeks ago,' said Martin's mother.

'When did the rash start?' I asked.

'About a fortnight ago.'

'And the wheeze?'

'About a fortnight ago.'

'I don't want to move,' said Martin.

'But you'll soon make new friends,' his mother pointed out.

'I don't want any new friends,' argued Martin with unbeatable logic. 'I've already got some friends.'

'Has Martin seen the new house or his new school?' I asked.

They both shook their heads.

'Well, I think that might be a good idea,' I suggested. 'See if you can arrange for Martin to meet some of the neighbours' children before you move.'

Martin and his mother left, and I stabbed the buzzer with my finger. I felt quite pleased with myself. The psychological strains and stresses on men, women and children seem responsible for more and more physical ailments as the years go by. Today a good half of all the patients who visit the surgery have psychological problems which either cause or contribute to their physical symptoms.

Children in particular seem to suffer from the modern style of living. Martin Brown was not the only child I saw that morning who displayed the symptoms of a pressure-cooker existence. Simon Wales was brought to surgery by his mother, who complained that he seemed unable to sleep properly.

'How is school?' I asked him, having investigated his home life without finding any sign of stress.

'All right,' said Simon.

'Do you get on with the teacher?'

Simon nodded.

'Have you got plenty of friends?'

He nodded again.

'Are there any bullies at school?' I asked.

'There was one,' said Simon, 'but I tripped him up and he broke his arm.' He grinned at me proudly.

'Do you have a lot of work to do?' I asked, more or less sure that the conversation was leading nowhere.

'We haven't a lot of homework,' said the boy, who had not reached his seventh birthday.

'Homework?' I queried, assuming at first that he had been given some mild task to perform. Perhaps, I thought, he's got to collect some wild flowers, draw his pet animal or cut pictures out of the newspaper.

'We have sums to do every evening,' Simon told me.

I looked at his mother. She nodded confirmation. She looked proud of him.

'What about sport?' I asked. 'Do you get any time to play games?'

'We play football,' said Simon, 'and cricket.'

'Do you like football and cricket?'

'Yes,' said Simon, 'but I lost my place in the team this week.'

'The team?' I asked.

'The sports master said I wasn't trying properly,' said Simon. He swallowed quickly. 'But I was,' he added, his jaw jutting.

'The school team plays in a county league,' said Simon's mother.

I said goodbye to sleepless Simon and his mother with the sudden realization that schooldays would never again be described as happy and carefree. I could see the worry-creases developing around his eyes.

Mrs McNamara, the wife of a successful executive at a major car-component factory, came in next.

For more than half of her married life she had been struggling to keep up with her ambitious husband. As he marched ahead, gathering promotion easily and consistently, she hurried along behind him, struggling ever less successfully to keep up with his astonishing progress. When they had married they had lived in a small terraced house and their friends had been ordinary folk. As the years went by they moved, first to a small detached house, and then later to a large comfortable home with two bathrooms, a double garage and a garden fence too high to lean over. Mrs McNamara had never managed to come to terms with her husband's success.

'You need something to keep you busy,' I told her, after listening to her bemoaning the fact that her husband would no longer allow her to clean, shop, cook or wash for him but insisted on having a housekeeper.

'He won't let me get a job,' complained Mrs McNamara unhappily.

'You need to involve yourself in charitable works,' I told her. 'Immerse yourself in good works and you will feel wanted and appreciated.'

I gave her the address and telephone number of the local organizers for a charity concerned with the welfare of unfortunate children and suggested that she give them a ring.

'You phone them,' I told her, 'and get yourself involved in something meaningful that gives you a chance to meet people who need your support.'

Dr Oaks had four or five hundred people over the age of sixty to look after, and that inevitably meant that neither he nor I could keep an eye on more than a tiny fraction of this particularly susceptible part of the practice. We were, therefore, largely reliant upon relatives, neighbours and friends to keep us informed about people needing help. Being independent, many old people refuse to accept help from anyone, so there is always the very real danger that some of them may slowly starve to death, cold and unnoticed. All this explains why I moved quickly when I had a telephone call just before surgery one evening to tell me that no one had seen seventy-three-year-old Mrs Bartholomew for four days.

Mrs Bartholomew lived on the ninth floor of a newly built

nightmare, a concrete tribute to twentieth-century inhumanity. I drove furiously across the town to get there as quickly as possible. No angel of mercy flying with supercharged wings could have arrived more quickly. The lift, of course, was stuck on the seventeenth floor, according to the indicator, so I took to the stairs. It was early dusk but already they were littered with couples losing their innocence and chilliness in each other's arms.

I hammered and banged on Mrs Bartholomew's door without any success. One of the many problems with multi-storey flats is that you cannot go round to the back to peep in and check. Nor are there any windows that can be forced open by honest or dishonest visitors. The only thing you can do is to bang on the door and wait for a reply. When none came I moved across the hall to try Mrs Bartholomew's neighbours.

'Have you seen the lady who lives across the hall?' I asked a middle-aged man with greasy tousled hair, a pair of grubby pyjamas and a ferocious look that would have disheartened even the most enthusiastic encyclopaedia-salesman.

'Piss orf,' he snarled.

Chastened but not disheartened, I tried the next door. This time the occupant turned out to be a child of no more than four or five years, with a chocolate-smeared face and not a stitch of clothing.

'Where's your mum?' I asked.

'Gone to the launderette,' replied the child, a boy. Before I could ask any more questions he had rushed back into the flat. In the distance I could hear a television set chattering to itself. I waited another moment and then pulled the door to and went back to Mrs Bartholomew's flat. There was still no reply.

Every winter there are several horrifying stories in the newspapers of old people who have died alone and unnoticed. I was not prepared to let any of Dr Oaks' patients achieve such notoriety. I decided to take the law into my own hands and break down the door to the flat. I felt confident that any damage I did would be excused by the fact that I had saved Mrs Bartholomew's life.

Unfortunately the door proved a greater obstacle than I

would ever have suspected. Unlike the doors in all the films I've ever seen, it stoutly and bravely resisted my attempts to force it open. Clearly determined to protect Mrs Bartholomew and her possessions to the last splinter, it remained tightly shut. My shoulder, however, hurt so much that I felt sure I had broken it.

I raced down the stairs, interrupting once more the experimental biologists on the seventh and fourth floors, and rushed across the road to a nearby telephone-kiosk. Inevitably it was damaged, the receiver hanging down impotently. Furious and frustrated, I hammered the coin-box with my fist. To my surprise my feet were showered with a stream of copper and silver coins. I looked round quickly. The street was deserted apart from a couple of boys. I hurriedly picked up the coins and tried to push them back into the fractured coin-box. They would not even go in through the official coin-slots. Left with no option, I stuffed them into my pocket.

Policemen, like taxis, are rarely about when you need them. Park in a prohibited zone just long enough to post a letter and one will appear. Drive two miles an hour above the stated legal maximum and you can be sure that there is a police car on your tail. But actually look for a policeman and you can be sure they will have gone for tea. Pausing only long enough to cuff the boys, who were now busy trying to remove the front offside wheel from my car, I rushed into a fish-and-chip shop.

'Hey, young man,' complained a sweet old lady heavily laden with parcels and shopping-bags, 'kindly take your turn.'

'It's a matter of life and death,' I explained to her. I turned to the proprietor. 'Would you ring the police station?' I said. 'Ask them to send a patrol car around to Lewis Road straightaway.'

I don't know what the fish-shop owner told them, but a police car squealed to a halt less than five minutes later. I introduced myself to the two beefy officers who clambered out of it and explained the problem.

'She's collapsed, probably suffering from hypothermia,' I said. 'Can you help me get the door down?'

The policemen, anxious to find themselves lauded in the local newspapers, followed me up the nine flights of stairs with great enthusiasm. We didn't even bother to wait for the lift, and the couples on the fourth and seventh floors raced ahead of us when they saw the uniforms approaching. Their clothes lay scattered behind them like clues on a paper-chase.

We paused outside Mrs Bartholomew's door for a minute or so while one of the policemen knocked to make sure that in my absence the old lady had not made a spontaneous recovery, and then the two men from the patrol car took it in turns to persuade the door to abandon its stand.

Eventually they succeeded, and it burst open. They stood aside to let me lead the way into the flat. Clutching my black bag in one hand I picked my way gingerly down the neat and tidy hallway. I peered first into the bedroom, then into the kitchen and the bathroom, and finally into the living-room. There was nobody to be seen anywhere. The flat was beautifully warm.

We didn't have time to try to puzzle out the mystery, for the silence in the flat was suddenly shattered by the screams of the old lady from the fish-shop. She stood in the doorway shouting abuse. Her parcels lay around her where she had dropped them.

'Mrs Bartholomew?' I asked.

I was surprised by her command of invective, which seemed inexhaustible. The policemen, of course, were anxious to blame the whole episode on me, but I excused myself with mumbled apologies, pointing out that I was already late for surgery.

I descended the stairs two at a time. This time there was no sign of the activity which had enlivened my previous journeys. The two boys had turned their attention to the police car, which had been left unlocked. Already both front seats were disappearing into a nearby house.

The first patient waiting for me when I got back was Mrs McNamara.

'Did you ring those people at the Children's Society?' I asked her.

She nodded. She still looked as miserable and discontented as she had done when I'd seen her previously. I felt rather disappointed.

'Did they give you something to do?' I asked.

'They asked me to help with a collection they were organizing,' answered Mrs McNamara. 'They wanted me to go round from door to door, delivering envelopes, and to pick them up a few days later.'

'Well, that sounds very worthwhile,' I commented.

'I suppose it is,' agreed Mrs McNamara, 'but I couldn't do it. I'm too shy to go and knock on a complete stranger's front door.'

'Well, just take the envelopes back,' I said. 'Ask them to find you something else to do. Perhaps you could help in the office.'

'I can't do that,' whispered Mrs McNamara. 'I was too embarrassed to tell them I didn't have the nerve to do the job, so I accepted two hundred envelopes.'

'Two hundred?' I cried.

'And then I thought I'd put money in them all myself, but I've already used all my week's allowance and there are still nearly fifty envelopes left,' she said, tears appearing in her eyes.

I reached into my pocket for a handkerchief and bruised my knuckles on the change I'd picked up from the floor of the telephone-kiosk. Instead of a handkerchief I brought out a handful of copper and silver coins. Then another handful and then another handful.

'Take these,' I begged. 'Fill up the other fifty envelopes.'

Mrs McNamara, very nearly smiled, but the tears didn't stop.

twelve

As a bachelor doctor Dr Oaks solved his domestic problems in a rather unusual way. His laundry, for example, was done by Miss Jelks, a middle-aged spinster who collected dirty shirts, socks, towels, sheets and so on every Friday evening and returned them clean and crisp on Mondays, apparently desiring no greater reward than the knowledge that thanks to her efforts Dr Oaks always appeared in public well laundered. Clothing requiring repair would not, however, be returned directly to the doctor's drawers but would be handed to another gentle spinster in her sixties who was employed by the income tax authority and whose name was feared by wage-earners all over the town whose surnames began with the initials O or P. This unusual soul, a Miss Elspeth Morris, looked after Dr Oaks' income tax problems and also provided, totally without charge, an efficient and effective repair service. It was she who kept the buttons on Dr Oaks' shirts and the holes out of his socks, and it was she who turned his collars and his cuffs.

On Mondays and Fridays Mrs Law, a widow of indeterminate years, came into the house to cook evening meals for Dr Oaks. On Wednesdays and Saturdays evening meals were cooked by Mrs Pincer, an octogenarian of astonishing fitness who had a way with spaghetti and ravioli which never failed to astonish those who were fortunate enough to dine with Dr Oaks. Evening meals on Thursdays and Sundays were provided by Miss Fenshaw, a spinster whose skils with seafood deserved wider acclaim. On Tuesday evenings Dr Oaks would either eat out or open a tin of something. While I was living in the surgery we ate in only once, and on that occasion we succeeded only in burning a can of baked beans into such a state of disrepair that even a Wimpy bar would have thrown them away.

The house and surgery were both kept clean by Mrs Timms, who was paid a small sum each week for her pains. Mrs Timms was the only member of Dr Oaks' household who actually received payment for her endeavours, though I suspect that the money she spent on purchasing cleaning materials, household goods and other miscellaneous items more than ate up the money Dr Oaks paid her. The garden was kept in good repair and fully productive by Mrs Sollace and Mrs Carter, both ladies whose husbands had been somewhat carelessly discarded somewhere along the line, and both ladies of considerable wealth who hired gardeners to look after their own acreage but who considered it a privilege to be allowed to dig in Dr Oaks' garden. These two ladies kept Dr Oaks' kitchen well stocked with fruit and vegetables, which they told him had been grown in his own garden, but which had in fact been grown in theirs and transported across the town in the boots of their capacious motor-cars.

When Dr Oaks' ancient saloon was in the garage for repairs (a not uncommon happening occasioned mainly by the car's tendency to get involved in minor traffic accidents at least once a month), a Miss Simpson, an assistant in one of the town's major department stores, would take time off to act as chauffeur, taking the good doctor about the town in her shiny Mini, which was always specially cleaned and polished for the honour.

Shopping chores were regularly performed by a neighbour with a stomach disorder, who had the unlikely name of Mabel Gorridge, and who had long cherished a desire that her name might one day be changed to Mabel Oaks. She received a list from Dr Oaks every Saturday morning and delivered cardboard boxes filled with groceries every Saturday afternoon. Miss Gorridge was also responsible for looking after Dr Oaks' impressive collection of house-plants; she it was who watered and pruned them.

These ladies made up the basic household, but there were many others who helped from time to time. A Miss Roberts, for example, would apparently come in at Christmas every year with mince pies, Christmas pudding, Christmas cake and decorations. She would even bring a tree with her and insist on staying to do the decorations for that as well. The windows of both house and surgery were kept shining and clear by Albert Quaverley, the obedient husband of Emma Quaverley, sent by his wife once a fortnight to ply his trade without charge at the doctor's residence. The doctor's drains were kept clear and in excellent repair by Edward Good, the slightly truculent husband of Phyllis Good, who once sent the doctor a bill for his services. The cheque, sent by Dr Oaks by return post, was brought back by an apologetic Mrs Good.

It would be nice to be able to report that all these folk got on well together with the single aim of keeping Dr Oaks in good repair and working order. It would not, however, be the truth. There were frequent quarrels and squabbles which disturbed the tranquillity of the household – although Dr Oaks was only aware of a small number of these.

The Monday and Friday cook, Mrs Law, was something of a stickler for perfection, and all too often she would complain that the others were not pulling their weight. In particular she would complain about Mrs Timms and Miss Jelks. She frequently moaned that the carpets were dirty and the table-cloths poorly laundered, and once insulted Miss Jelks by bringing fresh napkins and tablecloths to the surgery from her own home.

Miss Gorridge, who had expectations of her very own, would quickly let her objections be known if she fancied that any of the others was pressing suit. Once, when Emma Quaverley took a thermos flask of soup in to an ailing Dr Oaks, Miss Gorridge sulked for the best part of a month, leaving Dr Oaks to do his own shopping. She only returned when she heard that Dr Oaks had been building a friendship with one of the checkout girls at the local supermarket.

Dr Oaks, I should point out, never led any of these ladies on. He accepted their kindnesses with great humility, regarding their labours as a privilege rather than a right, and never once did he make demands of any of them. He thanked them profusely for everything they did but would never have dreamt of complaining or arguing. As a result the ladies worked much harder than they would have done for any employer. Most of them were desperate for an admonition, for that would have given them greater confirmation that their efforts were at least noticed. Dr Oaks' gentle acceptance of their presence merely spurred them on to greater efforts.

This strangely assorted harem provided Dr Oaks with just about everything he required. He was kept fed and clothed and clean and tidy, and never allowed to worry about household matters. I acquired no knowledge at all of how Dr Oaks satisfied his more fundamental desires.

thirteen

At the back of Dr Oaks' house there was a small secluded garden surrounded by a six-foot fence. The garden itself was designed along simple lines. There was a well-kept lawn and a small kitchen-garden. There were no gnomes, fishponds or ornamental borders. The fence at the bottom of the garden protected Dr Oaks from the gaze of pedestrians passing along the road which ran parallel to the fence. The fences down the two sides of the garden protected Dr Oaks from the inquisitive eyes of his neighbours.

Only an extraordinary gale could have caused so much damage to it. The wind slowly wound itself up over a dull and dreary Saturday, and by the early evening it was rattling windows and scattering slates. Eventually it efficiently and mercilessly spread pieces of fence across lawn and kitchen-garden.

For a week after the damage was done Dr Oaks pored over gardening magazines and catalogues from fence-manufacturers. He had a pocket calculator balanced on his knee, and with the aid of that and a large notebook he tried to work out the best way to replace the missing fencing. Eventually he must have reached some conclusion for, quite suddenly one Wednesday morning, the small front garden was turned into a builder's yard. A huge pile of posts and pieces of fencing appeared as if by magic.

'I tried to get someone to come and put the fence up for me,' Dr Oaks told me. 'The first people I rang said they could come in three months' time, the second honestly admitted that they could not cope with any more orders and the third lot just laughed cruelly.' He shrugged. 'I decided to do it myself.'

'I'll give you a hand,' I offered boldly, not bothering to add that my last work with a carpenter's tools had been concluded at the age of twelve and that the result of my efforts, a wooden spade-scraper, had attracted little praise.

We began work early to give ourselves a chance of finishing before dusk. Our first problem was to get the fences and the fence-posts through to the back garden. Unhappily this entailed carrying every single piece of wood through the house. Our next problem was the discovery that Dr Oaks' only spade had suffered, probably as a result of simple old age, an unfortunate fracture. The result of the injury was that its handle was about eighteen inches long.

Still, we managed to make some progress. I dug several large holes in the garden, working under Dr Oaks' strategic advice, and then while he held the posts in place I pushed the earth I'd removed back into the holes. The result was quite pleasing. By the time we decided to break for coffee we had managed to put five fence-posts into position, and the task was beginning to look easier than I dared to hope.

We were not so jubilant when we tried to fit the pieces of fencing into the gaps between the posts. Normally, of course, the fences will simply fit into the spaces and the workman will nail the battens on to the posts. Our difficulty arose from the fact that when we had put the posts into the ground we had measured the distance from post to post without much thought. We had not allowed for the fact that the posts themselves were several inches wide. Naturally this meant that the fences were rather too large for the spaces available.

We solved this problem by fastening the fences to the sides of the posts instead of to the usual parts. The resultant stretch of fence looked rather unusual but it did have a certain amount of character. However, the error stayed with us for the rest of the construction, and by afternoon it became apparent that we would be about four feet short when we put up the last piece of fencing. Dr Oaks insisted that it didn't matter very much and that he had always wanted a gate through which he could get on to the road behind the house.

As we put the last few nails into position I suggested that we celebrate with a beer or two each. Dr Oaks agreed and, leaving him pulling the lawnmower out so that he could complete his day's work by making the garden look worthy of the fence, I drove to the nearest off-licence. I was stuck in there for twenty minutes while I waited for a fat lady in a pair of blue denim jeans to buy in food and drink for a party. When she'd finished I was lucky to find a few bottles of beer left on sale. For a while I had expected the worst.

At first when I got back I thought that Dr Oaks must have given up waiting and gone upstairs to have a bath. I called to him but got no reply; I walked briefly round the garden but could see no one. Then, suddenly feeling that something might be wrong, I ran upstairs, again calling to him. Again I got no reply. I went back down the stairs and out into the garden again. And then I found him. He was lying in the garden shed, a small flimsily built wooden shack which had somehow managed to survive the storm and which was used mainly as a garage for the lawnmower.

At first I thought he was dead.

He was sprawled on top of the lawnmower, which he had obviously just carried back into the shed, and his face was pale and covered with perspiration. His pulse was weak but definitely palpable, and I could feel his heart beating when I pushed my hand inside his sweat-stained gardening-shirt.

He opened his eyes as I moved him away from the lawnmower and laid him on his back.

'It came on suddenly,' said Dr Oaks. I hadn't expected to hear him speak, and his voice startled me.

'Just lie still,' I told him. 'You've been doing too much.'

He nodded.

'I'll get my bag,' I told him, 'and give you an injection.'

'No,' said Dr Oaks. 'The pain is going off. I don't need anything.'

'Sure?' I asked.

'Sure,' said Dr Oaks quietly.

I'd dealt with scores of seriously ill patients, many of them very close to death, but never before with anyone I knew well. Like all doctors I found that my detached and calm clinical manner was in danger of being replaced by good old-fashioned panic.

'I'll call an ambulance,' I said.

'Take me in the car,' said Dr Oaks. 'I don't need an ambulance.'

'You can't walk,' I told him. 'You need to keep still.'

'You help me,' said Dr Oaks. 'I can make it.'

'You keep still!' I shouted at him.

'All right, all right . . .' he sighed, closing his eyes and keeping quiet.

'I'll bring my car around the back,' I promised, 'and take you out through the gap in the fence.'

He nodded but said nothing. I took off my jacket and covered him with it to keep him warm and ran through the house back to my car. I left in a tyre-burning skid and drove round to the back. Then I leapt out of the car again, dashed through the spacous gap in the fence and went back to where Dr Oaks was lying.

'I'm going to carry you out to the car,' I told him. 'You can lie in the back.'

I was surprised to find out just how light my employer was. I managed to lift him without any problem and I put him in the back of the car without difficulty.

'I knew that gap in the fence would come in handy,' he murmured as I quietly shut the car door on him.

The journey to the hospital took about six minutes when it would normally have taken a quarter of an hour. I tried to drive smoothly but quickly, and kept my finger on the horn in the vain hope that a police patrol would stop us. I had an idea that, if they did, they might give us an escort through the traffic.

When we arrived I leapt out and rushed into the casualty department to find a porter to help me lift Dr Oaks out of the car. At the same time I called to the clerk at the reception desk, telling her that I had a patient for the coronary care unit. Then I went back to the car with a porter and a stretcher. We went back into the casualty department, carrying Dr Oaks between us.

I stayed with my mentor while the medical registrar and consultant physician on call fussed around him. They fitted leads to his chest and to his arms and legs, listened to him with an electronic stethoscope and gave him an injection of something or other despite his protests. I say I stayed with him, but in fact I stood and worried outside the door, marching up and down like an expectant father whose wife is suffering a difficult birth.

Eventually they both came outside and I caught the consultant by the sleeve.

'How is he?' I demanded.

'I don't think there's anything more you can do here,' the consultant said. I had never seen him before and knew neither his face nor the name on his white plastic badge.

'He's all right?' I asked.

'He's had a heart attack,' the medical registrar told me. 'He's resting now. I suggest you come back tomorrow.'

'You think he'll make it?' I demanded.

'We must pray,' said the consultant with an earnest look on his face. 'But God is our ultimate superior. He will make the final decision.'

I could have managed without the sermon but did not have the spiritual energy to argue with the consultant. While he and the registrar stalked off I waited in the corridor. Ten minutes or so later a diminutive lady in a green overall darted past me.

'Hello, Mrs Faversham,' I said automatically.

'Oh, Doctor, fancy seeing you here,' said Mrs Faversham, a patient of Dr Oaks who had brought her varicose eczema along for me to study on several occasions. 'I didn't know you worked here.'

'I don't,' I told her. 'Dr Oaks is in there. He's had a heart attack.'

'Oh, no,' said Mrs Faversham with genuine concern.

'Have a look and see how he is, will you?' I asked.

Mrs Faversham nodded and darted into the coronary care unit. As she opened the door I saw for a brief moment an array of the instruments and machines which today are so much a part of hospital medicine.

She was gone for about two minutes and then she was back by my side.

'I've had a look at him,' she whispered conspiratorially.

'How does he look?' I asked.

'He's having a nice sleep,' said Mrs Faversham.

'Has he got a drip up?' I asked.

'You mean one of those tubes in his arm?' asked the cleaning lady.

'That's right,' I nodded.

'No,' said Mrs Faversham.

'Good,' I said. 'That's a good sign.'

'He really looks quite well, Doctor,' said Mrs Faversham. 'He's the best of the ones in there anyway.'

'You're sure?' I asked. 'You're sure he looks all right?'

'He looks fine,' said Mrs Faversham. 'I'm sure there's nothing to worry about, Doctor.'

'Thank you,' I said, pressing her hand. I made my way slowly back to the main entrance and from tehre I walked round to where my car was parked outside the casualty department. I had left it unlocked, and when I got there a porter was busy pushing it to one side.

'You can't leave this here, mate,' he cried. 'It's in the way.'

I apologized and drove slowly home.

fourteen

I telephoned the hospital the following morning and they told me that Dr Oaks had had a peaceful night. In the afternoon they let me see him for a few minutes.

'Just a warning,' he said. 'It was just a warning.'

'It was a waste of time standing in the queue to get that beer,' I said. 'Next time, tell me in advance if you're going to collapse, will you?'

'Sorry about that,' smiled Dr Oaks. He reached out and patted my arm. Our hands met for a moment, and I gripped his fingers tightly in my fist.

'I'll be home in a day or two,' he said.

'You'll be home when you're fit,' I said.

'No, really,' said Dr Oaks. 'It wasn't a bad one.'

'You stay here for a few days,' I insisted. 'I'm not bathing you.'

'There's a horrible thought,' he said, screwing up his face. 'I'l stay here a few days.'

We talked for a few moments about this and that. I told him how kind Mrs Faversham had been.

'Doctors sometimes forget what medicine is all about,' he said thoughtfully.

We talked a little longer about the practice, and then it was time to go.

'Is the fence still up?' asked Dr Oaks as I stood up.

'Still up?' I asked.

'It didn't blow down during the night?'

'Of course not,' I said, 'but the lawn grew.'

Dr Oaks grinned broadly, closed his eyes and settled back to sleep. I tiptoed out of the room.

During the course of the next ten days I telephoned or visited the hospital at least once every day. Dr Oaks continued to make slow but good progress, and even the consultant physician agreed that he was improving.

As luck would have it, while Dr Oaks was away Miss Whitby came back to the surgery. She asked me to prescribe her the contraceptive pill.

I began by studying her medical record.

'There doesn't seem to be anything here which would stop you taking the Pill,' I told her.

'Oh, good,' she said, with a wriggle.

'Is there any history of diabetes in your family?'

'No,' said Miss Whitby.

'Have you ever had any trouble with veins?'

Miss Whitby shook her head.

'Are your breasts all right?' I asked, feeling myself begin to blush.

'I've had no complaints yet,' said Miss Whitby. 'Do you want to look at them?'

'No, I'll take your word for it,' I said. 'I'll just have to take your blood pressure.' I stood up and walked round the desk. 'I'll have to go and fetch another stethoscope,' I told her. 'Mine isn't working.' I darted out and poked my head into the waiting-room to call for Miss Williams.

'Give me two minutes and then come and tell me there's an emergency call on the telephone,' I told her.

I went back into the surgery. As I'd expected, Miss Whitby had already stripped to the waist. St Anthony would have found the temptation testing and, not for the first time, I cursed the rules which differentiate between social and medical contacts.

'I thought you had to get another stethoscope?' said Miss Whitby.

'This one's apparently been mended,' I replied. I took her blood pressure with my eyes half-shut and then scurried back behind the desk.

'That's fine,' I said, writing out a prescription. 'I'll give you six months' supply of the Pill.' I took a small booklet out of a drawer. 'This will tell you all about the pills,' I said.

'Is that it?' asked Miss Whitby. She was still naked from the waist up and she made no attempt to hide the fact that when sunbathing she wore nothing. Her tan was quite perfectly even.

Miss Williams burst into the room just in time.

'Doctor,' she cried breathlessly. 'There's an emergency!'

I leapt to my feet and followed her out of the room. 'Thank you, Miss Whitby,' I shouted over my shoulder. 'Must rush.'

I hid in the lavatory until Miss Williams confirmed that the sun-worshipper had left the surgery, and then I crept back in to finish the evening's work.

'That was pretty realistic,' I told Miss Williams. 'You nearly had me fooled. I thought there really was an emergency.'

'Well, there was, wasn't there?' she said with a wry smile.

I was on duty again that evening. The surgery went on and on and, when I'd finished, two calls had already come in. One was for me to visit an elderly man who had collapsed and the other was to visit a pregnant woman who thought she was losing her baby. Both were genuine, and by the time I got back it was nearly ten. I ate a tin of spaghetti rings for supper and washed them down with one of the bottles of beer I'd bought the previous week.

It had been a long hard day and I fell asleep as soon as I had got into bed. I woke again what seemed only minutes later, although when I looked at my watch I saw that the time was nearly two in the morning.

'I'm sorry to bother you, Doctor,' said the caller, 'but I can't get off to sleep.'

'Have you got a pain?' I asked.

'No,' said the caller, 'I have no pains.'

'Do you normally sleep all right?' I asked.

'I've had difficulty once or twice recently.'

'Have you been to the surgery?'

'No, not yet. Do you think I should?' asked the caller.

'I think you should,' I said sleepily.

'Have you got any suggestions for tonight?' asked the patient.

'Not really,' I replied with restraint.

'Oh, well, never mind. I'll read a book,' said the caller.

'Could you give me your name and address?' I asked. 'Just for the record.'

The caller gave me his name, address and telephone number, and I jotted them all down on the notepad I keep by my bed.

Later in the night I was woken again. This time it was around five-thirty when the telephone rang, and the caller turned out to be a man working nights at a local factory who wanted to know what time the morning surgery started. I told him and put the telephone down again fairly quickly. As I did so I knocked my notepad off the bedside table. When I reached to pick it up I noticed the name and telephone number of my insomniac caller, and I couldn't resist the temptation which came my way.

The telephone rang for what seemed like a lifetime before it was answered.

'Hello,' I said, when the sleepy voice eventually greeted me. 'This is Doctor Vernon.'

'Doctor?' said the man I'd called. 'What do you want, Doctor?'

'You rang me earlier,' I said. 'You told me you couldn't get to sleep.'

'Oh, yes,' said the man.

'I thought I'd ring back and see how you were getting on,' I said.

'I was fast asleep,' said the man. 'You woke me up.' He sounded very hurt.

'Oh dear,' said I, 'what a pity. I just wanted to make sure that you were all right.' And then I put the telephone down again.

The following morning we heard that Dr Oaks was being allowed home from hospital. He had made a marvellous recovery from his heart attack. Miss Williams went out and bought two cream doughnuts and we had a small celebration after the morning surgery.

fifteen

During six and a half years working in hospitals, both as a medical student and as a doctor, I'd seen very little skin disease. Skin problems are not the sort of ailments usually brought along to hospitals. I had attended a few out-patient clinics where, along along with a dozen others, I'd caught glimpses of horrific rashes and frightening arrays of spots. But it wasn't until I started work as a general practitioner that I discovered just how much out-of-condition skin there is walking around the streets, well covered by nylon, wool, cotton or silk. I slowly began to realize that at every surgery I would see patients with eczema, dermatitis or simple acne. Gradually it dawned on me that, although patients with tremendous deformities and painful, chronic diseases may fight on bravely, many patients will fall apart mentally and spiritually when they find a small skin blemish marring an otherwise perfect complexion.

Joy, for example, came into surgery looking really glum. I suspected that she might have found a lump somewhere or that she might be worried about an unwanted pregnancy. I was quite wrong. When she'd settled down she reluctantly took off her gloves and held out her hands for me to examine.

'It's my hands, Doctor,' she said. 'They look awful. I daren't go out or even take my gloves off. I haven't been in to work all week. I feel so ashamed. What is it? Is it leprosy?'

I suppose to an ordinary proud owner the hands did look in poor condition. A bright red rash covered most of the fingers and the two palms.

'Does it itch?' I asked.

Joy nodded vigorously. 'I hardly slept last night,' she admitted. 'It's been driving me crazy.'

'What's your job?' I asked her, wondering if contact with some industrial solution could have caused the rash. I had already learnt that a good proportion of the people who visit a doctor have a disease or disorder which they have contracted at work.

'I'm an apprentice hairdresser,' the girl told me. 'I've only had the job for about three months and if I stay off work now I don't know what they'll say.'

'Do you have to do the shampoos and rinses and things?' I asked. I do not have a wide knowledge of what goes on in ladies' hairdressing salons.

Joy nodded. 'We take it in turns, but I spend quite a lot of time with my hands in water,' she agreed.

'It isn't the water that does the damage,' I told her, 'but it could well be the shampoo or one of the other substances you put in the water.'

Reluctantly, Joy took a few more days off work, and when she came into the surgery a week later her hands were almost completely cured.

'I hardly had to use the cream you gave me,' she said. 'They just seemed to get better by themselves.'

'I'm afraid that just about proves it,' I had to tell her. 'You're allergic to something you use at work. The only real way of proving that it *is* something at work is to go back to work and see what happens to your hands,' I went on. 'If they get bad again, then I'm afraid you'll probably have to give up hairdressing for good.'

Joy went back to work to give it another try, and within forty-eight hours she was back in the surgery. I had to sign her off work and advise her to change her job.

'What exactly was it?' asked Joy, as I wrote out the sick-note. 'Can I get it again or can anyone else get it off me?'

'It was a type of eczema or dermatitis,' I told her. 'It was in your case a contact dermatitis caused by some substance coming into contact with your skin. If you keep away from the sort of things used in hairdressing salons, then you certainly shouldn't get it again. You can't give it to anyone else, and you can't catch it off anyone, either.'

'There are lots of things to which people are allergic,' I told Joy. 'Some people are allergic to grasses and they have hay fever; some are allergic to the metal in watch-straps. I have met women who are allergic to the nickel buckles on their brassières and I have seen people who are allergic to certain dyestuffs. A disease called the Christmas syndrome was once reported in the

70

British Medical Journal; it's an allergy reaction which occurs after Christmas, when new gifts have been used for the first time. There are always a number of people who are allergic to the new soaps, clothes, talcs and perfumes they have been given.'

'I suppose it's pretty obvious, then, when someone is allergic to something,' said Joy, taking the sick-note from me.

'Not always,' I confessed. 'It's sometimes very difficult to track down the cause.'

'You make it sound like tracking down a criminal,' said Joy, 'as if you were a detective!'

We both laughed, but I sat for a moment after she'd gone and thought about what she'd said. She was quite right. Practising medicine is in many ways similar to being a detective. Conan Doyle, for example, the creator of Sherlock Holmes, based his character on a doctor at Edinburgh Medical School. His model was a man called Joseph Bell, who would make an invariably accurate guess as to a patient's occupation, birthplace and hobby. At my own medical school there was an elderly doctor who could not understand the many pieces of complex machinery used by younger physicians, but who used similar techniques to make many accurate diagnoses within very short periods of meeting patients. I remember once sitting in a clinic with him and watching him make a diagnosis of diabetes mellitus (sugar diabetes) as a man walked into the room. When I expressed amazement, the wise doctor pointed out that the man had a white stain on his shoe and his trouser leg which looked powdery, and was almost certainly caused by sugar-loaded urine spilling and falling short of its target.

That elderly doctor told me once about a forensic scientist called Sydney Smith who was sent three small bones by the police for his comments. The bones had been recovered from a disused well, and the police simply wanted to know whether or not they were human bones. 'The bones', Smith said, 'are those of a young woman. She was short and slim, aged between twenty-three and twenty-five when she died, which was at least three months ago. She had probably had at least one pregnancy, perhaps more. Her left leg was shorter than her right, and she walked with a pronounced limp. She probably had polio when a child. She was killed by a shotgun loaded with home-made slugs, fired in an upward direction from a range of about three yards by a killer standing or sitting in front of her and slightly to her left. She was not killed outright but died about seven to ten days later, probably from septic peritonitis due to the shooting.'

The report, part fact and part supposition, was correct in all details, and it is said to have later led to the arrest of the culprit.

The patient who followed Joy also needed a detective as much as a doctor. She was a nine-month-old baby whose parents had only recently come to live in the town. The husband had a job in a local car factory, and I had seen the wife once before when she'd come along complaining of a mild summer cough.

'Helen fell down the step into the kitchen,' Mrs Forrest began, when I arrived. 'She was lying in the dining-room watching me do the washing and she just seemed to roll down into the kitchen.'

I had a careful look at the girl and could find nothing much wrong. There were a few minor scratches and bruises but nothing else. I couldn't find any broken bones or signs of severe injury.

The scratches and bruises which were present, however, did not look quite right. They were not the sort of bruises and scratches which a baby would get after falling down a single step. After all, babies are fairly resilient creatures and are usually wrapped up in lots of shock-absorbing clothes.

'How many steps did she fall down?' I asked.

Mrs Forrest studied her fingernails intently.

'What were you doing when she fell?' I asked.

Mrs Forrest pushed her hair away from her eyes and scratched the side of her nose.

'Has she fallen before?' I asked, still trying.

'No, Doctor,' whispered Mrs Forrest.

'Was it slippery where she fell?'

Suddenly, to my surprise, Mrs Forrest burst into tears.

'I didn't mean to do it, Doctor,' she sobbed. 'Helen just wouldn't stop crying, and I lost my temper.'

I was flabbergasted and didn't say anything.

'I tore all her clothes off and pushed her into the sink which was full of cold water,' said Mrs Forrest. 'I thought it would stop her crying.'

I still didn't say anything. Mainly because I couldn't think of anything to say.

'Will I have to go to the police?' asked Mrs Forrest. 'Will they take my baby from me?'

'No, of course not,' I told her. 'It isn't my job to report you to the police. It's my job to try to help you both.'

I talked to her for a little while longer and, while she was there, fixed up an urgent appointment with a paediatrician so that she could get expert advice on how to handle her baby. It became quite clear that she herself was quite depressed, so I also started her off on a course of tablets which I hoped would help her. I also made arrangements for the health visitor to call round and offer assistance.

After Mrs Forrest had gone, promising to return in a couple of days, I breathed a deep sigh of relief. If that young mother hadn't broken down like a guilty witness being cross-examined by a belligerent and insistent Perry Mason, I'd have never realized just why Helen's scratches and bruises didn't seem quite right.

I saw a third patient that day who convinced me that Joy had been right when she'd talked about doctors being like detectives. This patient was a woman in her late fifties who was staying with a young mother of two who was on Dr Oaks' list.

'Can you come round straightaway?' asked Mrs Creighton when I answered the telephone that afternoon. 'I think my mother-in-law has had a heart attack.'

I rushed round there at tremendous speed, leaving dozens of motorists leaning on their car horns in anguish.

'Mother's had the pain for a couple of hours now,' said Mrs Creighton, leading me up the stairs of their smart semi-detached house. 'It came on at about lunchtime,' she told me as we passed the smallest of the three flying ducks, 'and it doesn't seem to have got any better at all.'

Mother-in-law was lying in bed surrounded by newspapers

and magazines. The television set was on and was clearly holding at least one viewer's attention.

'This is the doctor, Mother,' said Mrs Creighton.

Mother-in-law said nothing but watched carefully as the man on the television described how to make a passable imitation of a steam-engine with nothing more than an old washing-up liquid dispenser, an egg carton and a cornflake packet.

'The doctor's come to see you, Mother,' shouted Mrs Creighton. This attracted a brief flicker of attention. Mother-in-law looked away from the television for a moment, held out an arm and then turned back to the screen. I presumed that I was expected to take her pulse or blood pressure more or less *in absentia*. Since I'd left a boiling-hot cup of coffee and a few quid's worth of rubber behind, I didn't feel too much like waiting for the man to finish his speech, so I asked Mrs Creighton to turn the television off.

That didn't gain me much of a reputation as a charmer, but it did encourage Mrs Creighton's mother-in-law to take some slight interest in my presence. I took her pulse, measured her blood pressure, listened to her heart, examined her abdomen, studied her pupils and tapped her chest before finally pronouncing her quite fit and certainly able to make her steam-engine, should she ever find herself the proud owner of an empty washing-up liquid dispenser, egg carton and cornflake packet.

'Well, what is it, then?' demanded the old lady. 'I've got a pain, whether or not you can find anything wrong with me.'

I scratched my head and sat down on the arm of an easy chair which was positioned next to the bed. I was about to begin a series of questions about bowel habits, previous complaints and family histories, designed to give me time to think, when I suddenly found myself staring at a chamber-pot underneath the bed. The armchair, unaccustomed to such a badly distributed weight on one arm, had ejected me summarily as an interloper.

'Well, let's have another look at your chest,' I said, still lying half-hidden behind the upturned armchair. 'You show me just where the pain is.' I struggled to my feet as Mrs Creighton helped her mother-in-law to pull her nightie up again. Then I bent forward to examine the area under dispute. It was only then that I saw the small red vesicles which gave me the clue to the answer. Mrs Creighton's mother-in-law had *Herpes zoster*, a disease more popularly known as shingles.

I'd made the mistake of allowing Mrs Creighton's amateur diagnosis to put me off the track. She had told me that her mother-in-law had had a heart attack, so I'd been looking for evidence of a heart attack. It was only at the second attempt that I saw the evidence which led to the correct diagnosis. (Shingles, of course, can mimic almost any kind of pain. Similarly there are other diseases which can confuse and mystify. Pain in the shoulder, for example, can be caused by a gall bladder problem. Pain in the leg can be caused by a lesion in the back. Pain in the hand can be caused by something in the chest.)

I told the patient what was wrong with her, prescribed some suitable pain-killing tablets and then started to leave. I was within a yard of the bedroom door when I caught my foot in the edge of a bedside rug. I went crashing forward and landed on my side in the wardrobe, the door of which had been left open. I hastily untagled my head from the wide variety of underthings with which it had been mixed up, and got on to the stairs without further ado. As I descended I heard the patient talking to her daughter-in-law.

'He's very nice,' she said, 'but he's a bit clumsy, isn't he?'

sixteen

'There was a telephone call from a Mr George Partridge,' said Miss Williams when I'd finished the morning surgery. 'He wanted to know if you'd be able to see him this evening.'

'Well, there is a surgery,' I said, 'so if he comes to that I'll see him then.'

'I rather think he was hoping that you would be able to give him an appointment,' said Miss Williams.

I sighed and grunted something rude. One of the problems

with running an open surgery is that there are so many people who feel they should be excused the indignity of having to wait that, if they were all given appointments, there would hardly be anybody present at the open surgeries.

'Do I know him?' I asked. 'Or does Dr Oaks know him?'

'I don't think either of you knows him,' said Miss Williams. 'He's Mr Bennett's new partner.'

'Mr Bennett?' I asked. 'Who's Mr Bennett?'

'The vet,' replied Miss Williams with great patience.

'Do vets rank with nurses, dentists and clergymen, and merit special treatment?' I asked.

'I think they might,' nodded Miss Williams. She had clearly been impressed by the young vet. I asked her to ring him back and get him to come along at the end of surgery.

'There's only one urgent call for this morning,' said Miss Williams when I'd finished signing the repeat prescriptions, letters and miscellaneous forms with which I had become so familiar. 'It's for Mr Sunderland. His daughter-in-law is getting worried about him.'

I'd got to know Mr Sunderland quite well over the previous week or so. He had been slowly deteriorating for some time since his release from the local hospital, where they had diagnosed a cancer of the pancreas. The hospital doctors had attempted to treat the growth without success and they'd sent him home to spend his last few days in peace and in his own surroundings.

It was a decision which had pleased the old man, who'd insisted from the start that he be told the truth, and who had accepted the fact that he was dying with the mental strength you'd expect of a man who had almost singlehandedly built up a scrap-metal business worth a small fortune.

It had been three days since I'd seen him and I was surprised at the change which had taken place. He seemed much paler, much more haggard and much weaker. And yet at the same time he looked quite contented. I sat on the edge of his bed and took his hand.

'You're looking pleased with yourself,' I said, feeling for his pulse, more as a matter of habit than out of any genuine medical interest.

Mr Sunderland nodded.

'You look like the damned cat who's drunk the cream off the top of the milk,' I told him.

A grin slowly spread across the parched and wrinkled face before me. 'I've been here a long time, Doctor,' he said.

'Well, you've got to get your strength back,' I said. Even though I knew that he knew he was dying, and I knew that he knew that I knew that he knew he was dying, I still persisted with the age-old lies. They were a help to me, and I think they were probably a help to him. They helped us to brush under the carpet an ugly truth which we could manage without.

'They stopped me drinking and they stopped my cigars,' said Mr Sunderland. 'They told me they weren't good for me.' He spoke with the heavy irony I'd come to know so well.

I didn't say anything. I'd tried to persuade his son and daughter-in-law to let him have a drop of whisky and a cigar whenever he wanted. There is little point in banning the cause when the damage has been done.

'But they were out last night at some dinner organized by the Round Table,' said Mr Sunderland with a wink.

'Don't tell me you had a party!' I laughed. 'Didn't they remember to lock the cocktail cabinet?'

'I don't know,' said Mr Sunderland. 'I had some brought in.'

He reached down beneath the bedclothes, and a moment later produced a pair of bright red panties, edged with black lace and decorated with small pink flowers. 'A friend of mine brought them in,' said Mr Sunderland. 'I kept them as a last souvenir.'

'Did they come like that or as a wrapping?' I asked incredulously.

'As a wrapping,' said Mr Sunderland. 'I still have some friends who are ready to do me favours.'

Not being able to think of anything to say, I just took him by the hand and congratulated him silently.

'You don't think any less of me, Doctor, do you?' asked Mr Sunderland.

I shook my head.

'The fellow with his scythe is beating you lot with your scalpels,' said Mr Sunderland. 'I wanted to refresh my memory a little before I died.'

I reached out and picked up the red panties. They seemed delightfully out of place.

'I'll be back to see you later in the week,' I promised.

'I'm not going anywhere,' said Mr Sunderland, stuffing his souvenir back underneath the bedclothes.

When I had finished the evening surgery I put my prescription pad and pen back in the desk drawer, having forgotten my appointment with Mr Partridge. Fortunately, Miss Williams had a far more reliable memory and she managed to catch me before I left. Moaning a little, I settled down and read one of the medical journals while I waited.

I was about to give up and leave, when Mr Partridge finally turned up.

'I really am most dreadfully sorry,' said the vet. 'I was stuck with some damned Pekinese which had a gash on its forehead.'

'That's all right,' I lied cheerfully. 'What can I do for you '

'There isn't anything really *wrong* with me,' sighed Mr Partridge, 'but nothing much seems to be right either.'

I said nothing but prepared myself for a lengthy tale of woe.

'Things aren't very good at home,' he complained. 'I don't seem to get on very well with my wife.'

'How long have you been married ' I asked.

'Seven years,' said Mr Partridge. 'They say seven years is the danger point, don't they?'

'Any children?' I asked.

'Two,' said Mr Partridge, 'a boy aged three and a girl aged four.'

'Do you argue a lot?'

'The wife and I?'

I nodded.

'We seem always to be arguing. She doesn't seem to care about anything very much. The house is always dirty, and I'm ashamed to bring anybody home. When we're going out she always moans and complains that she's got nothing to wear, despite the fact that I give her as much to spend on clothes as I can, and then she takes so long to get ready that it's rarely worth going out. The pictures will have started or the dinner will have reached the last course by the time we get there.'

78

'Mmm,' I nodded thoughtfully.

'We used to have a good relationship,' said the vet. 'When I met her she was full of life and always bright and cheerful.'

'How long had you known her?' I asked.

'Before we married?'

'Before you married.'

'About a year, I suppose,' the vet answered. 'We met while I was working as an assistant just after I'd qualified. Life seemed to be all fun and laughter in those days.'

'How about the physical side of your marriage,' I asked, using the well-tried euphemism.

'You mean sex?'

'Sex,' I confirmed.

'It used to be very good,' said Mr Partridge, 'but these days we don't bother. She's usually got the proverbial headache.'

'How about work?' I asked.

'I'm a vet,' said the vet.

'Yes, I know you're a vet,' I explained. 'What I wondered was, do you enjoy your work?'

'Not really,' said Mr Partridge. 'My senior partner is a tartar. He always makes sure I visit the crotchety old women with sick poodles while he visits the farms and does all the decent jobs. I hate old ladies and I detest poodles.'

'What about hobbies?' I asked, desperate to keep the conversation going. I find it difficult to act the part of father-confessor, and I survive unhappily in the knowledge that in the wrong ears even the lightest and most flippant comment can cause chaos.

'I used to play rugby,' said Mr Partridge, 'but my wife complained after having to wash my shorts and shirt, so I packed it in.'

'Nothing else?'

'She complained about the socks as well.'

'No, I mean, no other hobbies?'

'I have a radio-controlled aeroplane,' said the vet, 'but I tried it out in a field in the country once, and afterwards a farmer complained to Mr Bennett that I'd frightened two of his cows and ruined their milk yield.'

'I can see that wouldn't do you any good,' I agreed.

'I sometimes think life isn't worth living,' said Mr Partridge suddenly.

'Do you ever feel like doing anything silly?' I asked, carefully using another euphemism instead of the fearful word 'suicide'.

Mr Partridge brightened a little. 'I do sometimes,' he said. 'Sometimes I think I'd like to murder my wife.'

Startled, I leant forward, and the pencil with which I was doodling on my prescription pad snapped in two.

'Of course, I wouldn't,' said the vet. 'I'd have to sit in court while her mother gave evidence for hours and hours. To cap it all, my car wouldn't start this morning,' he went on, after a pause.

I sat perfectly still and said nothing.

'I had to do my calls on an old bicycle I borrowed from Mr Bennett,' said the young vet.

'How about food?' I asked.

The vet looked at his watch and shook his head. 'The wife will have cooked,' he said.

'I meant your appetite,' I said. This seemed to be another conversation I was losing control of, and I was desperately looking for a symptom I could treat.

'My appetite is fine, but my wife's cooking is terrible,' said Mr Partridge. 'She ruins cornflakes.'

'Do you sleep well?' I asked, still putting off the moment when I would have to make a contribution to the conversation.

The vet nodded.

'You don't wake up early in the mornings?'

The vet shook his head.

The conversation was grinding to a halt.

'You don't wake up in the night?'

The vet shook his head again.

The conversation had reached its nadir.

'You don't have difficulty in getting off to sleep?'

The shake of the head was almost imperceptible.

We stared across the desk at each other for about an hour and a half, or so it seemed, and then the vet suddenly banged his fist down on the desk, making my fountain pen roll off the blotter on to the floor.

'You're absolutely right, you know,' he said as I tried to repair the bent nib of my pen. 'I've been far too negative about all this.'

I looked up in surprise.

'I've really been rather weak about everything,' Mr Partridge continued. 'I simply need to take a firmer line. I need to be firm with my wife and with old Bennett.'

I nodded.

'I must make it clear to them both that I've had enough of being used as a doormat,' said Mr Partridge.

I abandoned my fountain pen and nodded again vigorously.

'Thank you, thank you,' said the vet, leaping to his feet and extending a hand across the desk.

I reached out and shook it.

'I'm extremely grateful, Doctor,' said the vet. 'You've saved my wife's life.'

I shrugged my shoulders in self-deprecation.

'I shan't forget your help,' he promised hurriedly, leaving the surgery. I heard him curse as he leapt on to his bicycle, and then he was gone.

I forgot the vet's promise immediately but the vet didn't. Ignorant of the fact that I'm so fearful of anything on four legs that can bark that, unless Cerberus is kept on a very short lead, I'll be stranded for ever more on this side of the Styx, Mr Partridge sent me a very large and hungry-looking hound as a gift. At first I thought it was a full grown dog. It was only when I showed the gift to Dr Oaks that I discovered that I'd been given a Great Dane puppy. Miss Williams earned my everlasting gratitude by persuading her neighbour, a retired major, to give the animal a home.

seventeen

In ancient Egypt a list of herbs was made which included no less than 975 recipes for medicinal compounds. In the first century AD a Greek wrote a book listing 600 individual plants, and in ancient Arabia physicians mixed up to sixty or seventy plants in each compound.

By the seventeenth century rhubarb was so popular that it cost three times as much as opium. It was brought from Asia to Europe and considered so important that eventually the Royal Society awarded an annual prize to the man who could grow the most British rhubarb. Inevitably, seas of rhubarb swayed in the British wind, and the prize had to be withdrawn.

In the nineteenth century Sir William Gull, an eminent physician, worried by the claims being made by many quacks who believed that they had discovered cures for rheumatic fever, published a tongue-in-cheek paper extolling the virtues of mint as a cure for rheumatics. He chose mint at random and was amazed and dismayed to see that his 'joke' became a fashionable treatment.

Today many people believe in the efficacy of herbs. They use seaweed, grapes, beetroot and lettuce to help get rid of their ailments. Dandelions are used for getting rid of excessive fluid, marigolds are used for depression and foxgloves help heart conditions. There is a great deal of sense in the general use of plants as treatment.

Betty Bourne was an enthusiastic herbalist; she believed wholeheartedly in the power of the plant. I knew her only because she tempered her belief in the powr of herbs with an appreciation of the value of science. She would happily accept a prescription for a bottleful of pills or medicine.

She lived with her three sons in a condemned terraced house which adjoined a temporary car-park in the centre of the town. The town planners had hopes of turning Mrs Bourne's two-up-and-two-down into a forecourt for a twenty-storey building designed to give a home to every rubber plant and administrator in the county. Their ambitions had been thwarted by Mrs Bourne's reluctance to accept the council's offer of a home on the sixteenth floor of a block of flats two miles out of town.

Though she looked as if she had long since seen the onset of middle-age, Mrs Bourne was in reality nearer to thirty than forty. Her husband had disappeared after siring three sons, leaving the family to fend for itself. Betty never gave anything away about her former spouse, but Miss Williams once told me that he had been sorely missed by the local constabulary after his disappearance. They had looked to him to help them keep their arrest figures looking good. His criminal adventures rarely went unrewarded by the courts.

Mrs Bourne's three children all attended a local school. The youngest, William, was just six, yet he had already proved himself a capable and admirable artist. His work had been displayed in the town hall after he had won first prize in an art competition organized by the local newspaper.

Maurice, an eight-year-old, was musically talented. He played piano in the school orchestra, and the music teacher had strongly assured me that with a little luck Maurice could win a scholarship to a major music academy. The third brother, Peter, was no artist, but he was a footballer with more than average skills. He had played for the school and for the junior county side, and Betty had told me she felt convinced that he would play for England.

Despite Betty's appreciation of the healing powers of plants, all three sons were regularly brought along to the surgery whenever they had anything wrong with them. Betty Bourne had too much faith in her sons to risk their future on a single philosophy. She would feed them herbs and expected Dr Oaks or myself to prescribe for them as well.

Not that she confined her faith to these two theories. Betty Bourne was eclectic and catholic if nothing else. It was she who told me that amulets made of coffin nails, hinges or handles have curative properties and will get rid of the cramp. She also claimed that epilepsy can be cured by persuading the sufferer to pick peonies! She believed that cobwebs stop severe bleeding, that flowers in the bedroom at night are dangerous, that brown eggs are more nutritious than white eggs and that it is desperately unlucky to call the doctor on a Friday.

She was quite prepared to spread her beliefs to cover any sugggestion likely to promise her children greater health. For herself, however, Betty Bourne was strangely uncaring. She rarely asked for advice about her own health, and preferred to buy bottle after bottle of medicine either from the herbalist's shop in the town or from the local chemist. She had visited the surgery regularly for her children, but only twice for herself, as far as I could see. On both occasions she had required help of what she insisted on calling 'a delicate nature'. I was rather surprised, therefore, when I had a note from her asking me to call round and see her.

The house was tiny, surrounded by old bicycle frames and the remains of a dozen demolished shops. Outside, it looked pitiful, lonely and almost totally abandoned. The paintwork was peeling, and the front door was almost totally without colour. The roof had several tiles missing, and the gaps in the roof gave the whole building an even more temporary appearance. On both sides of the house, wallpaper still clung to the walls, showing where neighbouring houses had stood in the past. On the right the shape of a bedhead could still be made out; on the left there was a poster still pinned to the half-smashed plaster. The picture, a busty girl on a motorbike with flowing hair and inviting smile, was all that remained of the rest of the neighbourhood.

Inside, the house was well cared for. The carpets, though threadbare and worn in patches, were clean and neat. The furniture had seen better times, but the cushions were made from bright material, and the two easy chairs by the fireside were covered in a cheerful chintz.

I was met at the doorway by Maurice, the eight-year-old musician. He led me upstairs to where his mother lay in bed. She looked weaker and older than I had ever seen her before, and I felt a cold chill inside me. She was clearly ill. It had only been a matter of weeks since I had last seen her, and then she'd been plumpish and cheery and good-looking. Her adventures since her husband's departure had not been confined to skirmishes with the local social security department. Her income from the State had almost certainly been supplemented by night work of a very specialized nature.

Now she was frail and paper-weak. Her bones stuck through her skin in a grotesque mockery of her former figure. Her cheeks were hollow. I've heard that phrase many times, but Betty Bourne had cheeks you could fill with marbles. Her breasts, once voluminous, had become sad drooping sacks of skin draped across protuberant ribs. Her stomach was wrinkled and creased like an old paper bag. There was not enough flesh to fill the skin.

I sat down on the edge of the bed and held her hand.

'How long have you been in bed?' I asked, my voice hardly more than a whisper.

'Ten days,' came the reply. I could hardly hear it.

'Why didn't you call me before?' I asked.

'The boys have been looking after me,' Betty replied. 'They've been getting me medicine from the shop.'

'How much weight have you lost?'

'I don't know, Doctor,' she sighed wearily.

'Have you got any pains?'

'My tummy aches sometimes,' said Betty, rubbing her abdomen just below her umbilicus.

'Have you had any diarrhoea?' I asked.

'For a while,' said Betty. 'But it cleared up. The medicine got rid of it.'

'And now?'

'I've been constipated for a week,' came the reply. 'So I took some opening medicine, but it hasn't done any good.'

'Have you been sick?'

'I've felt sick, but I haven't eaten anything much,' said Betty. 'That's probably why I've lost so much weight.'

I nodded agreement.

'We ought to get some tests done on you,' I told her, palpating her abdomen gently and trying to pretend to myself that the hard lumps I felt there were nothing to worry about.

'As long as I can stay here,' said Betty, 'I'm not going into hospital.'

'But you'll have to go into hospital,' I said firmly. 'You need looking after.'

85

'I'll not go and leave the boys,' she said, equally firmly. 'You can't make me go.'

'No, of course I can't make you go,' I agreed. 'But I want you to.'

'I don't care,' insisted Betty defiantly. Her eyes were blazing, with a mixture of fear, defiance and fury.

I stood up and looked down at her. 'If you won't go into hospital,' I said, 'there isn't anything I can do for you.'

I started towards the door, hoping that my bluff would work. It didn't. Betty lay back and closed her eyes. I stood still, not knowing what to do.

'I'm going to die, aren't I, Doctor?' she said quietly.

'What do you mean, die!' I said, trying to sound convincing.

'That's why you want to get me into hospital, isn't it?' said Betty.

'I want to get some tests done,' I insisted. 'To see what we can do to get some weight back on you.'

'I've got cancer, haven't I?' asked Betty.

'You need some tests done,' I said.

'Well, I'm not going into hospital,' said Betty.

I stumbled down the stairs with tears in my eyes. Somehow I admired Betty for her pride, her individuality, her refusal to bow to society, her ability to bring up three boys under hopeless circumstance and to turn them into promising, successful students. At the bottom of the stairs, Maurice stood waiting for me.

'How is she?' he asked.

'She's very weak,' I told him. 'She needs to go into hospital.'

'She doesn't like hospitals,' said Maurice. 'She doesn't trust them.'

'I know,' I agreed. 'She won't go.'

'Give her a day,' suggested Maurice with a wisdom which belied his years.

I nodded and left.

The next morning I went back, hoping that Betty would have relented and changed her mind. She was just as determined as she had been the day before.

'What would I do with the children?' she argued.

'They'd have to go into a children's home for a few days,' I told her.

'This is their home,' said Betty. 'This is where they belong.'

'But you can't look after them,' I argued.

'I can't look after them, but as long as I'm here they can stay,' said Betty, her brain sharp, as usual, having grasped the fundamental stupidity of social service legislation. The children could stay in the house with their mother incapacitated in bed, but if she went into hospital they would have to be taken away.

'If you don't go into hospital you will die,' I suddenly shouted at her, frustrated by her stubbornness.

'You're not tricking me into hospital,' shouted Betty back at me. 'You get out of my house. I'm not going into hospital.'

I said nothing for a minute, and then sat down and reached out for her hand. She pulled it away as my fingers met her wrist. I reached out again, and this second time she allowed my fingers to encircle her frail bones.

'Let me help you,' I said to her. 'Please.'

'I don't need your help,' sobbed Betty. 'Go away and leave me alone. I'm going to die.'

'If I bring another doctor round here, will you see him?' I asked her.

'No,' shouted Betty. 'You're trying to trick me again, aren't you?'

'I'm not,' I insisted.

'I'm not having any other doctors in this house and I'm not going into hospital,' said Betty.

'But why not?' I asked.

'I don't trust hospitals,' she argued. 'They do experiments in hospitals. They cut you open and give you drugs. I don't want to be turned into a guinea-pig.'

'They won't do any experiments on you,' I promised her. 'You needn't let them do anything to you that you don't want them to do. You can ask me to explain anything they want to do and then you can decide whether or not to allow them to do it.'

'I don't trust you,' said Betty. 'You wanted to bring another doctor here.'

'Only to help you,' I said.

'What about the children?' asked Betty.

'I'll arrange for them to go into a children's home,' I told her.

Betty said nothing for another minute or two.

'Will you go?' I pleaded.

'If you can get the children into a home together,' said Betty. 'I don't want them to be split up.'

'I won't let them be split up,' I promised.

I hurried downstairs and drove back to the surgery. There I telephoned the social services department. I explained the situation to them and told them that I wanted to have three boys placed in a children's home.

'How long will it be for,' asked the woman on the telephone.

'I don't know,' I confessed.

'How long can you give us on this one?' asked the woman.

'About four hours,' I said.

'Oh, that's no good,' laughed the social worker. 'We need at least four days.'

'But we haven't got four days,' I said. 'I need to get their mother into hospital.'

'She isn't in the hospital yet?'

'No,' I agreed.

'Well, I can't do anything urgently, then,' said the social worker. 'If there was no mother, then we'd have to move them out straightaway, but if their mother is living with them it's hardly an emergency, is it?'

'But I can't get their mother to go into hospital until the children are settled into a home,' I said, 'and you won't take them into a home until the mother is in hospital.'

'Oh, we will,' said the woman, 'but we can't take them in urgently. And we can't take them all into the same home.'

'Why can't you take them all into the same home?'

'It's out of the question,' said the woman. 'There just isn't room in any of our homes for three boys.'

I put the telephone down quietly and reached for the directory. I felt sure that there must be some sort of establishment where the children could be cared for together. Perhaps a voluntary organization or some religious group? An hour later I was back where I started.

I rang the social worker again.

'The mother is in hospital,' I told her. 'Can you take these children into care? They are by themselves.'

'We'll organize that straightaway,' said the social worker. 'We'll have a car round there within the hour and we'll take them into our homes.'

'By the way,' I said, 'they've got scabies.'

'Scabies!' repeated the woman.

'So it might be a good idea if you kept them all in one place,' I suggested.

'We'll certainly do that!' affirmed the woman. 'We don't want scabies spread around all our children.'

I put down the telephone and raced back round to Betty's home. I told Miss Williams to ring for an ambulance to meet me there.

'I've arranged for someone to pick the children up,' I told Betty, 'just as soon as they get in from school.'

'I'm not going until the children are being looked after,' she said.

'All right,' I said.

'Are they going into a home together?' she asked me, tears filling her eyes.

I nodded, picked up her hand and held it while we waited.

The ambulance arrived first, but waited until the social worker had taken all three boys off to a nearby children's home. I told Peter to explain to the others that in order to keep together they should pretend to itch a little. They understood at once, and left doing a dance worthy of St Vitus. The social worker kept her distance.

I drove behind the ambulance taking Betty to the hospital and waited while the consultant physician examined her.

'She's not got long,' he told me. 'There's nothing much we can do for her.'

I nodded. I couldn't say anything.

'We'll have to give her a colostomy, to relieve the pain she's got,' said the physician. 'I'll get a surgeon to see her.'

'Can I tell her?' I asked him.

'Please, do,' he agreed.

I explained to Betty just what was involved. She shivered slightly but said nothing.

'It will ease the pain,' I said gently.

'I've had piles for years,' said Betty with a tiny smile. 'At least I shan't have any more trouble with them.'

That was the last thing she ever said to me or anyone else. She was asleep when the anaesthetist came to prepare her for the operation, and she was just too weak. She never woke up again.

eighteen

I visited the local hospital to see a patient whom I had admitted with a perforated duodenal ulcer. I arrived just after lunch-time, content in the knowledge that as a general practitioner, or at least an assistant general practitioner, I was entitled to visit my patients outside the usual hours.

The girl on the reception desk told me how to find the ward where I knew my patient was recovering, and I walked along the corridors with some nostalgia. Working in hospitals can be tedious and tiring, but it can also be tremendously rewarding and companionable.

There was no one about when I arrived on the ward. The office, usually the centre of activity, was quite deserted. I wandered in and looked at the notices on the walls for a few minutes. There were, as usual, half a dozen cartoons from daily newspapers pinned up alongside circulars from the hospital secretary, the principal nursing officer and the medical committee. None of the circulars made very exciting reading.

I was studying a notice telling me about the danger of throwing rubbish out of the window when a girl in a pretty blue uniform came into the room. She had a smart cap perched precariously on top of a bouquet of blonde hair, and a gleaming badge pinned to her apron front marked her out as a staff nurse.

'Mr Barton?' she said to me.

'No—' I began.

'You're supposed to wait outside,' she said. 'This is the office.'

'Yes—' I began.

'Go behind the screens round the first bed on the left and take your clothes off,' she said snappily.

'I think—' I tried again.

'Come on,' said the staff nurse. 'We've got a lot to do. You aren't the only patient we've got.'

'Really,' I began again, 'I came to—'

'There's no need to be frightened,' she said. 'It's a simple operation; it'll be over in a minute.'

'But I didn't—'

'Please,' she insisted, taking me by the arm and gently propelling me towards the ward, 'if you don't hurry I'll have to get two of the porters to come along and undress you. Now, you don't want that, do you?'

'Of course—' I attempted.

'Of course you don't,' said the nurse, 'so just get your trousers off and lie on the bed, and then I'll come in to you.'

'That's very nice of you,' I said.

'That's not original,' said the staff nurse, with a very tired scowl.

'You're mistaken,' I said.

'Do you or don't you want to have your operation?' asked the staff nurse, with hands on hips. 'There is a waiting-list, you know.'

'Hello, Doctor,' said the man I'd come to see, suddenly appearing in the corridor. 'I was just going to the bathroom. Have you come to see me?'

'Yes,' I said. I leapt away from the staff nurse and followed the fellow back into the ward. The nurse, mouth now opened wide, simply stood and stared.

I visited the hospital again several times after that, to see patients, to take blood samples and to study X-rays. I'd been working in the town for three months, however, when I received a telephone call from the hospital secretary asking me if I'd be kind enough to help out one morning.

'We've got a bit of a problem, Doctor,' said the hospital secretary.

'We've got two doctors away on holiday, and somehow I find that two theatre lists have been booked for next Wednesday. Mr Barker, our consultant surgeon, will manage one, but the other list, which should have been done by the house surgeon, will be left undone unless we can persuade someone to come in and help.'

'Well, I've got the surgery to do,' I pointed out.

'That's all right,' said the hospital secretary. 'Come along when you've finished.'

'And the visits,' I said. 'They've got to be done as well.'

'I'm sure you could fit them in later,' said the hospital secretary. 'Shall we expect you at about eleven?'

'Well . . .' I began. I really didn't want to annoy him.

'Splendid,' he said. 'And thank you, Doctor.'

I arrived at the hospital at about twenty past eleven, and the theatre team was waiting for me. It had only been a few months since I''d been working in theatre, but I'd still managed to forget that you don't walk into the operating-theatre with outdoor shoes on. I got quite a dirty look from the sister, but she didn't say anything.

The first patient had come in to have a cyst removed from the back of his head, and he'd been lying on a hospital bed for about three hours. Three hours is plenty of time for the most unimaginative patient to start thinking the worst. The porter brought him in on a trolley and helped him climb off it on to the operating-table. As the cyst was towards the back of his head, we had to get him to lie on his face, resting his chin on his hands. It looked most uncomfortable.

I carefully picked up one of the smart green towels which they use in operating-theatres for draping over patients. It had a neat hole in the centre through which I could operate. I placed it very carefully over the man's head, and then jumped back as a tuft of greasy black hair sprang up through the hole. I sat down for a minute or two while the porter found a razor and shaved a convenient area around the cyst.

He must have been an unusually enthusiastic porter, for, when I looked again, he'd shaved a huge circle in the middle of the man's head. The poor fellow would only have needed an old dressing-gown and he'd have been able to go to a fancy-dress ball as a monk.

I put the towel back and accepted the scalpel which the nurse offered me. I was just about to start cutting when the man reached up and scratched his scalp, pulling the sterile towel off. I took another one from the nurse and reached forward again. The blade was only about a quarter of an inch away from the man's head when I realized that I still hadn't put any local anaesthetic in. Wearily I handed the knife back to the nurse.

'Can you feel anything?' I asked, a few minutes later, prodding the area around the cyst with a needle I'd used to inject some anaesthetic.

The man shook his head, dislodging the towel yet again.

I picked up a third towel and the knife, and began to cut through the skin. The room was hot, and it had been a long time since I'd been in an operating-theatre at all. Mind you, I think I'd have been sweating if I'd been working in a fridge. It was a big cyst and it seemed to be getting bigger every minute.

I couldn't help thinking that if I removed it I'd have a huge flap of spare skin and the man would have a hollow skull. My mask was sticking to my mouth, the back of my neck was beginning to itch and there was so much sweat in my boots that I felt certain that my feet would drown.

Eventually, however, I got the cyst out. For the first few minutes of the operation the patient kept up a steady stream of chatter, and then he slowly quietened down, perhaps silenced by the nurse's gasps of surprise as the cyst slipped out. Where the cyst had been there was now a hole about an inch deep and an inch across. I was looking at it, wondering how best to close it, when one of the anaesthetists came in.

'Gawd!' he cried. 'What a big hole!' He called to one of the porters. 'Come and look at the enormous hole in this guy's head!'

I tried to catch his eye, to let him know that the patient wasn't unconscious. But he had already gone. Desperately I tried to sew the hole up. 'Are you all right?' I asked tentatively as I put in the last stitches. There was still no answer, so I bent down until I was only about a foot away. 'Are you still there?'

I called. I took the green towel off and swabbed away some of the thicker rivulets of blood. The man still didn't move. 'It's OK,' I said. 'I've finished. You can move.' Still he didn't budge.

I was getting frightened, and wondering just what it was that I'd removed. It had looked like cystic material . . .

'It's all over,' I shouted.

With a yawn the patient pushed himself up on one elbow and rubbed his eyes.

'Are you all right?' I asked.

The man blinked at me and tried to sit up properly.

'I can't move my left hand,' he complained. 'I think it's paralysed.'

My mouth suddenly felt very, very dry, and I could see myself struggling to explain my incompetence to the President of the General Medical Council. 'Paralysed?' I croaked.

'It feels all numb,' explained the man. He massaged it gently with his right hand while I stared at him, immobile.

'It seems to be getting easier,' he said a couple of minutes later. 'I think it must have just been the way I was lying on it.'

'Cramp?' I asked.

'Yes. It's fine now,' he smiled, sitting up and hanging his legs over the side of the operating-table. He continued to massage his left hand, but now he was moving the fingers as well. Relieved, I helped him down off the table.

'Oh, I almost forgot, Doctor,' he said, scrambling back on to the operating-table. 'While I'm here, you couldn't do my piles for me as well, could you?'

'I'm afraid not,' I told him, backing away. 'That's an operation that needs to be done by a proper surgeon.'

The man looked at me in absolute horror. As luck would have it, the anaesthetist wandered back in and heard my comment. He tapped me on the shoulder. 'When you've finished here,' he said, 'there's a sink that needs unplugging in the out-patients' department.'

The man without a cyst fainted.

nineteen

To celebrate my third month in general practice, Dr Oaks had
some notepaper printed with both our names on it. He left the
printer's package on the surgery desk one morning and, when I
pulled apart the thick white wrapping-paper, I just stared for a
moment or two at the sight of my name embossed in black. It
was another small milestone in my career, and that morning I
used nearly twenty sheets of notepaper in the course of seeing
as many patients. Pretending to have lost the pad of sickness
certificates which was usually kept on the desk, I wrote them
out on pieces of notepaper. I wrote three letters recommending
patients for council accommodation and two letters giving children permission to avoid school sports. I wrote a letter to the
local newspaper complaining about the smell emanating from a
car factory in the centre of town, and I wrote a letter to introduce a patient who wished to leave his body to medical science
to the professor of anatomy at my old medical school. The
patient wished to visit his last resting-place ahead of time to spy
out the land, and I did not feel inclined to discourage his request, since it gave me an opportunity to use a sheet of notepaper.

I had for some time been in need of a new suit more appropriate to my new status, and so when I had finished surgery and
completed the morning visits I called in at a local tailor's.

The tailor fussed around for over half an hour, taking
measurements in great detail. He measured the distance between every two points I possessed and then checked them all.
His care and attention to detail impressed me, and made me
wish I'd thought to ask the price of the suit before I'd made
myself available to his tape-measure.

When the measurements had all been taken and noted down,
the tailor, a small gnarled gnome of a man, pulled out some
small books which, instead of pages, contained pieces of cloth.
I couldn't help thinking that, sewn together, the leaves of these
unique books would have made eye-catching garments.

'Do you have any special requirements, sir?' he asked when

we had finally decided upon a heavyweight cloth in traditional pin-stripe, which I felt certain would add considerable weight to my position in the community.

'Lots of pockets,' I insisted. 'I always like lots of pockets.'

'Certainly, sir,' he agreed. There will be the usual four in the waistcoat, the two flap pockets in the coat and a breast pocket in the coat as well. Then there will be two inside breast pockets, a pen pocket and a ticket pocket. In the trousers there will be two front pockets, two hip pockets and a ticket pocket. What else would you like?'

'That sounds like quite a lot of pockets,' I said.

'Yes, sir,' said the tailor. 'Pockets are an integral part of a gentleman's suit, we always think.'

'Do you think I could have a stethoscope pocket as well?' I asked, inspired.

'Ah, certainly, sir,' said the tailor. 'Several of our clients have stethoscope pockets.'

'That would be wonderful,' I murmured enthusiastically.

'We would suggest that you have the pocket below the left inside breast pocket,' said the tailor, rubbing his hands in delight. 'A button will fasten it, and we will give you plenty of room there for all your instruments.'

'Well, just the stethoscope, really,' I said, not particularly wanting a suit jacket with a pocket big enough to carry an electrocardiograph machine, sphygmomanometer and ophthalmoscope.

'Would you like the cuffs to button back, sir?' asked the tailor, clearly warming to his task.

'Why would I want the cuffs to button back?' I asked, puzzled.

'For your obstetrical work,' he explained. 'We used to make suits for a grand practitioner forty years ago. He always had his jackets made so that he could roll up his sleeves and attend to his patients without removing his jackets.'

'No, I don't think that will be necessary,' I said. The tailor looked rather disappointed.

I arranged to return the following week for a fitting and walked out into the daylight.

As I unlocked my car door the tailor came rushing out to catch me.

'Doctor Vernon!' he called. 'Doctor Vernon!'

I abandoned the key in the lock and turned back towards imagined that a problem had arisen. Perhaps, I thought, there him, fearing the worst. My mind was still on the suit, and I is some difficulty with the number of buttonholes, which we have not yet discussed.

'There's a Miss Williams on the telephone for you,' panted the tailor when we met.

'There's an urgent call to a Mr Gladstone at 34 Hampton Court,' said Miss Williams. 'I don't know what the trouble is.'

'Do you know where Hampton Court is?' I asked.

'It's on Riley Street, just past the library,' whispered the tailor, standing beside me.

'It's on Clements Avenue, near the multi-storey office block,' said Miss Williams simultaneously.

'Thank you,' I said to them both, hurrying off outside. After a look at the map which I kept in the glove compartment, I found that Riley Street and Clements Avenue met at the site of the multi-storey public library, and that Hampton Court was next door to it. I accepted this is simply more evidence that local planning officers spend much of their time in trying to ensure that inhabitants as well as visitors to towns have the greatest possible difficulty in finding the spot they seek.

No. 34 turned out to be on the third floor at Hampton Court, so to save time I ran up the stairs. I was quite breathless when I reached the flat. I leant against the doorbell and waited. The door was opened a few minutes later by a young woman in a quilted dressing-gown. At the neck of the dressing-gown I could just see a few wisps of nightdress. Her attire surprised me, to say the least, since it was still early in the afternoon.

'He's in the bedroom,' she said with tears in her eyes. I followed her down the corridor.

The patient lay on his back in the bedroom. A glance was enough to tell me that never again would he worry about finding a tie to match his shirt, never again would he curse as he struggled to find the partner to a single sock, and never again would he put on a pair of trousers and find half the fly-buttons missing. Apart from the sheet which covered him, he was as naked as he had been at the other end of his life.

The question I asked as I turned to the young woman in the doorway still haunts me occasionally. It was a question based on the assumption I would no longer dare to make, and I still suffer when I think of it.

'Had your father been ill?' I asked. It was a natural question. The man was clearly in his late fifties or early sixties. The woman could be no more than thirty. They both looked quietly respectable. The woman in particular looked more like a daughter than a mistress. Ask me what a daughter looks like, and what a mistress looks like, and my answer will be to draw stereotyped pictures of fictional characters. The truth is that in life people very often do not fit the patterns we expect them to fit. The Don Juan turns out to be a rather grubby little man with a thin moustache and a spray of dandruff on his shoulders. The wife-beater turns out to be a plump, jovial-looking man with bifocals and a slight stutter.

Still thinking about my pin-stripe uniform, I'd left my mind on automatic pilot, and forgotten to switch on the piece of cortex responsible for intercepting stimuli before they can trigger off automatic responses, suspicions and conclusions. The doctor has to start each consultation and investigation with an open mind.

'He wasn't my father,' whispered the young woman.

In an attempt to disguise my embarrassment at my own thoughtlessness I fussed around the dead man. I took his pulse, or rather held my fingers where I would have expected to feel one if the heart had not stopped beating; I placed my stethoscope on his chest, and I examined his fundi, looking for the changes which finally convince the unbelieving that the body they are examining has suddenly been devalued and, instead of being the physical manifestation of a human being whose value cannot be estimated, has become a largely useless and rapidly deteriorating collection of minerals and elements worth no more than a few shillings on the open market.

'He used to come here two or three times a week,' whispered

the young woman. She sat on the other side of the bed and took his hand in hers.

'Had he been ill?' I asked quietly.

'No,' she said. 'He was always quite well.'

'What happened?' I asked.

'We were making love,' she said, 'and suddenly he cried out in pain. He fell back, clutching his chest, and he was dead within a few minutes. He didn't even have time to say anything.'

'Had he had any chest pains before?' I asked.

She nodded. 'I never thought they were anything serious,' she said. 'He used to get little twinges of indigestion sometimes, but he always said it was nothing to worry about.'

'And he didn't take any pills or tablets?'

'He took some patent indigestion pills occasionally,' said the young woman, 'but they never seemed to do much good.' She looked across at me. 'It was his heart, wasn't it?'

'Probably,' I nodded.

'What are we going to do?' asked the woman. She looked lost and lonely, like a child in a crowd whose mother has moved ahead too quickly. She never had been and never would be beautiful, but she had undoubtedly loved her man, and his death had left her very much alone.

'Where will his wife be?' I asked. It was my second mistake in less than ten minutes. The second conclusion I'd drawn, and the second time I'd been too slow to stop the automatic response.

'He wasn't married,' said the woman. She saw my confusion and continued, in explanation, 'His mother would never allow him to marry. She told him she'd cut him off without a penny if he did.'

'How old was he?' I asked.

'Fifty-seven,' she said. 'His mother is the chairman of Daisy Chain Stores.'

'The grocery chain?' I asked.

She nodded. 'David was on the board of directors,' she said, 'but he was never really a businessman.' A tear slipped down her cheek. 'He was too kind and generous,' she said. 'He would never hurt anyone.'

'Is that why he didn't marry you?' I asked. It was my third conclusion, but this time I'd got it right.

The woman nodded. 'He couldn't upset his mother,' she said.

'Where does his mother live?' I asked.

'She has a house in the country,' said the woman. 'She conducts most of her business from there.'

I should have telephoned the police, I suppose. I didn't know the woman or the dead man. I had no idea whether she had been telling me the truth. For all I knew I might be chatting to a murderess over her victim's body.

Instead, I helped her dress her lover and then telephoned the coroner.

'I've got a bit of a problem,' I told him. I explained the situation in abbreviated detail.

'You say it's his mother who doesn't know about this liaison?' said the coroner.

'That's right,' I agreed.

'Well, how old is he, or was he?' asked the coroner.

'Fifty-seven,' I told him.

'Fifty-seven!' repeated the coroner. 'And I thought I'd never be surprised by anything again.

'What do I do with him?' I asked.

'Ring for an ambulance,' said the coroner, 'and get them to take him along to the morgue. Is he dressed?'

'Yes,' I replied.

'Well, as far as we're concerned, he just happened to be passing the flats when he collapsed,' said the coroner. 'There's no point in upsetting everyone.' He paused. 'I'll get the pathologist to make sure your little lady hasn't been pulling the wool over your eyes,' he added with a little laugh.

Together with the dead man's mistress, I watched the ambulancemen take the cadaver away.

'Will Mrs Weinstein have to know?' she asked quietly.

'Mrs Weinstein?' I asked.

'David's mother,' explained the woman.

'I don't think so,' I said. 'There's certainly no reason for her to have to know that David died in your bed. At worst she may have to know that he died in your flat, but I'm sure you can produce an explanation.'

She nodded.

I left Hampton Court feeling quite exhausted. I looked at my watch. It was still not yet three o'clock in the afternoon, and the day seemed to have been blundering on for weeks. My stomach began to rumble, and I hurried away down the entrance steps heading for a nearby café where it looked as if I might be able to buy a meal and a hot drink. The proprietor could only offer me a rather worn-out-looking bun, and a cup of very weak tea served in a chipped cup.

twenty

Every Wednesday morning I had to do an ante-natal clinic. Every week half a dozen expectant mothers would turn up to be weighed, measured, tested and prodded. At the average clinic there would be a couple of women almost due, getting impatient as they waited for the final few weeks to pass by; there would be a couple in the middle of their pregnancy who had nothing much the matter with them and nothing very much to show that they were pregnant; and there would be a couple who had still not got over the fact that they were pregnant at all.

At each clinic I would ask them all whether or not they had any problems, ask about their iron tablets, confirm that they didn't have any ankle swelling and that their wedding rings were not too tight, and check up on blood pressure and on the urine samples which most women brought with them faithfully every time.

I remember one particular clinic very well. It was the one I did after my performance in the hospital theatre. At that time I still didn't know many of the women well. Most had been diagnosed as pregnant by Dr Oaks before I arrived. Later on, there would be women attending whom I had seen first when they had come along to see whether or not they were pregnant.

The first woman I saw that day complained that she was having a lot of heartburn and being sick several times a day. I prescribed some medicine for her and assured her that the symptoms were normal enough and would disappear with time. The second woman had no complaints, but I could see from the blood test which we had had back from the hospital that she was quite anaemic.

'Haven't you been taking the iron tablets Dr Oaks gave you?' I asked her.

'I'm afraid not,' admitted Mrs Bruce. 'They made me feel a bit sick, so I threw them away.'

I tried to explain to her that, without iron tablets, she would grow weaker and weaker and her baby would not develop properly. 'I'll give you a different kind of iron tablet,' I told her, 'and you must let me know if these make you sick.'

The third woman was having trouble with her piles. These had developed during her first pregnancy, grown during her second, continued to get bigger during her third and reached their present extraordinary size during the first half of this, her fourth. I prescribed some ointment and some suppositories for her and warned her not to let herself get constipated, whatever else she did.

Then I saw two women who needed absolutely nothing at all doing. They were both managing their pregnancies perfectly well and needed no expert advice. As I took her blood pressure one of these women smiled at me. 'It's almost a waste of time my coming here, isn't it?' she said.

'Well, it is and it isn't,' I replied. 'It's a waste of time when you're as well as you are now,' I told her, 'but it wouldn't be a waste of time if there was anything wrong, and we wouldn't know if there was anything wrong if you didn't come along here!'

'I think I see what you mean,' laughed the woman.

When she had left I rolled up the sphygmomanometer cuff, put away the urine-testing equipment, the weighing scales, and all the forms and special sets of notes which are as much a part of ante-natal care as the other forms and notes are a part of ordinary medical care. I was about to leave the surgery and set off on my morning visits when the door burst open and a large woman in a flower-print dress and a green velvet coat appeared in the hallway.

She was such a large woman that she looked as if, but for her dress, she would have flowed around the hall and lapped gently around my ankles. I told her to come into the surgery and sit down. She looked at me for a moment as if I'd made an indecent suggestion, and then shook her head vigorously. When she'd stopped, she hiccuped loudly.

'What can I do for you?' I asked her.

She looked at me very carefully and bent forward.

'Are you the doctor?' she asked.

I nodded.

'You're not Dr Oaks, are you?'

I shook my head.

'But you are a doctor?'

I nodded again.

'I want to talk to you,' said the woman.

'Fine,' I said, and waited. I wondered how long it was all going to take. I had a long string of visits to make.

'Can I sit down?' asked the woman.

'Of course,' I agreed. 'Come into the surgery.'

She followed me and sat down.

'It's very personal,' she said.

'That's all right,' I said. 'You can tell me. I'm a doctor.'

'But you're not Dr Oaks, are you?'

I shook my head again.

'I want one of these things,' said the woman, reaching inside her coat pocket and feeling around for a few seconds.

'What was it?' I asked. 'A pill?'

The woman shook her head and continued the hunt in her other pocket with equal lack of success. Then, inspired, she plunged her hand down the front of her dress. It disappeared completely and reappeared half a minute later clutching a small piece of tattered newspaper.

'There it is!' she said triumphantly, handing it to me. She coughed, and a ripple flowed down her body, to be swallowed up by her legs.

I looked at the sheet which had clearly been torn from a popular daily newspaper. There was a small advertisement for tooth-cleansing powder and a photograph of an almost naked girl carrying a flute and a piece of sheet music.

'Not that side,' said the woman impatiently, reaching across and pulling the paper from my hands. She turned it over and handed it back to me.

On the other side there was a delightfully descriptive and even erotic report of an American experiment conducted by a couple of middle-aged transatlantic sexologists. The cutting described how successful they had been at teaching American women and men how to have orgasms.

'I want one of those,' said the woman, 'one of those orgasm things. They sound wonderful.'

I looked at her.

'I don't want a lot,' said the woman quickly, 'just my rights.'

I just looked at her.

'Haven't you got any?' she asked.

'Well, it's not that simple,' I replied.

'Well, if you've got some, why can't I have a few, and, if you haven't got any, why haven't you, if the Americans have?' asked the woman angrily.

'Don't get cross,' I pleaded.

'I've paid my contributions,' she argued indignantly.

'Have you tried the chemist's?' I asked her.

'Of course not,' said the woman.

'Oh, well, I should try the chemist's,' I suggested hopefully.

'Don't be silly,' she said. 'Will the chemist's have any to sell?'

'No, I suppose not,' I had to admit.

'Well, then,' said the woman. She looked settled for the day, and I kept remembering the length of my morning visiting-list.

Then I did something of which I afterwards felt quite ashamed. I took a piece of notepaper out of the letter rack in front of me, wrote on it, 'This lady tells me she wants an orgasm, can you please help?', put the note in an envelope, addressed it to the casualty officer at the local hospital and handed it to the woman.

'Take this to the hospital,' I told her. 'They may be able to help you.'

'Thank you, Doctor,' she beamed, leaping to her feet. She scurried off expectantly.

I spent the rest of the day wincing every time the telephone rang, lest it be a call from the casualty officer. I didn't hear from him, so I must assume that he somehow managed to satisfy her demands. I never did find out what happened.

twenty-one

'There's a call in from Mrs Doughty,' said Miss Williams. 'She lives in the Old Vicarage at Cranbridge.'

'Where's that?' I asked.

'Cranbridge used to be a small village north of the town centre,' Miss Williams told me, 'but about ten years ago the town council bought several acres of farmland and built a small housing-estate there. The estate joined the village of Cranbridge to the town.'

'Right,' said I.

'There was another call for you,' added Miss Williams, 'from a Mr Evans.'

'Mr Evans,' I repeated. 'A patient?'

'No, from Dickson the tailor's,' said Miss Williams. 'He wanted to tell you that your suit was ready.'

'Ready?'

'That's what he said.'

'I only went for the second fitting last week,' I exclaimed.

'Well, you'll pass the tailor's on your way to Cranbridge,' said Miss Williams. 'Why don't you call in and collect it?' She smiled at me. Having accepted me as Dr Oaks' aide, she had taken a maternal interest in my welfare. She clearly felt that a new suit could only improve my image. Looking down at my worn checked trousers and my elderly sports coat with leather patches on both elbows, I could not disagree with her.

Mr Evans, the tailor, welcomed me with open arms when I arrived at the shop.

'Do come in, Doctor,' he said. 'We have your suit ready for you.'

He led me into the fitting-room and produced his master-piece. I gently reached out and touched the heavy material and fingered one of the real horn buttons. The tailor backed out, leaving me alone with my new image. Two minutes later, slacks and sports coat abandoned on the back of a wooden chair, I stepped out of the fitting-room for a second opinion. I felt fit to take up an appointment in Harley Street and spend my days signing my name to proclamations announcing the latest news of the monarch's illness.

Mr Evans fussed about me for a few minutes and then step-ped back, hands clasped in front of him.

'You're a credit to your profession, Doctor,' he said. 'Quite magnificent.'

He sighed deeply.

'It is rather smart, isn't it?' I agreed.

'Does the stethoscope pocket meet with your approval?' asked the tailor, leaning forward confidentially.

'The stethoscope pocket?' I asked, temporarily forgetful.

'Here,' said the tailor, patting the left side of the jacket.

I reached inside and found a capacious button-fastened poc-ket, large enough for a poacher to carry a brace of pheasant.

'Splendid,' I agreed.

'Would you like me to wrap the suit for you, sir?' asked the tailor.

'I think I'll keep it on,' I said. 'Perhaps you'd toss my old jacket and slacks into a bag?'

'Are you sure, sir?' asked the tailor, clearly unhappy.

'Oh, yes,' I agreed. 'I need the suit for my day-to-day work.'

'Yes, sir,' said the tailor. He looked down at my feet, and a pained expression replaced his professional smile. I followed his gaze, and couldn't help agreeing with him that my battered suède shoes did not do the suit justice.

'I'll get some new shoes,' I said.

'Black?' asked the tailor.

I nodded.

'Leather?' he asked, still unhappy.

I nodded.

'Could I ask if you'll be buying the shoes soon, sir?' asked the tailor.

'I'll get them straightaway,' I promised.

'I could pop across the road and fetch you a pair,' he suggested. 'Black brogues?'

'That would be very good of you,' I said, rather taken aback.

'I'll bring you half a dozen pairs to choose from,' promised the tailor, hurrying off. He returned moments later carrying a huge pile of shoe-boxes.

'That's very kind of you,' I said.

'Not at all, Doctor,' he said, and leant forward to whisper to me. 'We couldn't let you go out with those shoes on,' he confessed.

I chose a pair of black brogues, and he packed my suède shoes, jacket and trousers into a large white carrier-bag.

'I expect I owe you some money,' I said to the tailor as he handed me the parcel.

'I'm afraid so, sir,' he agreed. He reached into a drawer in his desk and took out a small piece of white paper on which he scribbled something. Then he folded the paper in two and pushed it across the desk to me. He smiled while doing it, and tried to look detached from something he obviously found a rather demeaning chore.

I opened the piece of paper like a party guest unfolding a motto out of a Christmas cracker. I didn't have the faintest idea what to expect, but I had a horrible feeling that I wasn't going to like what I saw. I didn't, and I signed the cheque as quickly as I could, so that I would not have to think for too long about the sum involved. I folded it in two and pushed it back across the desk. The tailor, without looking at it, then slid it straight into the drawer in his desk. It was a major financial operation, but done with great skill, and in a way designed to reduce pain and sorrow to a minimum.

The tailor escorted me out of the shop and followed me across the road to my car. He stared with some disbelief at the inside of my vehicle, and I felt it a duty to promise him that I would be cleaning out the rubbish before long.

He nodded gratefully and shuffled off back to the shop. I decided that I might as well get the task done there and then, so I immediately began to clear out the mess of miscellaneous papers and rubbish which had accumulated in the various corners of the car.

It is really quite surprising what one can collect in a small motor-car, without actually appearing to reduce the amount of space available, and without really trying to accumulate goods. There was a rubbish-basket attached conveniently to a nearby lamp-post, and during the next quarter of an hour I managed to fill it completely. I found three old newspapers, one still containing a few broken chips, half a dozen unopened medical magazines, a couple of dozen sticky sweets in various stages of undress, a half-eaten packet of crisps, two plastic coffee-cups, endless advertising leaflets and brochures produced by drug companies, a copy of a book I'd started to read and lost, a pen I'd assumed I'd abandoned at a patient's home, a half used prescription pad, a box of syringes for emergencies, a variety of small bottles filed with pills which had faded in the sunlight, a pair of broken sunglasses, a postcard from my mother, a couple of leaking torch-batteries, a lollipop-stick and a sock.

When I'd finished, the car looked quite smart on the inside. The problem, of course, was that the outside still looked dirty. I decided to solve this problem by driving through a car-wash on my way to Mrs Doughty.

I never do have much luck with machines of any kind. I'm quite convinced that there are some people who are genetically unable to get the best out of inanimate aides. I am one of them.

I managed to drive into the car-wash area successfully and I inserted the necessary coin into the necessary slot without mishap. My troubles started when the water began to spray over the car. I should never have taken the car there at all, for what I didn't know was that in an automatic car-wash the jets are extremely powerful. My car was not proof against such cascades. I leaked.

For the first minute or so I sat quite still, amazed at the noise and impressed by the machine's skills in manoeuvring its brushes to suit the contours of the car. And then I noticed that my right arm was beginning to feel damp. I saw with absolute horror that the whole sleeve was dark with water. And then I noticed that around my feet a small lake had appeared.

I quickly moved into the middle of the car, nearly damaging myself with the gear lever, and managed to perch up in between the two front seats. The water was spraying into the car through the two front windows and through the thin gap which I could see between the doors and the doorposts.

I reached across and attempted to tighten up the windows. Naturally I moved the window-winders the wrong way on both sides of the car and only succeeded in allowing larger, more powerful sprays of water into the soggy interior. A small river had collected on the dashboard and was cascading down into the area beneath my feet. Under other circumstances the cataract of water would have seemed amusing.

When the rotating brushes had reached the back of the car, I breathed a sigh of relief which was so enthusiastic that the interior of the car steamed up, and I didn't notice that the brushes were coming back for a second attack. I assumed that the noise the machine was making was simply in celebration, and I opened the offside front door to try to push out some of the accumulated water. My opening of the door more or less coincided with the arrival of the rotating brushes, which took great advantage of the opportunity to clean the inside of the car. In panic I slammed the door shut, trapping several dozen bright blue nylon bristles as I did so. The brush continued without its bristles, abandoning them as a lizard abandons its tail, but the bulk prevented the door from shutting properly. The result was that there was an even bigger gap through which the following jets could fire solid streams. The floor was a veritable reservoir of silghtly soapy water.

When the machine finally halted and left me alone I was sitting uncomfortably on the ledge at the back of the car. The water level inside had reached the door-sills, and the surface layer was dribbling out again. When the noise of the brushes stopped I rubbed at the steam on the window to look out. After making sure that the machine had definitely abandoned its malicious attack I clambered back into the front. It was then I noticed that, in between my black damp brogues and my smart pin-striped trousers, there was an incongruous stretch of damp brown nylon sock. Mr Evans, the tailor, had missed my socks.

I drove out of the car-wash with my heels dipping into a soapy sea and spent twenty minutes trying to mop out the car. The brushes had broken off my aerial as a final and victorious salute.

It wasn't until I drew into the drive leading up to the old vicarage that I saw the funny side of the disaster, and even then it didn't seem all that funny. Before I left the car, however, I did remember to put my stethoscope into my stethoscope pocket.

It quickly became apparent that Mrs Doughty was one of those patients who collect new treatments. When she'd shown me into the sitting-room and frowned at the puddle of water which quickly collected around my feet on her expensive carpet, she produced a large jewel-box which she opened with some pride. It was filled to the brim with boxes, bottles and tins of tablets, capsules and spansules. Some patients collect doctors, some like to try new tests and some like to try new pills. Mrs Doughty was clearly in the third category. She didn't even try to hide her speciality.

'I've really only asked you to come along, Doctor,' she began, 'so that I can ask you what's new in the treatment of rheumatoid arthritis.'

'Well, there's always something new,' I replied, 'but new drugs aren't necessarily the best.'

'How can we say that unless we try them?' asked Mrs Doughty with a certain amount of logic.

'Well, what have you tried?' I asked.

Mrs Doughty began to read out the labels on the drugs in her cabinet. The list was comprehensive, and I couldn't think of any product on the market not represented.

'You seem to have got a few of everything,' I had to admit.

'Well, I don't take any of them,' said Mrs Doughty. 'None of them works.'

'I don't really know what I can suggest,' I confessed, reaching forward and sorting through Mrs Doughty's private pharmaceutical store.

'Have you got any of those new purple capsules?' I asked.

'Oh, I don't know what I've got,' said Mrs Doughty. 'I just have what's in the box.'

The telephone rang as I lifted out bottle after bottle of pills, and Mrs Doughty, with a sigh, hurried off to answer it.

'You be thinking of something new I can try,' she cried as she disappeared. 'I have Mrs Roberts coming to tea tomorrow and I must have something new to show her.'

To get a better look I pulled the box towards me. Unfortunately the table on which it was resting was not as big as I had thought, and the box passed over the edge of the table, slipped from my grasp and hit the carpet. The boxes, bottles and tins inside it fell in a heap with quite a considerable crash.

The tins and boxes of pills were undamaged, of course, but seven of the glass bottles were smashed and their contents spread across the carpet. Frantically I put the unbroken containers back into the jewel-box, and then gathered the broken bottles and their contents together. Mrs Doughty's collection had been badly depleted but the box still seemed fairly full. I felt quite certain that she wouldn't notice that any items were missing, but I didn't have the faintest idea what to do with the broken bottles. I couldn't leave them in the waste-bin. Mrs Doughty would never forgive me.

However, in the end I did manage to find a hiding-place, and when Mrs Doughty returned I wrote out a prescription for her and confidently assured her that it was for something she'd never tried before. She accepted it with great enthusiasm, having no idea at all that I'd written out a prescription using the chemical name for common or garden aspirin. And then I shook her hand and left – the broken bottles and their contents being safely stored in my capacious stethoscope pocket.

I don't think my suit ever recovered from its first day in general practice.

twenty-two

At the end of my third month with Dr Oaks' practice I was asked to visit an old people's home in the town. I hadn't been there before and, when I arrived, I was very impressed to see that most of the inhabitants were wandering around the grounds, taking advantage of the fair weather to get a little fresh air.

I found the matron sitting in the garden on a swing hammock, busy with several folders stuffed with paper.

'These circulars come round in thick brown envelopes every day,' she complained, holding a bunch of them high in the air and shaking them furiously as if convinced that the circulars themselves had been responsible for their destination and that, if a few were punished, the next batch would choose another destination in the interests of self-preservation.

'I feel guilty if I just throw them away,' she admitted, 'so I keep them for a fine day, then I bring them all out here and look through them.' She quickly read the titles of the circulars in her hand, satisfied herself that she didn't want to read any more and then dropped them carefully into a large wastebasket by her chair.

'Isn't it rather daunting having that many to read through?' I asked her.

'Not at all!' she replied. 'In fact, it's much better. There are so many that I can't possibly read them all properly, so I don't read any of them properly. It's fairer that way.'

I had to agree that she might have a point.

'I asked you to come round to see a new patient we admitted yesterday,' said the matron. She stood up and led the way back indoors. 'I told him to stay in his room until you came so that you could examine him if you wanted to. Mr Paisley had a stroke about two months ago,' she explained, 'and he's been in hospital since then. According to the letter we received, he's made a good recovery, despite the fact that at one point they thought they might lose him.'

'He can walk about?' I asked.

'Oh, yes,' said the matron. 'He can walk about, move his arms, feed and dress himself, and look after himself. He misses the target sometimes when he's eating, but as long as we don't give him too much gravy he seems to manage quite well. The only problem,' she went on, 'is that he can't speak. He's had a

112

great deal of attention from the speech therapists but he is still totally unintelligible.'

We stopped outside Mr Paisley's door and the matron lowered her voice confidentially. 'He seems to get rather frustrated,' she whispered, 'because we can't understand him. We try to humour him as much as possible.'

I followed her into the tiny but smartly furnished bedroom where Mr Paisley was lying in his pyjamas on top of the bed.

'This is Doctor Vernon,' said the matron. 'He's your doctor.'

'Pleased to meet you,' I said.

'Grkl jknk hkjg klld kjkl ghtrk,' said Mr Paisley.

'Ah ha,' I said noncommittally.

'Mr Paisley was in the general hospital in Buckingham for three weeks,' said the matron, 'and they did a great deal of work with him to try to help him regain his speech.'

'But no success,' I said.

'Gklk hry kjhtk nknhd,' said Mr Paisley furiously.

'They did write us a note asking us to carry on trying to get him to practise with simple words,' said the matron.

'Hgtk nklh kjhgk!' shouted Mr Paisley.

'But he doesn't really seem to have the necessary patience,' said the matron.

I talked to and examined Mr Paisley for about ten minutes, confirmed that apart from his speech difficulty he had made a splendid recovery from his stroke, and announced myself well satisfied with his condition.

'You can get dressed and go outside now,' said the matron to the unfortunate man.

Mr Paisley nodded and smiled at us both. He didn't bother to try to say anything but, as I left, he gave me a letter to post. I took it from him with a smile, noticing absentmindedly that it was addressed to someone living in the Highlands of Scotland.

My next call was to the local hospital where I wanted to see a patient I'd sent in who had had all the symptoms of an acute peptic ulcer. The patient was something of a national celebrity, although his name, Lionel Hardman, wouldn't mean much to many people. Like many singers, actors and popular authors, Mr Hardman operated under a pseudonym. As 'Hawkeye' he was one of the best-known racing tipsters in the country. His tips appeared daily in one of the major newspapers.

I'd first met Mr Hardman during a morning surgery when he'd complained of a stomach pain. He told me then that it got worse when he ate, that it woke him up at night from time to time, and that if he drank anything stronger than milk he suffered terribly. I had diagnosed a stomach condition and prescribed an antacid. Unfortunately my prescription had proved less than adequate, and the following morning I was called to see Mr Hardman at home. He was lying in bed looking very unhappy, and I'd sent him into hospital for treatment there.

Mr Hardman had explained his job to me on my visit to his home.

'I haven't missed an edition of the paper for seven years,' he told me proudly. 'Every evening I telephone my tips in from wherever I am. Lots of people would like to be tipsters, but they don't realize just how much work it involves. I have to read the form-books and the racing-pages every day. I can't afford to pick too many losers or else my paper would soon find another tipster.'

He was sitting up in bed on the male medical ward when I arrived. Fortunately for me the ward sister was in her office and, when I explained that I was the doctor who had sent him in, she was quite happy for me to slip on to the ward.

'How are things?' I asked him.

He scowled at me. 'Dreadful,' he sighed. 'Absolutely dreadful.'

'Well, it can't be that bad,' I insisted. 'Don't you feel any better?'

'I feel really miserable,' complained Mr Hardman. 'It's not done me any good at all coming in here.'

'Why on earth do you say that?' I asked him. 'I sent you in here to have a rest.'

'Well, you should have left me at home,' said Mr Hardman rather angrily.

'What on earth is the trouble?' I asked him. 'Aren't they looking after you?'

'They're looking after me well enough,' he admitted reluctantly. 'I can't complain about the nurses.'

I felt sure that if I just let him simmer quietly for a moment or two he'd soon tell me what the trouble was. Sure enough the silence didn't last more than thirty seconds.

'It's Dr White,' said Mr Hardman.

'The consultant?' I asked him.

He nodded.

'What's he done?' I demanded.

'He's stopped me ringing my paper,' said Mr Hardman.

'What, stopped you sending your tips in to the paper?' I asked.

Mr Hardman nodded vigorously. 'When I came in here I thought I'd just be able to ring up the newspaper office from the hospital bed,' he told me. 'There's a phone on the ward which they wheel around from bed to bed. Well, I used it the first night, and then someone told Dr White that I was Hawkeye the tipster, and he came round and told me that I was in hospital for a rest and that he didn't intend to have me using up a hospital bed and still working,' reported Mr Hardman, all of a rush. He was quite red with anger, and I tried to calm him down.

'Well, the paper will hold your job, won't they?'

'No, they won't!' said Mr Hardman. 'There's a list of about sixty or seventy people who want to get jobs as tipsters. If I don't ring in every day they'll find someone else.'

'Well, I don't know what to suggest,' I said. 'I can see your point of view, but I certainly see Dr White's point of view too.'

'You sent me into hospital so that my stomach would settle down, didn't you?' asked Mr Hardman.

'That's right,' I agreed.

'You wanted me to have a rest?'

I nodded.

'And that's want Dr White wants me to have?'

I nodded again.

'Well, I'm not resting. I'm worrying,' snapped Mr Hartman. 'I'm worrying about how I'm going to pay the hire-purchase payments on my car when I lose my job on the newspaper.'

'I'm sure that if you explained all this to Dr White he'd understand,' I said.

'I tried to, but he wouldn't listen,' he said. 'He just told the ward sister that I wasn't to be allowed near the telephone and made her lock my form-book up in the ward safe.'

'Just how much is there involved in picking winners?' I asked him.

'There's a lot of work!' said Mr Hardman. 'I have to find out about the conditions and the weather, in addition to everything else.' He paused, and blushed. 'Well, it isn't really a lot of *work*,' he said, 'but it does take a fair amount of skill.'

'It seems to me that you have a simple problem,' I pointed out. 'You need to have your tips phoned in and yet you can't do it yourself. Why don't you get someone else to do it for you?'

'I can't trust anyone to do that!' he said. 'I wouldn't trust any of my mates that far! They'd try to steal my job!'

'Well, there must be *someone* you can trust!' I said. 'It's only for another week at the most. Get them to ring up for you. It doesn't really matter if they don't pick winners, as long as some horses' names appear in the paper.'

'I suppose you're right,' said Mr Hardman, a glimmer of a smile appearing on his face. 'I don't like doing it, but it is a solution.'

'Good!' I smiled back at him. 'I'm glad we sorted that out.'

'Would you do it for me, Doctor?' he asked.

'Me?' I asked unbelieving. 'I don't know the first thing about horses.'

'You just pointed out to me that it doesn't really matter for a few days,' said Mr Hardman. 'You just have to reverse the charges and call the sports desk.'

'But how do I pick winners?' I asked.

'Just pick horses for all the major races,' he told me, 'and telephone the names in.'

So that evening I telephoned the newspaper and gave them my selection for the Hawkeye feature. I explained that Mr Hardman had a sore throat and had asked me to make the call on his behalf. No one seemed to mind.

The following morning I was called back to the old people's home where I had met Mr Paisley. The matron had said on the telephone that another patient, a Miss Smith, had developed a chest infection which she though might need treatment. Miss Smith, a lively octogenarian, had, so the matron told me, insisted on cavorting about the grounds in her bathing-costume well into the dark of the evening.

I'd just finished examining and prescribing for a flustered and rather breathless Miss Smith, and was passing Mr Paisley's room with the matron at my side, when I heard voices from within.

'Has Mr Paisley got a visitor?' I asked the matron.

'I believe he has, Doctor,' Matron replied. 'We're very informal here. The residents are allowed to have visitors whenever they like.'

'Perhaps I ought to explain that Mr Paisley has had a stroke,' I said to her, 'just in case the visitor is worried.'

Matron opened the door and led the way in. We both stopped dead about a yard inside. Mr Paisley was sitting on the edge of his bed with a happy grin on his face. Sitting in the armchair underneath the window was a man of about the same age. The visitor was just finishing a tale of some sort, and Matron and I both stared at one another as he moved on towards what was obviously the punch-line.

'Grkh knjk khkjg likgkh hej hfgjg!' he said, roaring with laughter.

'Gjn hrm kjghk?' asked Mr Paisley.

'Khgj khfg ltejk?' nodded the visitor, in an only marginally more intelligible Scottish accent.

twenty-three

My night on call the following week was Friday and, to my surprise, the telephone had not rung once by midnight. Indeed, I was beginning to get worried that the machine might have broken down, and I was just about to telephone the exchange to ask them to check the line when it did ring, and I quietly cursed myself for having distrusted the silence.

The call was from someone who sounded as if she was in her

late teens. She recited an address and simply asked me to call round straightaway. I tried to ask her for more details, but she'd rung off. I hurriedly wrote down the address before I forgot it.

I was reaching for my coat when the telephone rang again. I picked it up straightaway, hoping that the caller might be the girl, ringing back with more information. It wasn't. It was a middle-aged man who was ringing to ask me to visit his wife, a chronic asthmatic. He told me that her condition had slowly deteriorated over the previous two or three hours. I told him that I had a call to do which had sounded urgent but that I would be with him as soon as I possibly could.

The address the girl had given me was for a house on a new estate to the north of the town. Most of the houses there were large, detached edifices with two garages and spacious gardens. The house I was looking for was named 'Eldorado', and I spent twenty minutes carefully examining gateposts, front doors and garden signs, with the aid of a powerful hand-torch held out of the car window, before I found the right house.

It was a smart two-storey house, with a separate garage which looked big enough for two cars at least. Nevertheless, the drive was packed with cars, and alongside the kerb outside the house another three or four smart vehicles were parked. It looked very much as if the people I was visiting were having a party.

I eventually managed to park my Mini a little further along the road and I walked back to the house listening appreciatively to the music which seemed to bathe the whole street. I doubt if I would have been as appreciative if I'd been living in the neighbouring house and trying to get some sleep.

The doorbell rang all right when I pressed the button. I could hear it chiming away inside. But no one came, and indeed I was hardly surprised. The noise was tremendous and you could have fired a cannon in the front garden without attracttng any attention. When I pushed at the front door I found that it was unlocked, so I nervously stepped inside. I still hadn't got used to the fact that many people expect their doctor simply to walk in when he arrives.

The hallway was deserted and so was the kitchen. The dining-room looked as if it had been occupied by a football crowd for an hour. There were empty crisp-packets, beer-cans and spirit-bottles spread across the floor. The expensive-looking thick-pile carpet, fitted from wall to wall, was unpleasantly decorated with cigarette-butts, cigar-butts and dead matches. An empty ashtray lay on its side underneath the dining-room table.

From the dining-room I went into the lounge. That too was deserted, but I had at least found the source of all the noise. An expensive hi-fi set was switched on with the volume at maximum. A dozen or so records were strewn around the carpet in the vicinity; mixed up with their covers I saw a shiny black LP with a beer-glass sitting wetly on top of it.

Since there was no one downstairs I assumed that everyone must be upstairs and, hesitatingly announcing my arrival in as loud a voice as I could manage, I began to climb the stairs. I hadn't dared to interfere with the music since my ignorance of hi-fi equipment is rivalled only by my ignorance of motor-cars. I was halfway up the stairs before I heard any reply. There was a cheery shout and, looking up, I saw a curly-headed fellow staring at me over the banisters.

'Doctor,' I shouted in explanation. 'Doctor Vernon.'

'What?' shouted the curly-headed fellow.

'Doctor!' I repeated, feeling distinctly foolish and waving my black bag at him.

'Joyce, it's the doctor,' he yelled, turning away from the banisters and calling to someone out of sight. The girl he'd summoned appeared by his side as I reached the top. She had long black hair which was parted neatly in the middle of her head, but apart from that there was nothing in the slightest bit conventional about her. She had several ounces of make-up plastering her eyelids, and bright red hearts painted on her cheeks with lipstick. She wore a long, completely diaphanous dress which allowed observers to admire the decorations painted on her body.

'Thank you for coming, Doctor,' said Joyce. 'Would you like a drink?'

'No, thank you,' I said. 'I've got another call to make. Could you tell me what the problem is?'

'Well, we really want your advice,' said the girl called Joyce. 'Come on in.' She turned and walked into one of the bedrooms. The only lighting was provided by a small bedside lamp over which a pair of pale pink ladies' panties had been stretched, giving the room a reddish hue. The light was enough, however, to show that the room was packed with people in various stages of *déshabille*.

'We're having a party,' said Joyce, quite superfluously.

'Goodee!' cried someone from a far corner.

'Do your parents know you're having a party?' I asked.

'Of course not,' replied Joyce. 'We want a cure for a hang-over.'

'You want what?' I asked incredulously.

'Who is it, Joyce?' called a girl wearing a pair of men's pyjama trousers and nothing else.

'It's the doctor,' replied Joyce, answering her guest first. She turned back to me. 'We need a cure for a hangover,' she repeated. 'We're all going to have awful hangovers. What can we take?'

'Is that what you rang me for?' I asked her.

'Well, who else would we ring?' asked Joyce, with perfect logic. I couldn't think of a suitable answer, so I retreated while my temper was still more or less under control. Joyce and her guests watched my departure without much interest or obvious disappointment.

The second call was to the south side of town. As I drew up outside the house, the hall light was switched on, and a man who had obviously been watching for me came marching out into the driveway carrying a rubber-coated torch.

'Thank you for coming, Doctor,' he said. 'I'm sorry to have to get you out, but the wife isn't very well. Dr Oaks usually gives her an injection.'

'Right,' I said. 'Let's have a look at her.'

'I didn't mean to suggest to you what you should do,' said the man hastily. 'What I meant was that I thought that it was worth calling you, since I know your profession can help.'

I turned and grinned at him. 'That's quite all right,' I said. 'I expect I shall give her an injection as well.'

The man's wife, Mrs Belmont, was sitting in the kitchen with her head resting on a pillow on the kitchen table. On the table in front of her there were five small brown bottles half-filled with tablets.

'I put her tablets out for you to see, Doctor,' said Mr Belmont. 'I wasn't sure whether you'd know what she was on.'

'That's very good of you,' I said, picking up the nearest bottle. 'It's a great help.' I examined the other bottles. Mrs Belmont was wheezing badly.

'What happened to bring this on?' I asked.

'Well, we'd been out to dinner, celebrating,' explained Mr Belmont. 'We'd been to the Hare and Hounds restaurant – do you know it?'

I shook my head, and opened my black bag.

'It's a lovely place,' said Mr Belmont, 'very good food.'

'Did your wife have something to disagree with her?' I asked.

'No, nothing like that,' said Mr Belmont. 'I think it was just the cold night air which started it off when we came out of the restaurant.'

'It does sometimes,' I agreed, taking out an ampoule and a syringe.

'Mind you, it could have been the excitement,' confessed Mr Belmont.

'The excitement?' I repeated breaking the ampoule successfully.

'We'd been celebrating a little win of mine,' said Mr Belmont. 'I'm not a great betting man but I occasionally like a little flutter.'

'Really?' I said. 'Was it a good win?' I unwrapped the needle.

'Very good odds,' said Mr Belmont. 'Fifty to one.'

'My word,' I said. 'How did you pick a horse at odds like that?'

'The tipster in the paper,' explained Mr Belmont. 'I always have a bit of a flutter on the last Saturday of the month and I always bet on the first horse that Hawkeye tips in our morning paper.'

'Hawkeye?' I said, fitting the needle on to the syringe.

'I won a fiver by betting on a horse he tipped five years ago,' said Mr Belmont, 'so it's a sort of tradition with me.'

I drew the aminophylline up out of the ampoule and made sure the syringe was empty of air. I wondered what Mr Belmont would say if he knew that the horse he'd backed had been a horse I'd chosen with the aid of an empty syringe and needle I'd thrown at the newspaper from a distance of twelve inches. I put my hand round Mrs Belmont's arm and squeezed until a vein at the elbow stood up, plump and ready for pricking. Then I pushed the needle in, released the pressure on Mrs Belmont's upper arm and slowly injected the drug into the vein.

'This should start to work in a few minutes,' I told her. 'Don't try to talk.' I felt her pulse, keeping a close watch on her heart rate. Aminophylline can cause heart problems if given too quickly.

When I'd finished the injection I wrote out a prescription for some extra tablets I wanted to add on a temporary basis to Mrs Belmont's tiny pharmacy, and then I refastened my drug-bag and sat and waited. It took about five minutes for any noticeable effect to appear and then, slowly, the wheezing began to diminish and Mrs Belmont began to look better.

'Thank you, Doctor,' said Mrs Belmont, when her breath began to come with less effort. 'I feel much better now.' The distasteful memory of the abortive visit to Joyce and her friends had gone and was now replaced with the much more pleasing sight of Mrs Belmont's slow improvement.

'Are these flowers likely to be making you worse?' I asked Msr Belmont, suddednly noticing that there was a large vase of flowers on the dining-room table and that the door between the kitchen and the dining-room was wide open.

'No, I don't get any trouble with flowers,' said Mrs Belmont, 'and I'm very grateful for that.'

'You like flowers?' I asked her.

'I love them,' said Mrs Belmont. She was beginning to breathe much more easily, and her colour had improved tremendously. 'Did you know,' she said, 'that there is even a language of flowers?'

'Well, I know that red roses are supposed to denote true love!' I laughed. 'Is that what you mean?'

'That's what I mean,' said Mrs Belmont, 'but it's much more than that. It started a couple of hundred years ago in Turkey when women would send long and complicated messages to one another by making up bunches of flowers.'

'What a beautiful thought,' I said.

'Different colours and varieties of roses have different meanings,' Mrs Belmont told me. 'There are over thirty different messages that can be sent with roses!'

She proceeded to tell me some of the details of the language of flowers, explaining to me that the deep red rose denotes 'bashful shame', that the red rose bud suggests that the recipient is 'young and beautiful' and that the York rose stands simply for 'war'. She explained that the bilberry means 'treachery', the snowdrop 'hope' and the bluebell 'constancy'. I listened to her, fascinated by it all.

It was half-past two before I left the house, and we had both benefited from the visit. I drove back to bed idly dreaming of the various types of bouquet I could make up for the people in my life.

twenty-four

It is fairly well known in medical circles that things go in runs. If you are woken up at night, then you'll probably be woken up for the next three or four nights. If you see a patient with a fairly unusual disease, then the chances are that you'll see another patient with exactly the same disease at the next surgery.

I hadn't seen much breast pathology until, one morning in late autumn, I did a surgery which seemed to consist of nothing much else. The first patient I saw was a young woman in her mid-thirties who had two young children with her. She arrived at the surgery looking very strained and worried. She could hardly wait to tell me her problem.

'It's my breast, Doctor,' she said. 'The right one. It feels swollen and painful, and I think I can feel a lump there.' She told me that she had noticed the lump the previous day.

'I'm glad you came along so quickly,' I told her. 'Take off your jumper, blouse and brassière and let's have a look at it.' I ushered her behind the screen and tried to comfort the two small children, who seemed to think that their mother had disappeared for ever. Dr Oaks kept a jar full of sweets in his desk, and I'd been replenishing it, so I was able to give them both a handful of sticky sweets. I know of no better way of keeping small children quiet.

I examined her carefully and comprehensively, although I was sure fairly quickly that she had no need to worry.

'There isn't anything at all to worry about,' I told her. 'You can sleep properly tonight.'

The look of relief on her face made it worth getting up that morning.

'What is it, then?' she asked when she'd dressed.

'The lumps you felt are due to a condition variously known as fibroadenosis, hyperplastic cystic disease and mastitis,' I told her.

'I've heard of mastitis,' she said. 'What causes it?'

'It's probably some hormonal change,' I told her. 'I don't think anyone really knows what causes it. I certainly don't.'

'Do I need an operation?' asked the woman.

'Good heavens, no,' I assured her. 'I'll give you some pain-killing tablets which you can take if the pain become very severe, but the best thing you can do is to buy yourself some well-supporting brassières.'

'You mean those with wire in?' asked the patient, blushing.

'That's right,' I said.

'I never wear bras like that,' she said. 'I'm too big.' She blushed again.

'It's because you are fairly big that you need to wear a good supporting bra,' I told her.

'You don't think I'm *too* big, do you?' asked the woman.

'Of course not.'

'They're not unusually large?'

'No, they're very nice,' I told her. 'Quite perfect.'

'Oh,' said she, looking down and adusting her youngest child's hair, 'thank you.'

'If it doesn't settle down in ten days or so, come back and see us again,' I suggested. I scribbled out a prescription and handed it to her quickly. I couldn't understand quite why, but once again the conversation seemed to have got a little out of hand.

The next patient I saw who had a breast problem came in about half an hour later. This was a young girl who wasn't on Dr Oaks' list but who was a student at the local college, training to be a schoolteacher. She too looked desperately worried when she came into the surgery. She told me a similar story, explaining that she'd found a lump in her breast by accident.

Telling her to get undressed was almost superfluous, for she was wearing nothing but a thin jumper which did little to disguise the outline of her extensive mammery equipment. However, in order to preserve professional decorum I asked her to go behind the screen and strip to the waist. I suppose there are some advantages in being a doctor. In what other profession can you meet a young girl and then, within seconds, ask her to strip to the waist for you? *And* be obeyed?

I spent a few moments scribbling on a pad on the desk in front of me. I'd thought about buying a pair of spectacles with plain glass in them to give me an added air of authority, but had abandoned the idea eventually, and whenever I was suspicious of my own ability to appear professionally calm I spent a little time scribbling on forms. That always brought me down to earth with a squiggle.

The girl was waiting for me when I got behind the screen. She was really quite extraordinarily pretty. Tentatively I extended a few fingers and began to palpate one of the proffered breasts. The girl's nipple reacted naturally and I tried to convince myself it was chilly in the surgery. Then to my horror I found that there was something happening in my trousers. I bent forward a little to provide some disguise and necessary cover, but that merely took me closer to the girl.

I could feel her heart racing a little and felt sure that she could feel mine from where she was sitting. Her lips were moist and her eyes looked quite fascinating.

I didn't hear the surgery door opening, and the man's voice

startled me out of my wits. I leapt backwards, releasing the girl's breast and cannoning into the screen. The screen and I ended up flat on our backs, leaving the girl exposed to the public gaze. The public turned out to be a tiny man with a small moustache, who apologized profusely and rushed out of the room. He never returned, as far as I know, so I'll never know what he came for. I can only assume that either he'd bypassed the waiting-room and found himself in the surgery, or that he'd mistaken my heartbeat for the buzzer summoning the next patient.

It wasn't the same after that interruption. I continued my examination in cold blood, found nothing at all and reassured the girl. She smiled and left with a quiet 'Thank you.'

After she'd gone I sat quite still for a few minutes and thought about the General Medical Council, the British Medical Association Ethical Committee and the Community Health Council. But I still hated the little man with the small moustache.

The first visit after surgery was to a large house on one of the main roads out of the town. I knew from a previous visit that it contained several dozen separate rooms in which old people, mainly women, lived alone. I'd been called to the house by a niece of one of the inhabitants, a woman who'd travelled up from London, spent a day visiting and then travelled back to London again, leaving requests for other people to attend to the needs of her elderly and frail relatives.

Mrs Hart lived in a small room right at the top of the house. To get there you had to climb four flights of stairs and, by the time I knocked on her door, I was feeling exhausted. I wasn't surprised to find out later that Mrs Hart hadn't left her prison in the sky for nearly nine months.

'Hello, Doctor,' whispered a quiet voice when I entered the room. Mrs Hart was lying on her bed. She looked quite awful – she was pale, and her skin looked paper-thin. She wore a grey dress through which I could see bones sticking.

'Hello, my dear,' I said, sitting down on the edge of the bed and holding her hand. 'How are you feeling?'

'Very weak, Doctor,' said Mrs Hart, 'very weak. I just seem to be getting weaker and weaker.'

'How long have you been living here by yourself?' I asked her.

'Two years,' replied Mrs Hart.

'You must have lots of friends here, I suppose,' I said.

'Mrs Gibson does my shopping for me twice a week and collects my pension,' said the old lady, 'but I never see anyone else.'

'But the place is full of old people,' I said.

'No one ever seems to talk to anyone else,' said Mrs Hart. 'I suppose we're all too proud and stubborn to admit that we're lonely.'

'Can I examine you?' I asked her.

'Yes, if you wish,' said Mrs Hart, 'but you won't send me into hospital, will you?'

'I'll try not to,' I agreed.

'You mustn't,' said Mrs Hart.

It took me less than two minutes to discover that Mrs Hart had carcinoma and less than a minute more to find that the cancer had originated in her left breast. The whole of the breast was a solid lump of cancer tissue. There was nothing anyone could do about it.

'You must have had this lump for some time,' I said to her.

'Oh, yes,' said Mrs Hart. 'That's been there for a long time.'

'Why didn't you tell anyone?' I asked.

'I'm eighty-six now,' said Mrs Hart. 'I just wanted to live in peace. Don't send me into hospital, will you?'

'Well, I can hardly leave you here, can I?'

'Why not?' she asked.

'Well . . .' I began. Then I looked around the tiny room. The walls were covered with framed photographs and pictures in old gilt frames. The furniture was old and well worn but loving tended. The bookcase was crammed full of novels which had been collected over many years. The mantelpiece was crowded with mementoes.

'Well, who is going to look after you?' I asked.

'I don't know,' said Mrs Hart, with tears running down her cheeks, 'but I don't want to die in hospital.'

'Who said anything about dying?' I asked her.

She looked at me with affection and reached out to hold my

hand. She knew she was dying. I knew she was dying. We both knew that each other knew, and yet that simple gesture told me that the subject was closed.

'Have you got no relatives?' I asked.

'I've got a niece in London,' said Mrs Hart, 'but she runs a boutique. She hasn't time to look after me as well.'

'I'll try to fix up a nurse to come in and see you every day,' I promised, 'and I'll come back tomorrow.'

'Thank you,' said Mrs Hart simply.

'You've no pain at all?'

She shook her head.

As I pulled away from the house in my Mini car, a huge saloon roared past. Its driver hooted imperiously. I accelerated after it furiously, and when I caught it at the next set of traffic lights I tooted my horn. The driver turned his head and looked down at me. Very deliberately, I raised two fingers in rude salute, and waved them at him slowly and clearly. He snapped his seat belt undone, opened his door and started to come round the back of my car. Just then the traffic lights changed colour and I accelerated away from him, leaving him enveloped in a cloud of exhaust smoke. The motorists behind him hooted impatiently and he waved his fists at me. It made me feel a little better.

twenty-five

When my name had finally appeared on the medical-school noticeboard to tell me and the world that I had been passed as fit to practise medicine, I had innocently imagined that I was done with education. Naïvely, I thought that at last, after an educational career which had spanned two decades, I was free of the world of obscure syndromes, clever questions and witty answers. I had left medical school and the associated academics without a qualm, looking forward to practising my profession in the real world outside.

During my junior hospital appointments I had found myself once or twice joining teaching ward rounds organized for the doubtful benefit of those enthusiasts seeking higher qualifications and hoping to become specialists. I had regarded myself as an outside observer on these intellectual jaunts, for I had no desire whatsoever to spend my life peering into one specific cavity of the human frame, only occasionally getting a glimpse of the body around the cavity.

After I had finally cut the cord connecting me to the comforting warmth of the hospital service, with all its advantages of shared responsibility, I knew of course that in order to keep up with the day-to-day advances in the medical world I would need to keep an eye on the *Reader's Digest* and other medical journals, but I honestly thought I'd done with ward rounds and case presentations. I was wrong. A few months after being hired by Dr Oaks, I found myself once again treading the wards in the wake of an eagle-eyed, razor-tongued consultant.

It was all Dr Oaks' fault. Before I'd taken the job, he had arranged for his future assistant to join the teaching rounds organized once a fortnight by Dr White at the local hospital. He had made the arrangements in the mistaken belief that any young doctor would welcome the opportunity to learn with a well-qualified specialist. When I'd taken the job, and proved far less enthusiastic about the academic arrangements Dr Oaks had made, it was too late to do anything about it without offending Dr White.

And so, on alternate Thursdays in autumn, I found myself struggling into a borrowed white coat at the local hospital and shuffling along behind a mixed team of medical and surgical registrars, senior house officers and junior housemen. Dr White had clearly always wanted to be a teaching hospital consultant and to have a procession of medical students and qualified acolytes following him wherever he went. Since such success had proved to be beyond him, he'd satisfied himself by arranging for junior doctors from four local hospitals to travel to his side once a fortnight.

Each teaching round would start with nauseating milky coffee served in the hospital library. Then we would all follow

Dr White as he made his way to some spot in the hospital where his registrar had prepared suitably interesting patients. Some unfortunate young houseman would be given the job of interviewing the patient, eliciting the salient facts, and then, by means of a clinical examination, finding any significant signs. As a general practitioner, albeit an assistant general practitioner, I was relieved to find myself immune from the embarrassment of such a public trial of skill. Perhaps conscious that his private patients came on the recommendation of general practitioners, Dr White carefully avoided making fools of the general practitioners who attended his round.

Dr White would dress up for these occasions, presumably aping some studenthood hero. He wore a faded but startling medical-school tie, an immaculate but severaly out-of-date pinstriped three-piece suit, a starch-stiff white coat and, around his neck, a tarnished and dented brass stethoscope which had tubing of partly perished red rubber instead of the more usual and useful black plastic. This uniform was never varied.

The registrars would play the game with Dr White, deliberately reading out-of-the-way journals and memorizing extraordinary anecdotes and out-of-the-way eponyms, so that they would be better able to exchange banter with their chief.

Dr White very nearly tripped over his own ingenuity the very first day I attended one of his rounds. It was his usual practice to read up the notes concerning the patients chosen for public discussion. The night before, his registrar would tell him the names of the patients selected as being of most clinical interest, and White would therefore be able to arm himself with all the titbits of information about the patient and about the disease itself. He would, for example, be able to tell us which historical celebrities had suffered from the same disorder as the one disabling Mr Kent, the local sweetshop-owner. A case of haemophilia would enable him to describe the members of the European royal families who had also been sufferers, a case of porphyria would lead him on to members of the British royal family, and even an ordinary case of senile dementia would give him the opportunity to talk about the errors made by similarly afflicted international statesmen. I must confess that personally I never find it all that interesting to know that Sir Anthony Eden had gall-bladder disease and that General de Gaulle had problems with his prostate gland.

What nearly tripped Dr White up was his own determination to humiliate whichever young doctor was struggling to examine the next patient on his list. The doctor concerned on this occasion, a young house surgeon, was getting absolutely nowhere with his questioning. The patient seemed quite fit and healthy.

'I think that perhaps you had better begin your examination, Doctor,' suggested Dr White coldly. 'Your present contract with the hospital has only another five months to run, and I'm sure you'd like to see one or two more patients before you have to leave us.'

The hapless house surgeon blushed, and pulled back the bed-sheets, revealing a perfectly fit-looking abdomen and a healthy pair of legs. The examination was proving similarly unproductive when Dr White, eyes raised heavenward in search of celestial support, decided to intervene.

'Allow me, Doctor,' he said, gently pushing the house surgeon to one side, and placing one hand on the patient's abdomen. He searched around for a moment or two, as if he'd no idea what he might be looking for, and then stood back.

'Examine the left hypocondrium,' he said, 'and you'll find a swelling which is mobile, smooth and unattached the skin.'

The house surgeon moved forward again and had hardly got his hand on to the patient's abdomen when Dr White pushed him to one side.

'Now examine the groin,' he suggested, placing his own hand in the man's left groin, 'and you will find a number of palpable nodes.' He stood away from the bed. 'This patient has lymphadenopathy,' he announced. 'Let us therefore discuss the possible causes of lymphadenopathy.'

It was then that I noticed that Dr White's registrar, a weedy-looking individual who had a pair of sharply pointed sideburns and shifty eyes, was looking very worried. In fact, he was looking positively desperate.

As Dr White began a long discourse on the many varied causes of lymphadenopathy, the registrar struggled to attract his attention. He coughed nervously, waved his hand in the air for a few seconds, hopped on one leg, started to move away from the bedside, and did every thing else except actually say what was troubling him.

'What's bothering you, Jackson?' demanded Dr White at last.

'I think we ought to be moving on, sir,' said Dr Jackson. 'We're getting behind time.'

The ploy was a clever one, for Dr White could never stand getting behind time. He would get most upset if his arrival on a particular ward was delayed and if, as a consequence, the ward sister and her staff were not ready waiting for him. He considered it a personal insult if anyone on the ward used a bedpan or did anything discourteous, like bleeding, while he was conducting one of his teaching rounds.

'What the devil was the mattter?' I asked the registrar as we moved away from the patient with lymphadenopathy.

'Wrong patient,' hissed the registrar. 'That chap's got an unexplained raised erythrocyte sedimentation rate and we've brought him in for tests. We haven't got the faintest idea what's wrong with him. The chap with lymphadenopathy is in the next bed.'

Unaware of his narrow escape, Dr White continued on his academic journey.

At the end of the teaching round we were treated to a lecture by a gentleman from one of the country's major research laboratories. A specialist in drugs used to counteract blood-clotting problems, he talked to us about a single new drug which he and his colleague felt had a great future in the treatment of patients with deep vein thrombosis.

The speaker told us that the drug, prepared in minute quantities from several hundred thousand gallons of human urine, actually did dissolve coagulations and that, in consequence, it should be prescribed for all patients whose lives were threatened by vascular clots.

After the lecture was over I returned to the real world outside, inspired with the thought that, with the aid of this magnificent new drug, I would at last be able to treat those patients suffering from venous thrombosis. I was almost delirious with delight when I at last found one with a suitable clot for treatment.

'Stay in bed,' I told him, 'and get your wife to take this prescription to the chemist.'

I returned to the surgery puffed with pride and pleased that I had attended the teaching round. My joy was short-lived, for the telephone rang shortly after I arrived home. It was one of the local chemists.

'Did you prescribe this urokinase?' he asked me.

'Yes,' I agreed. 'It's marvellous new stuff. It clears up clots.'

'I haven't got any of it,' said the chemist.

'You haven't got any!' I said unhappily. 'Why haven't you got any?'

'Two reasons,' said the chemist. 'First, they aren't making it commercially yet, and, secondly, if they were, I'd have to mortgage the shop to buy a single dose.'

'Oh,' was my feeble and disappointed reply.

'Sorry about that,' said the chemist. 'I rang the wholesaler about it, and they don't think it's likely to come on the market for a few years yet.' He paused. 'What would you like me to dispense instead?'

'Have you got any crêpe bandages?' I asked him sadly, my faith in the value of continuing medical education badly damaged.

I attended several more ward rounds, but I never managed to forget my disappointment and regain my trust in those determined to educate me. Eventually I arranged an immunization clinic to clash with the rounds so that I could offer Dr White a good excuse for my absence. Dr Oaks didn't mind. He shared my lack of enthusiasm.

twenty-six

Artificial legs have been used as replacements for missing lower limbs since the year 600 BC, and metal hands have been provided for handless patients since the sixteenth century. The artificial-organ business is now well established. Kidneys and hearts are transplanted from one human being to another, and artificial eyes and teeth have been used for centuries. A twenty-four-year-old Californian had a false right arm made for him by a team of engineers which enables him to squeeze with twice as much force as an average healthy male.

Ophthalmic surgeons are said to be working on artificial eyes made like small television cameras, which will fit into the eye sockets of the blind and transmit signals directly to the brain. There is no reason why these cameras should not be fittted with zoom lenses. Surgeons all over the world now use elastic, seamless, corrugated, indestructible artificial materials to replace diseased blood-vessels, and long-life metal is used to produce replacements for bones and joints in arthritic and accidentally damaged patients. It is possible to look through an instrument-maker's catalogue and buy knees, hips, elbows, fingers and toes.

Medical researchers do not spend all their time pulling habits out of rats; many spend their time on work that Dr Franken-stein would have enjoyed.

Dr Oaks had no such patients on his list, but he did have Gerald Renton, the proud possessor of an artificial heart-valve. Mr Renton had been a weak and rather spindly child, according to his medical records. His parents, eager to help him achieve a stature more in keeping with the family tradition of sporting heroes, ensured that young Gerald took part in as many sporting events as possible. The perhaps inevitable result was that he became an Olympic high-jumper, several times representing his country and frequently leaping higher than any of his competitors.

In his middle years Gerald became increasingly breathless, and it slowly became apparent that his heart was failing. A visit to a local specialist resulted in his being referred to a thoracic surgeon working at a nearby teaching hospital. The teaching hospital surgeon decided that the provision of an artificial heart-valve would solve most if not all of his problems, and in due course the valve was fitted. Gerald Renton arrived home in a blaze of glory again.

Since that day he had not moved from his living-room. A bed and commode had been installed to save the retired athlete from unnecessary effort, and an electrically driven wheelchair had been purchased to enable him to move about the living-room and attached sun-lounge without putting too much of a strain on his plastic heart-valve.

It was not at all what the surgeon had intended should happen. He had expected that Gerald would regain some of his youthful fitness and vitality; indeed, Dr Oaks' record folder was full of letters from the surgeon and from the local physician, pointing out that they saw no reason at all why Gerald should not resume his normal activities as soon as possible.

Gerald Renton, however, was strangely satisfied with his new-found status. He had inherited the family fortune at the age of thirty-three, and had bought a large mansion on the outskirts of the town. The mansion, surrounded by four or five acres of well-kept gardens and by an orchard much loved by youthful apple-hunters, was decorated from top to bottom with cups, medals, trophies and certificates of sporting endeavour. The hallway was covered in photographs showing Gerald winning a medal here, a cup there and 'a plaque elsewhere, and being presented with prizes by members of the Royal Family, eminent politicians and show-business personalities.

In this museum of sporting trophies lived Gerald Renton and Sophie, his second wife. They were frequently visited by other former athletes, who made the trip to Gerald's house more or less a pilgrimage. They brought more photographs from Gerald's former competitors around the world, and they all expressed sympathy and concern over his confinement to a wheelchair.

Gerald loved it all. He ran the house and gardens from his chair, using his wife as an extension of his own personality. It was she who was given the job of ensuring that visitors were made welcome, that new photographs were properly framed and hung, and that the furniture was kept spick and span. Even though Gerald never left the living-room with its sun-lounge, he took an active, even unnatural interest in the management of the rest of the house.

The first time I met him I had not studied Dr Oaks' records. I assumed that his condition must be more serious than it at first appeared, and I listened attentively and sympathetically as he explained to me the problems of being a former athlete in a wheelchair.

'It's a living nightmare,' he moaned dramatically. 'I only have the past to keep me alive.'

'Have you taken your pills today?' I asked, examining the array of pills which surronuded his chair. Most of them were vitamin pills bought from the chemist's shop. None of them was prescribed.

'It's not pills I need, Doctor,' said Mr Renton with a sigh, 'it's a new heart.' He reached down the side of his wheelchair and pulled out a rather tattered copy of the local newspaper.

'Have you seen this?' he asked.

I took the paper from him and examined it carefully, frightened lest the well-thumbed pages should fall apart.

'It's all right,' he said. 'I've got another half-dozen copies.'

Inside, spread across two centre pages, there was an illustrated feature describing the bravery and undoubted courage of Mr Renton. There were photographs of the young athlete, dressed in knee-length white shorts and England vest, and there were photographs of the veteran invalid sitting up in his wheelchair with a proud and determined look on his face.

'How has your husband been?' I asked Mrs Renton, who until then had stood patiently just inside the doorway to the room.

'Oh, don't bother asking her anything,' said Mr Renton quickly, before she could reply.

I must have looked puzzled.

'She's my second wife,' he said. 'We've only been married ten years; she doesn't know anything about me.'

I looked at Mrs Renton, encouraging her to speak. She stood silent and unashamed.

'My first wife was a right corker,' said Mr Renton, pulling out a photograph of a slender blonde dressed in a gown which gave ample opportunity for the inspection of her secondary sexual characteristics.

'We had some good times,' he said with a wink.

I looked at him in amazement.

'Mind you,' he went on, 'we weren't always faithful. I didn't mind her having a bit of fun and she never asked where I'd been on a Saturday night. Some of those shot-putters were pretty keen on indoor sports in those days,' said Mr Renton with another heavy wink. 'They didn't take all those hormone tablets then.'

'Of course, Sophie is a good wife,' he said, nodding in the direction of the doorway. 'She looks after me and the house.'

'Well, I don't think there's anything to worry about, Mr Renton,' I told him, standing and moving away quickly.

I smiled at Mrs Renton as I left, but she said nothing, and was clearly not in the least disturbed by her husband's unusual behaviour.

I met them both a second time about a fortnight later. Mr Renton's son by his first marriage, a well-known cross-country runner, was visiting his father with his wife and four-year-old son. I was called because the young boy was found wandering round the gardens clutching a handful of orange tablets.

'He's picked up some of his grandfather's pills,' the unhappy mother told me. She was near hysterics.

'Get him to the hospital straightaway,' shouted Mr Renton senior, red-faced with rage. 'If my blasted wife had moved those tablets this wouldn't have happened.'

Mrs Renton was nowhere to be seen.

I studied the bottles of pills on the table. None of them seemed to match the pills in the young boy's clenched fist. I decided that the old man was undoubtedly right and that the boy should go into hospital.

Just as I was about to lead him out to the car, Mrs Renton senior appeared. She walked across the room, ignoring her stepson and his wife, and came straight to me. She placed a small cardboard packet in my hand.

'I found this in the garden,' she said. Inside the packet there were still half a dozen orange tablets identical to the ones in the boy's hand. The outside of the packet explained that they were in fact cinnamon-flavoured sweets.

Having thus been saved from a great deal of potential embarrassment, I felt grateful towards the apparently unfortunate Mrs Renton when I left after my second meeting with that unusual family.

Our third meeting occurred just a couple of days afterwards. I was called during the evening surgery to go and see Mr Renton. The call was made by his son, still a guest in the house.

Mrs Renton met me on the doorstep.

'I'm sorry to have troubled you, Doctor,' she said. 'I didn't want them to call you, but they insisted. He often has little turns like this, and I really don't think there's anything to worry about at all.'

She led me into the living-room, where the former Olympic high-jumper was lying full-length on the floor, his head propped up on two cushions, taking great gasps of air as if rationing were about to begin.

I pulled my stethoscope out of my pocket and began to listen to his chest. His heart and lungs were working perfectly and, apart from the clicking made by the heart-valve, there was nothing at all abnormal to be heard. I looked at his ankles, which were not swollen, and examined his neck veins, which showed no sign of cardiac failure.

As Mrs Renton had suggested, I could find nothing at all wrong with her husband. I decided to give him an injection of a sedative to help him to calm down a little.

'Just one moment,' I said to the family group. 'I'll have to pop out to the car to fetch my drug-bag.'

The black bag was in the back of the car. Regulations insist that the bag should not only be kept in a locked vehicle when not in use, but that it should also be kept locked itself, and so, as I walked back into the house, I felt in my pockets for my keys.

I felt in both trouser pockets and in a total of five jacket pockets. I didn't have the keys with me. I was holding a drug-bag filled with all sorts of life-saving equipment, and it was locked. It seemed that I had little alternative but to break the lock open. It was a handsome, expensive bag which had been bought for me by loving parents shortly after I'd qualified, and I was

138

reluctant to destroy it. My reluctance showed. As I walked into the house Mrs Renton, who was waiting in the hall, called across to me.

'What's the matter, Doctor?' she asked.

I told her what had happened.

'Follow me,' she said without another word. She led me up the stairs and into the bathroom, opened the cabinet on a shelf above the bath, and took out a bottle of purgative tablets.

'Give him two of these,' she said.

'They won't do him any harm, will they?' I asked.

'Of course not,' said Mrs Renton. 'And he's never had them before, so he'll not recognize them.'

I examined the bottle carefully. The pills promised to do no more than match the power of half a dozen prunes.

Downstairs I handed the pills to Mr Renton with great ceremony, instructing him to take them both immediately. He sat up and nodded his understanding. I noticed that, as he reached for a glass of water with which to swallow the pills, he seemed to be breathing quite normally.

Mrs Renton saw me to the door, and the wink she gave me was almost imperceptible.

twenty-seven

I peered through the windscreen, searching for No. 35, but I could hardly see anything for the driving rain which was hammering down and proving too much for my feeble wipers. Suddenly, although my foot was still on the accelerator, the car came to an abrupt halt and I heard someone shouting. The car stalled, and then there was only the sound of the rain beating down on the roof. Pulling my rain coat tightly around my neck, I opened the door and stepped out into the rain. Summer had well and truly gone.

Small pieces of glass on the roadway told me without any

doubt that I'd collided with another vehicle. It wasn't difficult to see which one of the three men on the pavement was the owner, for the other two had their hands in their pockets and their cheeks decorated with grins. The plaintiff in any ensuing action stepped off the pavement and came over towards me.

'What the hell do you think you're doing?' he demanded. 'Why don't you look where you're going?'

'I'm sorry—' I began.

'Sorry!' exclaimed the unhappy owner. 'You've demolished my rear light!'

'And my headlamp,' I pointed out. 'I didn't do it on purpose.'

'What's the name of your insurance company?' demanded the angry man.

'How much will it cost to buy a new rear lamp?' I asked him. 'It's too wet to start scribbling down names and addresses.'

'A tenner should do it,' said the man quickly.

'A tenner!' I moaned. 'You don't need a new car!'

'It'll save you losing your no-claims bonus,' pointed out the aggrieved motorist. I was about to argue with him, but I could feel the rain beginning to stream down underneath my collar.

I reached into my pocket and found my wallet.

I'd been called to see a man who had fallen down a flight of stairs and injured his leg, and eventually, after driving on with one headlamp for another couple of hundred yards, I found No. 35. It was a three-storeyed terraced house in an older part of the town, where the accommodation had once been expensive and occupied by the wealthier business and professional men but where most of the rooms had now been turned into bedsits. If a landlord buys an old house and then purchases a dozen doorlocks, he can let the rooms for considerably more than he could obtain if he were to attempt to rent the house to a single occupier.

Like most of the other houses in the street, No. 35 had nearly a dozen bell-pushes on the doorpost. As usual, I had no idea which one to push, so I compromised – I pushed them all. Deep inside the house and far above me I heard faint ringings and tinglings.

The front door was opened by a middle-aged woman in a

dressing-gown who looked me up and down without a word.

'I'm the doctor,' I explained, holding my black bag up for her to see. A black bag doesn't make a caller a doctor rather than a brush salesman, but most people are impressed if the bag looks large enough and heavy enough.

'You've come to see Mr Stevens,' said the woman, standing aside to let me through. 'He's upstairs on the second floor.' She closed the front door behind me and led the way upstairs. The linoleum on the hall floor was badly cracked and torn, but the woman herself looked well cared for. Her dressing-gown was fringed with lace and she wore an expensive-smelling perfume. Or perhaps it was just a cheap perfume worn with a little subtlety. I really wouldn't know.

Mr Stevens was sitting on the top step of the fourth short flight of stairs. He was dressed only in his underpants, but had a thick grey overcoat draped around his shoulders.

'I was on my way to the toilet,' he explained, 'and I slipped.'

'Ah,' I said.

'It's my ankle,' he pointed out. 'I think I've broken it.'

At first I wasn't at all impressed by his diagnosis. People always think they've broken something, whatever the actual injury. To my surprise, however, he seemed to be right. Mr Stevens had indeed broken his ankle.

'Is there a telephone around anywhere?' I asked the woman in the dressing-gown.

She nodded.

'Do you think you could telephone for an ambulance?' I asked her. 'Tell them I asked you to call, and explain that there is a man here with a broken ankle.

'Amanda!' called the woman in a voice which would have perhaps been more at home in the body of a regimental sergeant-major.

A girl appeared on the floor above, peering over the banisters.

'Ring for an ambulance, would you, love?' called the woman in the dressing-gown. 'Tell them Mr Stevens has a broken ankle and that Doctor . . . she looked at me expectantly.

'Dr Vernon,' I responded.

'. . . that Doctor Vernon asked them to come round.'

'I'm assistant to Dr Oaks,' I explained.

'He's assistant to Dr Oaks,' repeated the woman in the dressing-gown.

Amanda nodded furiously, and an earring fell off and disappeared past us down the stair-well. Then she disappeared from view as well.

'We might as well get some clothes on you,' I said to Mr Stevens. 'It's freezing outside.'

'I'll fetch them,' said the woman, vanishing up the stairs. She reapepared a couple of moments later carrying a bundle of clothes and a brief-case. She helped me dress Mr Stevens, the only tricky bit being helping him into his trousers.

'Have you ever been a nurse?' I asked her. 'You're very good at this.'

The woman laughed and shook her head. Mr Stevens blushed, and I helped him put the shoe on to his good foot.

'These stairs are very dangerous,' I said, more for the sake of filling in time while we waited for the ambulance than because I really felt that they were dangerous.

No one answered, so I tried again.

'It's been really wicked weather tonight,' I said.

This time, I noticed that the woman in the dressing-gown was trying to tell Mr Stevens something. She kept rubbing her thumb and forefinger together and scowling furiously. Mr Stevens kept shaking his head. Eventually the woman seemed to win, for Mr Stevens let out a great sigh and reached into his pocket for his wallet. He counted out two five-pound notes and handed them to the woman, who quickly pushed them out of the way between her voluminous breasts.

I couldn't help wondering what the money was for, and hoping that his tenner had bought him more than a new rear light for someone else's car.

The ambulance men arrived a few minutes later. They brought a small collapsible stretcher up the stairs and, although Mr Stevens could probably have hopped down with a little help, it seemed a pity not to use the stretcher, so we carefully wedged him into place, and the two ambulance men carried him down the four short flights.

Their vehicle was parked in the middle of the road with lights flashing all over it. With a red light on the roof and orange and blue lights flashing on the corners, it looked like a glistening white Christmas-tree. The two ambulance men carried the unfortunate Mr Stevens out through the front door and towards the open back doors. The rain had eased off a little and I could feel the steam rising from my own soaked body.

They settled Mr Stevens in the back, and while one of the men stayed with him the other, the driver, came back out on to the roadway. I had half-expected the woman in the dressing-gown to come outside with us, or at least to stand in the doorway and wave the ambulance goodbye. She was nowhere to be seen, however, and the front door was firmly shut.

'Just passing, were you, Doctor?' asked the ambulance driver with a stage wink.

I stared at him uncomprehending.

'Just happened to be passing?' said the ambulance man again, this time nodding to the door of No. 35.

'No, I was called out,' I answered.

The driver looked at me very strangely, and it wasn't until he'd driven his well-decorated vehicle off into the night that I suddenly realized that one of the red lights which lit up the street had been fixed, not to the ambulance, but to the stone arch above the doorway of the house I'd just left.

twenty-eight

When I first started to train as a doctor I imagined that the black bag which general practitioners always carry must be filled to the brim with life-saving drugs, important pieces of medical equipment and perhaps a prescription pad and a pen. Even while working in hospital as a junior doctor I had no idea that the family doctor's bag must be packed tight with forms, forms and more forms, with the result that there is hardly any room left inside it for drugs or equipment.

In my first week as a general practitioner I signed my name about three hundred times, and by the end of the week my signature was almost unrecognizable. I signed a cheque on the Friday morning which was returned by my bank manager later.

The prescription form is the most widely used, of course. The average general practitioner signs about 13,000 prescription forms every year. Then there are the forms which patients need when they have time off work. The national insurance certificate is needed by those who hope to claim sickness benefit, so that just about every patient unfit for work needs one. In addition many patients signed off work need private medical certificates for their employers. The general practitioner is entitled to charge a fee for these certificates, and this provides a small extra income.

When he wants laboratory tests done or X-rays taken, the general practitioner has to fill in other forms. And, if a patient wants to have his eyes tested, the family doctor has to fill in a small green form which states that he agrees that the patient needs to have his eyes tested. The patient takes this form to the optician, who does the testing, and it is then sent off to some administrative office where it is stored.

No one seems to have yet realized that, if a patient feels his eyes need testing, it might be simpler, cheaper and wiser to allow him to go and get them tested.

When he has injected a patient against smallpox, protected him against tetanus or visited him at night between 11 p.m. and 7 a.m., the doctor has to fill in special forms if he wants to get paid. Some of these have to be signed by the patient as well. There are forms which entitle pregnant women to get free dental treatment, forms enabling women to have cervical smears, form which enable the doctor to prescribe contraceptives, and forms which can be used to supplement other forms which may not be suitable for patients in particular circumstances.

Many general practitioners fight furiously and continually to avoid being swamped by administration. One day Dr Oaks told me of a delightful battle he had once had with the senior local administrator in charge of form distribution and collection.

This man had one day telephoned the surgery and asked Dr Oaks if he might come along and sort through the patients' notes. 'I told him what he could do,' Dr Oaks told me with unexpected vigour. 'And he then pointed out to me that, on the bottom of each medical record, it is claimed that the record card itself is the property of the Minister of Health. That had me stumped for a minute or two, and I very nearly agreed to let him come along and check up on the notes. I still don't know exactly what it was he was planning to do.' Dr Oaks grinned at me. 'But then I had a brainwave. I told the chap that he could do what he liked with the record cards, but that the ink on them was mine, and he had no right at all to touch or look at that.'

But, although Dr Oaks may have won that particular battle, he knew as well as anyone that in the end the administrators always win. General practice these days is a jungle where more people are concerned with administration than with patients. There are administrators centrally, locally, and even in each general practitioner's surgery. The practice of medicine has become such a complicated affair that a number of general practitioners now employ people full-time simply to manage their business affairs. It's difficult to imagine how the general practitioner I used to visit when I was a boy could possibly have managed with just his own eyes and hands. He used to keep the records in his surgery, just above his desk, and when a patient came in he would take out the right one, write in it if necessary, and then, while waiting for the next patient to come in, he'd put it away. Today there are receptionists and secretaries and clerks, and the job still isn't done half as efficiently. Professor Parkinson should be pleased to see his law so well applied.

Of course, the administrative hierarchy doesn't only affect general practice. It also has a bad effect on hospital medicine. Doctors both within and without the hospital service waste much time dealing with administrative problems when they could be dealing with patients.

Mr Seymour, for example, was one patient who suffered from the administrative load which doctors carry. He had been a patient in the small local hospital, which has two surgical wards, one for men and one for women, two medical wards,

145

one for men and one for women, and one maternity ward. He had been admittted, I could see from his notes, after being found unconscious in his garage. While there, he had been diagnosed as a diabetic who had gone into a coma while still ignorant of his medical condition.

I was called to see him about three or four days after he had been discharged. The message came from his wife, who sounded very worried about him when she rang. I set off straightaway for the village two or three miles away where the Seymours lived. It was already getting dark when the call came through and, by the time I'd reached the village, it was completely black. Only a thin nail-paring moon provided light, and I discovered with dismay that the batteries in my torch had finally expired.

Mrs Seymour had given me directions over the telephone. 'Pass the Black Horse public house,' she told me, 'drive a little way further, and then take the track on the left. Ours is the third house on the right. You can't miss it.'

The directions sounded simple enough but, then, they always do. Before I became an assistant in general practice I had no idea just how difficult it can be to find some houses. A remarkable number of patients live in out-of-the-way places, in streets without names, in terraces without numbers and in suburbs without lights. A general practitioner's patients do not lie in neat rows in pyjamas, the way that a hospital doctor's patients lie. He has to work hard actually to find them.

Those people who live in blocks of flas are also impossible to find without great effort. Rarely are there any maps available to guide the newcomer, and there is never anyone around who knows where Flat 87 is hiding. Councils and private builders alike have some contempt for numbers and will never number flats sequentially. The doctor must stop at alternate flats to awaken the occupant and ask if anyone has ever come across 87 while out visiting friends. When he finally has found Flat 87, the doctor invariably finds that the caller made a mistake or that he misheard the number. The people living at flat number 87 are alive and very well, thank you, and they don't want a doctor at all.

146

The Black Horse public house had changed owners at some time recently, and the new owners had renamed it the Councillor Ackles, after some formidable local figure. Unfortunately, the locals still referred to it as the Black Horse, finding it difficult to make arrangements to meet friends and neighbours at the Councillor Ackles. The resulting confusion sent me driving several miles past the correct turning, and I spent an annoying half-hour trying to extricate myself from a tarmacadam maze into which I had inadvertently driven.

Eventually, with the aid of several customers in the Black Ackles or the Councillor Horse, I discovered my mistake. The barman drew a map for me on a fresh beer-mat, and I soon found the turning which I'd been told I couldn't miss. Once in the correct lane it was not difficult to find the third house.

As I drew up outside the house another problem appeared out of the darkness. Standing on guard in front of it were two huge, ferocious Alsatians. I sat in the car and cowered, rather like a tortoise staying in his shell. Tentatively and bravely, like a tortoise in spring, I put a head out of the car door. Discretion overcame my valour with ease, and I pulled it back in quickly.

I sat there for several minutes, tapping the horn occasionally, as if I'd just driven up and was hoping that the noise would attract someone's attention and thereby save me the time involved in knocking on the front door. Still there was no sign of life, and eventually I decided that I'd have to do something. Either I would have to drive back to the Black Ackles and ring for Mrs Seymour to come and escort me to the house, or I would have to get out of the car, leave the security of my metal shell, and take my chance with the dogs. I decided to get out of the car. I picked up my defunct torch in one hand and my bag in the other, and stepped out of the car with my eyes fixed on the two dogs. Neither of the beasts moved a muscle, but I could see them licking their lips as I moved towards them. I gripped the torch tightly; it would make a useful weapon.

The puddle I stepped into wasn't deep, but it was damp enough to worry my socks. The mud, however, was the least of my problems. The two Alsatians were first and second in my league of difficulties. I reached the doorstep without so much

147

as a scratch, much to my surprise, and slowly stretched out a finger towards the doorbell. To my continued surprise the two dogs hardly seemed interested in my approach, and I idly wondered if they could be doped, blind or even harmless.

The door opened without much delay and, as it opened, the porch-light was switched on. Startled, I jumped backwards a foot or two and fell against one of the dogs. My weight sent the beast tumbling off its perch and away into the darkness. I heard the sound of bushes being broken and waited for the bite of revenge.

'Oh, thank heavens you're here, Doctor,' said a lady whom I presumed to be Mrs Seymour. 'Do come in.'

'I'm afraid I seem to have frightened one of your dogs away,' I murmured as I followed her into the hall. I hoped that it sounded as if my hobby just happened to be chasing Alsatians.

Mr Seymour was lying on the bed looking very pale and out of sorts. He was quite unconscious and made no reply at all when I spoke to him. His pulse was fast and his pupils were dilating. It looked to me as if he were suffering from low blood-sugar, but to make quite sure I pricked his left thumb and put a spot of blood on to a small strip of paper which I took from a special bottle in my black bag. The strip of paper turned light grey and confirmed the diagnosis.

I told Mrs Seymour to make some tea and to dissolve as much sugar in it as she could. Meanwhile I gave Mr Seymour an injection of a concentrated sugar solution. He woke up while I was actually giving him the injection, and I felt quite biblical. Mrs Seymour came back with the tea as I took the needle out.

'Here you are, Doctor,' said Mrs Seymour. 'Here's your tea.'

'No, it's not for me,' I told her. 'It's for Mr Seymour.'

'Oh, he never drinks tea,' she said. 'He can't stand the stuff.'

I explained that I wanted to get plenty of sugar inside him, and she agreed to make up a very sweet solution of orange juice. Meanwhile, rather than simply waste it, I took a sip of the tea. It was quite undrinkable.

When Mr Seymour had recovered enough to be able to talk, I asked him what insulin he was supposed to be taking. He told me that he had been put on tablets, not insulin, and that he'd been taking three a day, just as he'd been told to do by the doctors at the hospital.

'Well, something went wrong,' I told him. 'You had a very low blood-sugar, which is why you went unconscious.'

Mr Seymour shrugged. 'I don't know why it went wrong,' he insisted. 'I did just as I was told.'

'Well, tell me exactly what you were told, then,' I said.

'Not very much,' admitted Mr Seymour. 'I think the doctors were busy most of the time. They always seemed to have a lot of forms to fill in. They were always writing in folders or in small notebooks. They told me that I had diabetes,' he said. 'They told me that I'd need to take the tablets for the rest of my life, and that I'd have to go along to the hospital in three months for a check-up.'

Apparently no one had told him that he needed to keep to the diet he'd been started on in the hospital, no one had told him that he should eat more if he was working harder, and no one had explained to him exactly what diabetes is. I explained to him, as well as I could at that time of night, that the tablets had been given to help reduce the level of his blood-sugar, but that they had clearly proved too effective and too powerful for the amount of sugar he was eating.

'What have you been eating?' I asked him.

'Oh, nothing much,' said Mr Seymour. 'A friend of mine knows something about diabetes and he told me that I had to keep off sugary things. When I began to feel ill,' he continued, 'I thought it was because I was eating too much, so I stopped eating altogether today.'

'You've eaten nothing?' I asked incredulously.

He nodded. 'That's right.'

'Make him a feast,' I told Mrs Seymour, 'and then make sure he comes along to surgery in the morning. I want to have a long talk with him.' I started to the door. 'And one other thing,' I said. 'If he ever starts to look odd again, try him with a lump of sugar. That may well help.'

'Thank you for coming, Doctor,' said Mr Seymour. 'I know how busy you doctors are.'

'Don't mention it,' I told him, following Mrs Seymour to the front door. She opened the door and stood to one side to let me through. As I passed her I saw the one remaining dog, now brightly lit under the rays of the porch-lamp. It was a massive beast, but about as harmful as a cathedral gargoyle, for it was carved out of stone. I looked across the porch and saw the dog's stone partner nestling on its side among a pile of smashed rose-bushes.

'Oh dear,' I said, 'I'm sorry about the dog.' As I scurried back to my car I stepped in the puddle again, and this time I cursed roundly and vehemently.

twenty-nine

Diane first came to see me with a friend. Both aged fourteen, both full of giggles and both restless, they sat together in the surgery, refusing to be parted.

'She wants to go on the Pill,' said Diane's friend, pointing to her companion.

'She's been taking it for three months,' added Diane, pointing to her friend. 'Her doctor thought it was all right.'

'If you don't give it to her she'll only get pregnant,' said Diane's friend.

'I don't see why I shouldn't have it,' said Diane. 'It's a free country, and I'm old enough to have a baby.'

'Hang on a minute,' I cried. 'I haven't had a chance to speak yet.'

They both collapsed into a fit of giggles.

'How long have you been having sexual intercourse?' I asked Diane.

Both girls giggled even more hysterically.

'Look,' I said desperately. 'I'm happy to prescribe the Pill for you if I think you need it and are healthy enough to take it, but I must ask you some questions and I must examine you. I can't do that while the two of you sit there giggling.'

150

To my surprise, that quietened them down. The rest of the consultation went without any problems at all. Satisfied that without effective contraceptives she would soon be back requiring an abortion, I gave her a prescription for a supply of the Pill.

I next heard about her when I had a visit from her father about ten days later. He came along to ask for advice, complaining that she was becoming quite impossible to control.

'She stays out until midnight,' he told me, 'and if I try to tell her off she just screams at me and locks herself in her room.'

I listened to him for the best part of ten minutes and nodded wisely as the tale unfolded. I didn't like to admit that I'd been quite unable to control her myself. It all sounded very much like the classic story of a rebellious daughter struggling to find her feet in the world. I eventually muttered words of mild encouragement and assured him that eventually time would prove the most valuable healer. I privately congratulated myself for putting her on the Pill, since it was perfectly clear from what her father had told me that without it Diane would soon have found herself pregnant.

My next encounter with her occurred when I visited her mother, who had a chest infection which had failed to respond to a usual course of antibiotics. I had spent some time examining her mother and writing out a prescription, when there was a timid knock on the bedroom door, and Diane's head appeared.

'Come in, Diane,' said her mother.

I said hello and was greeted politely.

'She's been marvellous since I've been ill,' said Mrs Burns. 'I don't know what we'd have done without her.'

Diane blushed, picked up a tea-tray by the side of the bed and quietly left.

'We were very worried about her,' said Mrs Burns, 'as you know.'

I nodded.

'When my husband came to see you about her we really thought we'd never be able to control her,' said Mrs Burns, 'but during these last few days she's been quite a different girl. She's done all the shopping and cooking, the cleaning and the laundry, and she's looked after us all like a young mother.'

'Perhaps that's the secret,' I said.

'What do you mean?' asked Mrs Burns.

'Well, did you ever let her help you around the house before you were ill?' I asked her.

'No,' said Mrs Burns. 'I thought she had enough to do with her school work. I wanted her to enjoy herself.'

'But young girls often want to feel needed,' I explained.

'There's no telling with children, is there?' said Mrs Burns. 'I've been struggling to protect her from the realities of life, and now it appears that it's the realities of life which she wants to worry about.'

On the Wednesday after I'd seen Mrs Burns I had to visit Mrs Marsh, who had asked for someone to call round and see her young son, William. On reading through William's medical record I could see that Mrs Marsh was an overprotective mother. Unlike Mrs Burns, who had merely kept her daughter away from the household chores, Mrs Marsh had been fighting a losing battle for several years to keep her only son immune from all the perils of the world.

A close study of the records showed that William had been seen by Dr Oaks no fewer than twenty-eight times in the previous year. He had been to surgery about twenty times and been seen at home another eight.

Whenever there was any sickness at school William was kept at home. Whenever he had a slight cold William would be taken along to the doctor. Whenever it was raining the doctor would be called round to visit if William had been caught outside. William would suffer from mumps, chicken-pox and measles in adult life and would probably go through it protecting himself from all sorts of non-existent dangers.

From the notes I could see that he had grown accustomed to his rather unusual way of life. I noticed that he had been seen half a dozen times on Monday mornings before Dr Oaks had managed to convince Mrs Marsh that William simply didn't like going to school on Mondays. On each occasion he had complained of an abdominal pain, which had disappeared without trace halfway through the morning.

In the call-book Miss Williams had written a short note to

tell me that William was complaining of a stomach-ache and that his mother didn't think he was well enough to be brought out. I had put the medical record notes back in their envelope and shaken my head in amazement. When I had made out my visiting-list I had been tempted to ignore the call, and in the end I had put William at the bottom, since I knew that I could quite easily fit him in after I'd been out of town to visit a farmer with a pain in his leg.

It was lunchtime when I got round to Mrs Marsh. I was led upstairs into the bedroom where William was lying in bed, looking very sorry for himself. In a way I was surprised; I'd half-expected to see him playing about outside the house.

'I'm not sure what's the matter with him,' confessed Mrs Marsh. 'Last night he complained of having a bit of tummy-ache, and he had an attack of diarrhoea as well. Now this morning he's still complaining that his tummy hurts, although the diarrhoea has stopped.'

'Has he eaten anything that the rest of te family hasn't?' I asked.

Mrs Marsh shook her head.

'When's he due back at school?'

'Not for another three days,' said Mrs Marsh. 'They're on half-term holiday at the moment.'

I examined him and found, to my astonishment, that he really did seem to be tender. I looked a little more closely.

'Have you a telephone?' I asked.

Mrs Marsh nodded.

'May I borrow it?' I asked. 'William has appendicitis. I'm afraid we'll have to get him into hospital.' I rang the hospital, spoke to the doctor in charge of the children's ward and arranged for William's admission, and then telephoned for an ambulance.

I offered silent thanks to my guardian angel for helping me to resist temptation.

thirty

I used to think that disposables were one of the greatest boons of our time. After all, I thought, the introduction of paper handkerchiefs must have helped to cut down the spread of germs. But gradually, during the years, I have come to realize that disposables are not quite the wonderful invention they may once have seemed. When working in hospital, I realized just how wasteful they are. Every ward contains supplies of disposable drip sets, bottles, sputum-cups, paper towels, spatulas, surgical gowns and masks. Operating-theatres which used to be stocked in stainless-steel equipment now carry supplies of sterilized plastic instruments which are intended to be thrown away after a single use.

But it was only when I stared work in general practice that I really developed a sophisticated dislike of disposables. For it was only then that I realized just how difficult it is actually to get rid of them. Disposable syringes and needles, for example, cannot simply be thrown away like disposable plates. You can't just toss them into a dustbin. For one thing, the dustmen (sorry – refuse collectors) are likely to complain if they find a dustbin filled with sharp needles. When they star rummaging around looking for whatever it is that dustmen look for when they rummage around in dustbins, they are likely to inject themselves. And, for another thing, drug addicts are likely to pluck the syringes out of the rubbish and use them for their own evil purposes.

So the syringes and the needles have to be properly destroyed before they can be thrown away. Now, that sounds easy enough to say, but it just is not as easy in practice. Plastic syringes and needles are made to withstand enormous pressures. There would be complaints if syringes fell apart while in use. The result, therefore, is that smashing a syringe is just not possible.

One doctor recently wrote to the *British Medical Journal* and described a method he had evolved, which consisted of using a pair of sharp shears to cut the nozzle off the syringe. I tried this, but just couldn't manage to find any shears strong enough to

cut through tough plastic without cutting through my own fingers at the same time. You can't flush syringes down the loo
because they just won't go away. They bob up and down
defiantly for days afterwards, and eventually you just have to
fish them out and think of something else to do with them.

Miss Williams came into the surgery one morning as I was
struggling to cut up a syringe with a scalpel. The knife blade,
although sharp, seemed to make hardly any impression at all on
the plastic of the syringe, and Miss Williams stared at me in
astonishment.

'What on earth are you doing?' she asked. I assumed that the
question was rhetorical since there could be little doubt about
what I was doing.

'You'll cut yourself,' she said. 'If you want a smaller syringe
there are plenty in the cupboard under the desk.'

'I'm not trying to make it smaller,' I told her. 'I'm trying to
destroy the wretched thing.'

'Have you tried burning it?' she asked.

'That's a good idea!' I replied. I put the syringe in the metal
waste-basket which Dr Oaks kept under his desk, added a few
old envelopes and drug-company advertisements and, after
rummaging around for a few minutes, found a box of matches.
I carefully set fire to the paper and watched while the flames
slowly licked over the syringe.

The smoke didn't start to appear for two or possibly three
minutes but, when it did appear, it was thick, black and choking.
Miss Williams retreated immediately, promising to call the fire
brigade. I managed to pick up the big metal syringe used for
removing wax from ears, and fill it with water. Desperately I
fired it, full of water, at the now-blazing waste-bin. The fire
died down for a moment and then flared up again. It needed
two more squirts to extinguish it properly.

The firemen who arrived were very understanding. They told
me that the smoke from burning plastice can prove fatal. They
agreed that they just could not understand how a syringe could
just catch fire by itself in a waste-bin, and laughingly said that
it almost looked as if I'd started a bonfire in the surgery. I
laughed with them.

I did start burying old syringes in the garden but I had to give it up after two days because a neighbour's dog seemed to think I was playing a game with him. He delighted in watching me bury them and then, as soon as I'd gone back indoors, rushing down the garden and recovering them, leaving them later on the doorstep.

I tried simply stuffing the syringes in a drawer, but abandoned that idea when, after less than a week, it became apparent that I was using syringes up at such a rate that there would soon be no drawer space left in the house. I gave an elderly man a syringe and needle to use for oiling his grandfather clock, and I managed to persuade next door's dog to chew a few syringes into unrecognizable shapes, but I was still left with scores of the damned things to get rid of. I rang the local council, but they couldn't help, and the local hospital said they didn't know what to do with their own syringes, let alone anyone else's.

Eventually I asked Dr Oaks what he did with his.

'Oh, I just chuck them in the bin,' he told me. 'Always have.'

'But don't the dustmen complain?' I asked. 'You aren't allowed to throw syringes in the bin.'

'Oh, I don't just throw them in,' he explained. 'I put them in old paper bags and then stuff them into empty cardboard boxes and tin cans. Then I sprinkle potato peelings and tea-leaves over the lot. No one ever knows they're there.'

There is a lot more to general practice than meets the eye. and I am daily surprised about just how much there is to learn.

thirty-one

'I can't sleep,' said Miss Clarke.

'How long have you been unable to sleep?' I inquired.

'A couple of months now,' replied Miss Clarke.

'Do you get to sleep at all?' I asked. 'Do you wake up in the middle of the night?'

'I just can't get to sleep,' she said. 'I lie there all night.'

'Is anything worrying you?'

'Nothing particularly,' said the girl. She looked down as she answered, and it was obvious that she was lying.

'I don't have to know what it is that's worrying you, if you don't want to tell me,' I pointed out, 'but I have to know if you're worrying about something.'

'Everyone worries, don't they?' said the girl with unexpected anger. 'Everyone worries about something.'

I sat back and looked at her carefully. She was, according to her medical records, in her late teens, but she looked much older. She wore no make-up and no jewellery which, in a girl of her age, is unusual, and she wore only a grubby blouse and a pair of faded blue jeans. She quite clearly did not have a bra on underneath the blouse. Her face was lined and creased, and her eyes seemed dull and somehow empty.

I was about to ask her some simple basic questions about her appetite and so on, when there was a knock on the door. I excused myself and crossed the surgery. Miss Williams was waiting by the door.

'I'm sorry to bother you, Doctor,' she whispered, 'but we have a bit of an emergency.' She opened the door a little further to encourage me to follow her.

'Excuse me, I won't be a moment,' I promised Miss Clarke rashly.

She nodded unsmilingly.

Out in the hall there stood two small children, both draped in bath-towels, and two worried-looking parents.

'Sorry to bother you, Doctor,' said the father, whose face I felt sure I recognized.

'What's the trouble?' I asked. He looked very familiar.

'The boys were having a bath together and they had a bit of an accident,' said their mother.

'What sort of an accident?' I asked. I looked at the small boys. They both looked very guilty. But then some small boys automatically look guilty whether or not they have done anything wrong.

'Rodney was playing with a water-pistol in the bath,' said the father.

'We've told him not to play with it in the bathroom . . .' interrupted the mother. 'It makes an awful mess.'

'. . . and he fired at the light-bulb.'

'I wasn't aiming at the light-bulb,' said one of the bath towels.

'Oh, yes you were!' said the other one.

'You rotter!' yelled the first towel, thumping the second towel.

Their father pulled them apart and held one on each side of him.

'The bulb shattered,' explained the mother, 'and they've both been covered with glass.'

'We thought they were shocked,' said the father, 'but they seem to have recovered remarkably well now.'

'Children often do,' I murmured. I opened one of the bath-towels and looked at the boy. He seemed all right. Then I inspected the second boy. He too seemed unharmed.

'Isn't that always the way?' said their mother, inspecting them with me. 'When we came out of the house they were both bright red and bawling their heads off.'

'I hope you don't think we're wasting your time, Doctor,' said the father. 'We were worried about them.'

'That's all right,' I smiled. 'I can understand your being worried, but I think you've got away with it this time.'

'There won't be a next time,' said the mother. 'I threw the water-pistol away!'

'Sorry to bother you, Doctor,' said the father again, ushering his sons back towards the door.

'Cheerio,' I said.

'My lump's not come back,' said the father, grinning suddenly.

I looked at him without comprehension.

'You did the operation to remove it,' he said.

'Good heavens!' I cried, suddenly remembering. 'You're the fellow with the cyst!'

'And the big hole!' said the man, winking.

I turned back to the surgery and walked straight in without knocking. Miss Clarke was just sitting down again as I entered. She, too, looked very guilty.

'Sorry to have kept you,' I apologized. 'We had a slight emergency.'

'That's OK,' said the girl. She didn't lift her eyes from her lap.

I folded my hands in front of me and leant forward slightly on my blotting-paper. Something seemed to be missing. It took me a moment or two to realize just what it was. The prescription pad that had been sitting in the middle of the blotter, with my pen lying on top of it, had disappeared.

'You haven't seen my prescription pad, have you?' I asked, hunting around on the desk. I felt in my pockets and rifled through the pile of notes on the desk. The prescription pad had completely disappeared.

The girl across the desk said nothing. She just kept staring at her hands.

'Did you move it at all?' I asked. 'Perhaps accidentally?'

She said nothing.

'Please tell me now,' I said. 'It'll save a lot of problems for both of us.'

Suddenly the girl reached inside her blouse and produced the prescription pad. She slamed it on the table.

'You shouldn't have left it there,' she said.

'Why not?' I asked. 'Why shouldn't I have left my prescription pad on the desk? That's where it's usually kept.'

'You know why,' cried the girl angrily.

'No, I don't,' I insisted. 'You tell me.' I must confess I was beginning to guess why.

'I'm a junkie,' she yelled at the top of her voice.

'Oh,' said I. 'A junkie.' I'd been half-expecting it, but that didn't make it any less of a surprise.

'A junkie,' repeated the girl. 'Now do you see why you shouldn't have left your prescription pad there?'

'I'm sorry,' I said, meaning it.

'I really can't sleep,' she said.

'What are you on?' I asked her.

'Anything I can get,' replied the girl.

'Like?' I encouraged her.

'Downers and uppers,' she said.

'Downers and uppers?' I repeated rather stupidly.

'Barbiturates and amphetamine,' said the girl.

'Anything else?' I asked.

'Grass,' she said.

'Marijuana?' I asked.

The girl nodded.

'Have you ever . . .?' I began, searching for the proper terms.

'Used a needle?' she asked with a half smile.

'Yes,' I said gratefully.

'I've tried skin-popping,' confessed the girl, 'but I haven't shot up.'

'Shot up?'

'Injected anything into a vein,' she explained with remarkable patience.

'Do you know people who have?' I asked.

The girl nodded. 'One of my best friends is in an addiction unit in London,' she said. 'She's dying.'

'What of?' I asked. I had not realized that our quiet and simple town was in reality so close to the horrors of the real world.

'Heroin,' she said. 'She O.D.'d.'

'Took an overdose?' I asked.

The girl nodded.

'How much are you taking?' I asked her.

'As much as I can get,' she replied. 'Half a dozen pills a day, usually.'

'When did you start?' I asked.

'About six months ago,' said Miss Clarke, 'at a party.'

'Where was the party?' I asked.

'You were there,' she said.

'I was there?' I repeated, astonished.

'Someone called you,' said Miss Clarke. 'Someone telephoned you for a joke.'

I remembered vaguely the call to the large house full of drunken teenagers. At least, I had assumed that they were merely drunk.

'I remember,' I said quietly.

'Someone had taken along some dope,' said the girl. 'They gave it away that night.'

'And you took some.'

'Everyone took some,' she said.

I picked up her record card and looked at it casually. I could see that she and her parents lived in one of the most expensive parts of the town.

'Do your parents know about all this?' I asked her.

She shook her head. 'Of course not.' She looked up at me. 'Do you have to tell them?' she asked.

'I don't, but you do,' I said.

'I know,' said the girl. She looked at me again. 'I'm glad you know,' she said. 'It doesn't help much, but I'm glad somebody knows.'

'Have you got any brothers or sisters?' I asked her. I felt I needed to know her a little better.

'One of each,' said Miss Clarke. 'My brother is younger and my sister is older.'

'Your brother is Robin Clarke,' I said, suddenly remembering the name.

'That's right,' she said.

I knew Robin Clarke well. His mother had contracted German measles or rubella about eleven years ago, just as he was growing in her womb. The result was that Robin had been born deaf and partially blind. Robin's parents spent a great deal of effort, time and money on their crippled child, refusing to allow him to be cared for in a special hospital but insisting on looking after him at home.

'I don't know your sister,' I said.

'She's never ill,' said Miss Clarke. 'She's the brilliant one.'

'Brilliant?' I asked.

'She had a novel published last year, just after her twentieth birthday,' she said. 'She's only eighteen months older than I am.'

'And you're not brilliant?' I asked. It was a question that needed no answer.

'I'm not anything,' said the girl bitterly. 'I'm not good-looking or courageous or brilliant. I'm just me.'

'What do you want to do?' I asked her.

'I want to get away from home,' she said.

'Why don't you, then?' I demanded.

'What would I do?' she asked.

'You could get a job,' I suggested.

'I'd quite like to get a job,' said Miss Clarke.

'I think you ought to think about a job you'd like to do,' I said, 'and then I think you ought to do it.'

'Are you going to give me any sleeping-tablets?' she asked suddenly, standing up.

'No,' I said.

'I didn't think you would,' she answered.

'Will you come and see me tomorrow?' I asked her.

'Can I?' she asked, seeming pleased by the invitation.

'I'd like you to,' I said. Then she left.

She did not come into the surgery the next morning, and I waited until the end of the evening surgery before giving up hope for her. As Miss Williams put away the last patients' notes I reached for the telephone directory. I found Miss Clarke's telephone number and stood for a moment by the telephone. I didn't know whether to ring or not. Eventually I decided to try. I dialled the number quickly before I could change my mind again.

'Yes,' said the very brusque voice which answered.

'It's Dr Vernon,' I said. 'I'm with Dr Oaks.'

'Yes?' said the voice again.

'Your daughter came to see me last night,' I said hesitantly. 'The younger one, Sharon; she wasn't very well.'

'No,' said the voice. He frightened me.

'I wondered if she was all right,' I asked.

'She came in from seeing you all filled up with nonsense about leaving home and getting a job,' said Mr Clarke. 'Never heard such nonsense. She doesn't need a job. She's needed here to look after Robin. Her mother needs her help.'

'But—' I began.

'She doesn't need a job,' insisted Mr Clarke. 'I can look after her.'

'Is she there?' I asked.

'No,' he said.

'Oh,' said I.

'She ran out of the house last night. We'd had a row. She was knocked over by a bus.'

162

'A bus?' I repeated stupidly.

'She's in hospital,' said Mr Clarke. 'She's got a broken leg.'

'Oh, good,' I said. 'Thank heavens for that.'

'What the devil do you mean, "Thank heavens for that"?' he demanded.

'I meant, "Thank heavens she's alive",' I said.

The phone went dead.

I went straight over to the hospital after I'd put the telephone down. Eventually I managed to persuade the sister on the ortho-paedic ward to ring for the registrar. When he came down to the ward I had a few words with him in the sister's office.

'We'd wondered what was going on,' said the registrar, when I'd told him about Miss Clarke's problem. 'Thanks for telling us.'

'Can I have a few words with her?' I asked the sister.

She nodded.

'Hello,' I said when I'd found Miss Clarke. She was lying in bed with her leg in a plaster cast which hung from a metal pul-ley.

'Hello,' she said. She seemed surprised to see me.

'I hear you had an argument with a bus,' I said.

'Yes,' she nodded. 'I lost.'

'Is it hurting a lot?' I asked, nodding at the leg.

She shook her head.

'It's funny, really,' she said, 'but in a way I'm glad I didn't see that bus.'

I said nothing.

'At least I've got away for a while,' she said.

thirty-two

The town where Dr Oaks had his practice had, over recent years, developed a relationship with a twin town in Switzerland. Citizens of both towns travelled across the sea once or twice every year to stay in one another's homes. It was understood that while Swiss visitors were staying in England they would be treated by general practitioners as relatives of local citizens, should they be unfortunate enough to fall ill.

Which is how I came to visit a young seventeen-year-old Swiss boy one Friday afternoon. His hostess telephoned me when, while sitting watching television, her visitor had apparently slipped into what she could best describe as a coma. She sounded worried when she rang, so I wasted no time at all in getting around to her house on one of the newest and most exclusive housing-estates in the area.

The Swiss boy was lying on an expensive imitation-leather couch while a twenty-one-inch colour television muttered away to no one in particular. The hostess, her husband, her fifteen-year-old daughter and her eighteen-year-old son all sat around staring at their immobile visitor.

'What happened?' I asked.

'Nothing,' said Mrs Roberts, the hostess, with a slight shrug of her expensively tanned shoulders. 'He just seemed to drift off. I'm really rather worried about him.'

'He's our responsibility while he's here,' added Mr Roberts.

'My brother is a neurosurgeon in California,' said Mrs Roberts inconsequentially. I couldn't decide whether she was telling me that to give me confidence in her skills as a diagnostic aide, to encourage me to try harder, or merely to impress me. I didn't say anything.

'Do you speak English?' I asked the boy on the couch.

He shook his head and grinned at me. He raised a hand and half-opened his mouth, but then the hand fell away and his mouth shut again.

'He speaks a little English,' said the fifteen-year-old girl. 'He's picked up quite a lot since he's been here.'

I examined him carefully, but could find absolutely nothing wrong with him except for the fact that he seemed extraordinarily weak.

'He's not on any drugs, is he?' I asked. 'He didn't bring anything with him?'

'Good heavens, no!' said Mrs Roberts. 'What are you suggesting? That is outrageous! I've already told you my brother is a neurosurgeon in California.'

'I mean medically prescribed drugs,' I said coldly. I wondered idly how much money Californian neurosurgeons earned.

'Oh,' was all that Mrs Roberts could manage.

'No,' said Mr Roberts coolly.

'I think we'll have to get him into hospital,' I said. 'I'm afraid I don't know what's the matter with him.'

'Is there no one else we could call in?' asked Mrs Roberts. 'Where's Dr Oaks? Why didn't he come?'

'Dr Oaks is having a rest,' I told her. 'I'm his assistant.'

'Well, I really think that's too much,' said Mrs Roberts. 'It's a pity my brother isn't over here.'

'Why?' I couldn't help asking.

'He's a neurossurgeon in California,' said Mrs Roberts predictably. 'He's got a tremendous practice and three cars.'

'Have you got a telephone?' I asked.

'Of course,' said Mr Roberts.

'Can I borrow it?' I asked.

'You're going to ring for someone else?' asked Mrs Roberts.

'I'm going to ring the hospital,' I told her, 'and arrange for your visitor to be admitted.'

The ambulance turned up in about ten minutes and, less than ten minutes after that, the young Swiss was on the medical ward of the local hospital. I followed the ambulance in, since I was curious to see what the hospital doctors would make of the boy.

They examined him carefully for half an hour or so, and then came into the sister's office, where I was sitting with a pretty nurse and a pot of tea.

'Well?' I asked. 'What do you make of him?'

The medical registrar shrugged his shoulders. 'Heaven knows,' he said. 'We'll get some blood tests done.'

I went off to do some more visits and returned to the hospital a couple of hours later. The results had come back then, and the medical registrar was studying them in splendid solitude.

'Any help?' I asked.

'Very odd,' said the registrar, pointing to the slip of paper which listed the Swiss boy's electrolytes. 'He's got an extraordinarily low potassium. I can't find anything else wrong with him. I'm going to have to call in one of the biochemists to have a look at this.'

I left to do the evening surgery and returned at about eight that evening. The registrar and the biochemist were in deep consultation in the ward sister's office.

'Any news?' I asked.

'He's even weaker than he was before,' said the registrar, 'and his potassium is still dropping.'

'I think it's one of these rare hereditary hypokalaemias,' said the biochemist. 'I've seen one like it before. Years ago now, though.'

'We have to fill him up with potassium,' said the registrar, 'or else he'll just fade away and stop breathing before the night is out.'

'Can you get it in fast enough by mouth?' I asked.

The biochemist shook his head. 'It'll have to go in intravenously,' he said.

'It should be interesting,' said the registrar. He didn't look as if he found the prospect very inviting.

I went with him when he went to give the injection. Potassium is usually given intravenously only in very diluted solutions. The syringe which the registrar was carrying was full of a very concentrated solution containing a large quantity of potassium. As it was slowly pumped into the Swiss boy's arm I saw the sweat drip off the registrar's forehead. Half an hour later it was all over. The boy began to move a bit more easily, the syringe was empty and the registrar looked exhausted.

'His heart stopped twice while I was giving him that,' the registrar told me as we moved away from the bedside. 'I need a drink.'

'It's on me,' I told him. I waited while he changed out of his white coat and then took him across the road to a pub patronized largely by hospital employees. When I got back to the surgery to see if any more calls had come in, I found that there had been one from Mrs Roberts. She'd left a message asking me to ring back.

'Your young Swiss has a disease he's had since birth,' I told her. 'I think you'll find that he usually takes potassium tablets quite regularly. Somehow he managed to come away without them. It was lucky I got him straight into hospital, for if he hadn't been there he'd be dead by now.'

There was no sound from the other end of the line.

I called back in at the hospital the following morning to see how the boy was doing. He was sitting up in bed giving French lessons to the nurses, and seemed quite happy with the world. I saw the medical registrar talking to the sister.

'Hello there,' he cried. 'Come to see your Swiss?'

I nodded.

We talked about the case for a couple of minutes and then the registrar wagged a finger at me. 'You know,' he said, 'I couldn't help thinking last night that there is one way to ensure you get excellent service out of the NHS.'

'What's that?' I asked.

'Have an interesting disease,' he said. 'You think about it.'

I thought about it when I visited an elderly man with bronchitis, an eighty-year-old woman who was simply crippled with arthritis, and a young girl with multiple sclerosis, and as I left the bedside of a young man with a chest infection I suddenly realized just how right the registrar was. The patient with the unusual or exceptional illness gets much better attention and far more intensive medical care. The health service is designed to care for the haemophiliacs, the patients needing open-heart surgery, the ones with rare endocrine disorders and those with hypokalaemia.

It is not geared to care overmuch for the elderly, the mentally ill or the disabled. If you ever get a choice between trypanosomiasis and tonsillitis, choose trypanosomiasis.

thirty-three

The waiting-room was full to the brim with unhappy children sitting on their mothers' laps and nursing seasonable colds, all the readable magazines were in use, when Michael Robinson came into the surgery. Miss Williams suggested to me that he might deserve earlier attention than his time of arrival would otherwise merit. She had noticed that around his left wrist was wrapped a rather dirty handkerchief which was already a rich red in colour.

'What on earth have you been doing?' I asked the boy as he sat down, holding the wrist out in front of him.

'We was playing by the canal,' he said quietly. 'I went to pick up a piece of wood sticking out of the water, but it was stuck and I had to take hold of it underneath the water to try to get it free.' He winced as I slowly unwrapped the handkerchief from around his wound. 'There must have been a nail or something still in the wood,' he told me. 'I thought I'd just scratched myself until I saw the water turning red.'

He had a nasty-looking gash. It was only about an inch and a half long, but it was quite deep and wide. It had been bleeding fairly furiously, and it didn't look too dirty, but I told the boy to stand up, and walked him over to the sink, holding the now-sodden handkerchief underneath his hand to catch the drops of blood still leaving the wound. Then I turned on the cold water tap and washed the wound out properly. It looked quite clean but clearly needed a couple of stitches.

'Which stretch of the canal were you playing by?' I asked him as I rummaged around looking for a needle and some instruments.

'The bit behind the hospital,' said the boy.

'And you've walked all the way up here?' I asked him. 'Why on earth didn't you go into the hospital?'

'I did do,' said the boy, 'but they told me to go and see my own doctor.'

'They told you to do *what*?' I demanded, hardly believing my ears.

'They told me to come and see you,' he said.

I had managed to find a pair of sharp scissors and a needle-holder. I was still looking for a needle, however. Dr Oaks was not the tidiest of men, although he did keep his surgery fairly well stocked.

'Who did you see?' I asked him. 'One of the cleaners?'

'It were a lady in a blue dress,' the boy told me. 'She told me that the hospital didn't have a casualty department and said I'd have to come and see you.' The boy shook his hand and peered cautiously into the wound. 'It doesn't hurt very much,' he said. 'I'd have thought it would hurt more.'

'Got it!' I said, triumphantly holding out a ready-threaded needle neatly wrapped in a sterile package.

'You going to sew me up?' asked the boy.

'That's right,' I said.

'Will it hurt?'

'Not much,' I assured him. 'You only need two or three stitches. It won't take more than a couple of minutes to put them in.'

He was braver than I would have been, and I managed to sew him up quite neatly. When I'd finished I gave him a tetanus injection. 'Come back and see me in five days,' I told him, 'and don't get that wound dirty.'

When he'd gone I telephoned the hospital and asked to speak to the hospital secretary.

'I've just seen a young lad who was injured in your grounds an hour or so ago,' I told the administrator. 'He tells me that he was told that he'd have to see his own doctor to get treatment.'

'What was wrong with him?' asked the secretary.

'He'd cut his hand,' I said. 'Not badly, just a one-and-a-half-inch cut needing a few stiches, but a cut nevertheless.'

'Oh, well, a cut is a casualty problem,' said the hospital secretary. 'We've had to close our casualty department.'

'Close it?' I asked. 'Close the casualty department?'

'That's right,' said the administrator. 'All casualties have to go to the district hospital ten miles away. It's obviously better, however, if general practitioners can deal with minor problems.'

I was so astonished that I couldn't think of anything else to say, so I put the telephone down and pressed the button underneath the desk to tell the next patient to come in. To my surprise it was a nun.

'Good morning,' I said, not quite sure whether or not I ought to stand up.

'Good morning, Doctor,' said the nun cheerily. 'I'm pleased to meet you.'

I hastily looked through the pile of notes on the desk, searching for one emblazoned with a suitable-looking name. I could see nothing that looked a likely possibility.

'Could you tell me your name?' I asked her. 'I'm very sorry, but . . .'

'That's all right, Doctor,' said the nun, 'you can't be expected to know everyone's name. I'm Sister Agnes.'

'Ah, thank you,' I said, looking through the notes. I still couldn't find one that was marked with the right name.

'I used to be Thelma Bottomley,' said the nun, with the faintest hint of a blush appearing on her cheeks.

Sure enough, the top set of notes on the desk were in the name of Thelma Bottomley.

'Well, what can I do for you?' I asked, picking up her notes and pushing the others out of the way for the time being.

'A couple of little problems, Doctor,' said Sister Agnes.

I waited expectantly.

'I seem to be suffering from dandruff,' she said suddenly.

'Oh dear,' I said. 'How long have you had that?'

'Several weeks now,' said Sister Agnes. 'I've tried several different brands of shampoo, but it doesn't seem to be getting any better.' She paused and then giggled unexpectedly. 'It's so bad that I don't have to put sugar on my cornflakes,' she told me.

'Could I have a look?' I asked, uncertain as to whether or not I was allowed to see underneath her cowl.

'Of course,' said Sister Agnes without hesitation, pushing back her headgear and revealing a full head of deep black hair thickly flecked with white. I looked at it, made sure that there was nothing more than simple dandruff the matter and then wrote out a prescription for a powerful medicated shampoo.

'You'll have to use this two or three times a week for a month or so,' I told her, 'and then I suggest that you use it every week for another couple of months.'

'Thank you, Doctor,' said Sister Agnes, accepting the prescription, folding it and pushing it deep inside her habit.

'You said a couple of little problems,' I reminded her.

'Oh, yes,' said the nun. 'I think I've got piles.'

'Piles?' I repeated.

'I think that's what it is,' she said. 'They're very uncomfortable.'

'Do they bleed?' I asked her.

'Occasionally,' replied the nun. 'Do you want to look at them?'

'Er, well, er,' I answered, 'if that's all right.'

'Of course it's all right,' said Sister Agnes, peeling off her habit. 'You're a doctor, aren't you?'

She stripped quickly and lay down on the examination couch. It didn't take long to confirm that she did indeed have piles. In a strange way it was both disturbing and comforting to discover that nuns have piles. I wrote out another prescription for her, this time for some suppositories and ointment.

'You know what to do with the suppositories, don't you?' I said to her when she'd dressed.

'Chew them well,' replied the nun immediately, with a tremendous grin on her face.

'But remove the silver paper first,' I reminded her, pressing the button underneath the desk as Sister Agnes disappeared.

'Take your jumper and blouse off,' I said to Mrs Howlett, the greengrocer's wife, who came into the surgery complaining of a persistent cough and slight pains in her chest. She looked at me and allowed an eyebrow to wander northwards.

'I want to listen to your chest,' I explained, lest there be any misunderstanding.

'Oh,' said Mrs Howlett, surprised. 'Dr Oaks never needs to listen to my chest. He always knows what to give me.'

'Well, he's had a lot more experience than I have,' I explained. 'I'd be grateful if you'd let me just have a listen.'

Reluctantly she pulled off her jumper and began to unbutton her blouse. She unbuttoned it from the neck down to the point where her gold necklace came into view, and stood waiting.

'I need a little bit more than that, I'm afraid,' I said.

'Dr Oaks never—' began Mrs Howlett.

'Just unbutton the blouse, please,' I begged. She unbuttoned the rest of it and put it down on the examination couch. She still had a petticoat, a vest and brassière to protect her skin from my gaze.

171

'Oh dear,' I murmured. 'Do you think I could ask you to remove your underthings?'

'Well, really,' said Mrs Howlett, clearly shocked. 'I wouldn't have thought that was necessary.' Nevertheless, she pulled her petticoat down and pulled her vest up to her neck; finally she unfastened her brassière. She didn't remove any of these garments, however, and I was left with the problem of finding my way through a three-dimensional nylon maze.

Eventually I managed to manoeuvre the end of my stethoscope over the top of her petticoat, underneath her raised vest and behind the solid structure of her brassière. I listened for a few moments and then with difficulty retrieved my instrument. While she dressed I wrote out a prescription.

'Here you are,' I said, when we'd both finished. 'I'm giving you a prescription for a bottle of medicine and for some tablets.'

Mrs Howlett looked at the prescription carefully, then she looked up at me with a superior smile on her face. 'That's what Dr Oaks always used to give me,' she said, 'and he never needed to examine me.'

Even after working in the surgery for several months I was still very much aware that Dr Oaks was the real doctor and that I was merely a replacement, temporarily accepted because I'd been employed and therefore given the medical seal of approval by Dr Oaks himself. After a lifetime as a general practitioner he had learnt a great deal about his patients, and indeed about human beings in general. He knew what people's weaknesses were, he recognized their strengths and he had their confidence. In their turn his patients knew him, knew his strengths and weaknesses and welcomed him as a member of the family. They would come to the surgery to chat to him, to bring news of Grandma's legs and young Maureen's asthma, to ask advice about ailing and ageing friends and relatives.

Dr Oaks' patients talked about him with great affection, asking to be remembered to him, and leaving messages which I frequently failed to understand but which I reported faithfully word for word. It wasn't just in the surgery that his word was lore. Travelling around the town with him was a particularly memorable experience. He drove slowly and carefully, for he expected to be flagged down at regular intervals on any local journey. He kept a prescription pad and pen in the glove compartment of his faithful but battered Wolseley and in the pockets of all his jackets. His journeys around the town, whether by car or on foot, would be interrupted by a number of prescription-signing sessions which, to the outside observer, seemed to turn him into a celebrity. A visit to the cobbler would be lengthened by the need to give Mrs Townsend a prescription for something to deal with her mother's night cramps, a visit to the bookshop would be interrupted by a conversation with Mr Browne, anxious to discuss his errant daughter, and a visit to the town hall to complain about his rates would be extended by the need to accept the counter clerk's confidences about his neighbour's wife. When in a hurry, Dr Oaks would walk with head bowed and eyes averted; that way he could avoid all but the most determined patients.

There may have been many times when Dr Oaks was annoyed by this persistent invasion of what was left of his privacy, but there were also times when he was grateful for the fact that his face and name were as well known locally as those of many more celebrated national figures.

For example, I was once driving with him to a medical dinner in a neighbouring village, when we were stopped by a police car. Now, Dr Oaks had an original if perhaps careless approach to the whole business of driving. He would never park his car, but would simply abandon it wherever he happened to be; an amusing and even likeable trait in his own town, where the police and traffic wardens would simply put cones around it and direct the traffic around it, but an offence in other towns, where Dr Oaks would regularly be awarded tickets for his skills at impromptu parking. Similarly Dr Oaks drove as if he were the only motorist on the road. It would have perhaps been safer if his supposition had been an accurate one, for Dr Oaks had numerous unusual driving habits. He would, for example, use the white lines down the middle of the road as a guide between the hedgerows. He regarded traffic lights as simply warning lights suggesting extra care, and he would never dream of sitting parked at a red light if there was no traffic travelling from left to right or right to left. He would completely ignore all other road signs and travel at the speed he found most suitable.

We were stopped for some trivial offence like crossing double white lines on the main road out of town at a speed over twice the legal limit, and the policeman who had stopped us came round to the car with a particularly satisfied leer. He walked towards us with the exaggerated slowness which traffic policemen must practise.

'Good evening, sir,' he said, bending slightly and peering into the car.

'Hello, William,' said Dr Oaks, 'how's your Aunty Bertha?'

'Oh, she's fine, thank you, Doctor,' said William. 'I didn't realize it was you. I'm very sorry.'

'Is she out of hospital now?' asked Dr Oaks, concerned. I think that was probably why he was so popular – he was always so genuinely interested.

'She came out last Friday,' said William.

'And your mother?' asked Dr Oaks. 'How is she these days? I haven't seen her for six months now.'

'Not bad at all,' said William. 'She still gets twinges from time to time, but she gets about very well.'

'Oh, I'm so pleased,' said Dr Oaks. 'Well, we must be off; we have an emergency to attend to.'

'Of course, sir,' said William, unaware that the emergency was an expensive dinner spoiling. 'I'm sorry to have stopped you.'

'I'm glad you did,' said Dr Oaks. 'It was nice to see you.'

William saluted as Dr Oaks noisily found a forward gear and edged away.

'Nice young fellow,' he said.

'You forgot to ask about his grandmother,' I said, mischievously.

'Oh, no,' said Dr Oaks earnestly, 'his grandmother is fine. She had her operation months ago.'

thirty-four

It was nearly midnight on the day when I'd met both Sister Agnes and Mrs Howlett when Mrs Castle telephoned. She sounded apologetic, and began by explaining that she didn't usually like to bother doctors during the night, but that she thought one was really needed this time. She told me that her husband, a retired butcher whose name still adorned two shops in the centre of town, had been getting worse and worse all day.

'I kept thinking he would improve,' she told me, 'but now I'm sure that he won't last until the morning unless someone comes to see him.'

While listening to her I was already scrambling out of bed and into the pants, socks, trousers and polo-necked sweater which I kept by the bedside when I was on night call. Patients may prefer to see their doctor dressed neatly in an immaculate white shirt, a well-pressed pin-stripe suit and a pair of polished black shoes but, in the middle of the night, the patient who is ill doesn't really care what his doctor looks like, as long as he gets there quickly, and the patient who calls the doctor but isn't really ill doesn't count.

The roads were glistening with a film of water from a heavy shower which had fallen an hour or two earlier, and almost totally deserted. The post-closing-time rush had long since finished, and now the town was left for the night people. I doubt if I ever will get used to waking and driving across town in the middle of others' peaceful slumber, but there are compensations: the roads are free and uncluttered, the town is silent and relaxed, and there are always the stars for company.

Mr and Mrs Castle lived in a town house on a small estate. It was a smart three-storey house with the living-room and two bedrooms on the first floor, and the bathroom and two more bedrooms on the top floor. Mr Castle was in bed on the first floor.

When I examined him he was cold and sweating a great deal. His breathing was uncomfortable and he seemed to be having difficulty in getting air into his chest. His pulse was fast and not very strong. His lips and face were slightly blue. His blood pressure was low and his ankles were slightly swollen. He looked genuinely ill.

Mrs Castle gave me a handful of bottles which, she explained, contained the tablets which her husband was taking. I looked at them quickly, mentally thanking the people who had ordained that the names of drugs should appear on the bottles, and learnt a great deal about Mr Castle's past history from them.

'What's the trouble?' asked Mrs Castle. 'Is he going to be all right?'

'I'll have to give him an injection,' I told her, 'and then I think it might be wise to get your husband into the hospital for a day or two.'

'Oh dear,' said Mrs Castle. 'Has he really got to go into hospital?'

'I want to give him oxygen urgently,' I told her, 'and I think he'd be best off in hospital where they can give it to him straightaway.'

Mrs Castle sat down on the bed and held her husband's hand. I sat down on the other side of the bed and held his other hand. She was holding his hand in affection; I was holding his hand while I looked for a vein in his arm which I could use for the injection I was planning to give.

The human heart is a fantastic piece of machinery. It beats seventy times a minute every hour of the day for is long as its owner is alive. It doesn't have time off for holidays or maintenance. It never has a rest and it never goes on strike. Attempts to manufacture an artificial human heart have so far met with enormous technical problems, and the only artificial replacements which have been made are so complicated that they cost as much as a small house, and then then they are unlikely to last for more than a year or two at most.

It is not surprising that from time to time the heart grows tired and needs a little help. Mr Castle's heart just wasn't managing to get the blood around his body at the right pace. It was pooling in the lungs, with the result that Mr Castle was literally beginning to drown in his own blood. Blood and body fluids were also collecting in the legs, particularly around the ankles, rather than continuing usefully around the body.

There are a number of drugs which can help in a crisis like this. One of the most important is morphine. Another which is useful is a diuretic – a drug which encourages the kidneys to empty more fluid out of the body.

I took an ampoule of morphine and an ampoule of a diuretic out of my black bag and laid them carefully on the bed. Then I took out two syringes and two needles and fitted them together. Holding the ampoule carefully, I drew the morphine solution up into one of the syringes. Then I did the same thing with the diuretic, drawing it up into the other syringe.

Sticking needles into veins is a craft which is not difficult to master. The most difficult part about learning how to do it is overcoming one's natural reluctance to plunge sharp needles into other people whom one does not know. The novice tends to be too hesitant, too cautious, and therefore to inject painfully. With a little experience the needle can be stabbed neatly into the vein so that literally little more than a sharp prick is felt by the patient.

I'd prepared both the injections I planned to give, so that when I'd given Mr Castle the morphine I could use the same site to give the diuretic. I put the needle attached to the morphine-containing syringe into a suitable vein first and gave that injection; then I took the needle off the diuretic-containing syringe, and the empty syringe off the needle already in the vein, and re-attached the full diuretic-containing syringe on to it. The other needle and syringe I discarded.

Mr Castle recovered miraculously. He wasn't fit enough to go on a cross-country run or even walk downstairs by himself but, five minutes later, he was breathing much more easily. He smiled at me and nodded his head in approval. Most modern medicine is pretty slow and often fairly hit-and-miss, but there are some procedures which produce an almost miraculous recovery. Syringing ears, putting catheters into overfull bladders, and injecting morphine into patients with heart failure are procedures which very often prove immediately successful and satisfying for both patient and performer.

I left Mr Castle and went across the room to where Mrs Castle was standing with her hands over her face.

'It's all right now,' I told her. 'He's feeling a little better already.'

'Oh, thank heavens,' said Mrs Castle, ignoring the success of my own ministrations.

'Can I borrow your telephone?' I asked.

'Certainly, Doctor,' she said. 'It's in the kitchen.'

I telephoned the ambulance station first of all and asked them to send an ambulance round to the house straight away.

'What sort of case is it?' asked the ambulance man.

'A heart case,' I told him.

'Right, sir,' said the ambulance man, sounding excited. 'We'll send our cardiac ambulance.'

I was impressed by this, for I had always thought of ambulances as being very much of a muchness. They are white, large and filled with bits and pieces of medical equipment. They always have red blankets so that the blood doesn't show, and are manned by ambulance men who are invariably kind, considerate and courteous.

Next I telephoned the hospital, woke up the house physician and asked him if he had any beds for men. He told me with regret that all their beds were full and that they already had two put up in the corridors. So I had to telephone another local hospital several miles away. Fortunately they had a spare bed and, when I'd explained the situation, they promised to get ready to receive Mr Castle as soon as we could get him there.

No sooner had I put the telephone down than the ambulance drew up outside the house. In fact, to say that they parked it outside the house is something of an exaggeration. The truth is that it was such a huge vehicle that they had to park it on the verge forty or fifty yards away.

'What's this about a cardiac ambulance?' I asked the older of the two ambulance men.

'Haven't you seen it before?' he asked. Like all ambulance men, he seemed friendly and talkative.

I had to admit that I hadn't.

'Come down with us and we'll show you around,' he promised. 'There's no great hurry, is there?'

I shook my head. 'No great hurry,' I agreed.

I followed them down the stairs and then waited at the back of the ambulance while the two uniformed men loaded the stretcher into their vehicle. Mr Castle was now in good humour. He felt better and was even cracking jokes. The British are a great race for cracking jokes when they've just had a foot through the pearly gates.

They invited me inside when they'd settled the patient comfortably. The ambulance looked like an intensive-care unit in a busy general hospital. It was packed solid with expensive pieces of equipment.

'You've got some good stuff in here,' I told them. The two ambulance men beamed.

'What's this?' I asked, bending over a large machine in one corner.

'That's our electrocardiogram,' explained the older ambulance man. 'It's one of the best. Cost several hundred pounds.' He picked up a couple of leads and showed them to me. 'We've got a screen in the cab on which we can keep an eye, and there's a permanent recorder which keeps a physical record of the cardiac rhythms.'

'Ah,' I said. It was all getting a bit too much for me.

'We've got a cassette recorder on which we can keep sound records of everything that goes on,' said the younger man.

'And we've got an excellent defibrillator,' the older man went on, 'and equipment for intubating.'

'Anything for heart surgery?' I asked.

He ignored me, and opened a cupboard on the other side of the ambulance, displaying a shelf full of laryngoscopes, tubes and other pieces of anaesthetic equipment.

'Of course, we carry a wide variety of drugs,' said the younger man, opening another cupboard and showing me what looked like a chemist's shop. 'And several spare oxygen cylinders,' he continued, pointing out an oxygen store at the far end of the ambulance.

'We're in full radio contact with the cardiac unit at the hospital as well as with our own base,' said the older man. 'We can stay in contact with the specialist while we drive in.'

'Fantastic,' I murmured. 'Quite remarkable.'

'Of course, we all go on a six-month course,' said the younger man, 'and learn all about elevated S.T. segments and Q waves in V.4.'

I didn't know what he was talking about, so I nodded.

'We have a six-month course in anaesthetics, pharmacology and cardiology,' said the other man.

'Well, I suppose we'd beter be going,' said the younger man.

'Can I come with you?' asked Mrs Castle, who'd been waiting, patient but forgotten, on the pavement.

'Of course,' said the older man. 'Jump up, love.' He pulled down a seat from the wall and showed Mrs Castle how to use the safety belt.

'All right?' said the younger man.

'Fine,' I said. 'Thanks.'

They waved to me and climbed up into the ambulance.

'Very impressive,' I shouted.

They both waved cheerily, and nodded, content.

The older man turned the key and pressed the starter button. The engine whined for a moment and then died away. He tried again. The same thing happened once more. He pulled the choke out and tried once more, with no bettter fortune.

'We seem to be having a little trouble,' said the younger man, jumping out of the vehicle. He looked embarrassed.

I didn't say anything. I couldn't think of anything appropriate.

'There's a slight incline just here,' said the ambulance man. 'If you could just give us a bit of a push . . .'

thirty-five

Dr Oaks unexpectedly suggested one Friday that I should take a weekend away from the practice. 'Go and breathe some different air,' he said. 'Go somewhere with lots of bright lights for a change.'

'But who'll look after the patients?' I asked him.

'Me, of course,' replied Dr Oaks. 'I'm fit enough now. A weekend's work won't do me any harm.'

'Hey, now, wait a minute . . .' I began to argue.

'I'm perfectly capable of doing two days' work,' he insisted. 'Wrapping myself up in cotton-wool won't do anyone any good.'

Eventually I gratefully agreed with him that a weekend away would do both of us good. I went down to London to stay with friends. The two days I spent there confirmed more than ever my feeling that I am not a big-city man. The bright lights soon lose their attraction when bathed in clouds of smog, and I soon got bored with sitting around in traffic jams.

When I got back from London late on Sunday evening, Dr Oaks was sitting up in the surgery attending to his practice accounts.

'Hello,' he said, pushing aside a half-full cup of cold coffee and pushing a huge mound of papers and receipts off a chair. 'Thought I'd spend the evening doing something useful.'

'Why don't you get an accountant to deal with all that?' I asked him, nodding to the piles of paperwork.

'I've got an accountant,' said Dr Oaks, 'but I have to get the accounts into some sort of shape before he can start!'

'What sort of weekend did you have?' I asked, settling down and resting my elbow on half a dozen old cheque books and a paying-in book. I watched with fascinated awe as Dr Oaks played with a pocket calculator.

'Fairly quiet,' he said. The figures didn't seem to please him, so he stabbed angrily at his calculator again.

'No emergencies?' I asked.

'Mrs Lightwood called me at four this morning to look at her baby who had a cold,' said Dr Oaks absentmindedly.

'You've got your thumb resting on the percentage sign,' I told him.

He looked at me very strangely.

'Move your thumb,' I said. 'Your calculator is working out percentages.'

'Oh, thanks,' he grinned, suddenly comprehending. He moved his thumb.

'Do you fancy another coffee?' I asked him. 'I'm going to make one for myself. I've had a long drive.'

'I'd love a coffee,' said Dr Oaks. He hunted around on the desk.

181

'Are you looking for your coffee-cup?' I asked.

'Yes,' he nodded.

I picked it up from on top of an income tax assessment form. The coffee-cup had left a round brown stain on the form.

'I think I've been at this long enough,' Dr Oaks said wearily.

'I'll make the coffee,' I promised, moving to the door.

'Oh dear me, I've just remembered,' said Dr Oaks. 'There was something else. Mr Renton.'

'Mr Renton?' I said, my hand on the door.

'The long-jumper or pole-vaulter or something.'

'High-jumper,' I corrected him.

'High-jumper,' agreed Dr Oaks.

'What about him?' I asked.

'He died,' said Dr Oaks. 'On Saturday night.'

'My God,' said I.

Mr Renton, it appeared, had been holding a dinner-party for a few former sportsmen who had shared the spotlight with him several decades ago. He had, according to his wife, been anxious to impress, and had flirted outrageously with the wife of a former middle-distance runner. After dinner he had insisted on pushing back the furniture and attempting to clear the cocktail cabinet. Years of immobility had not prepared him for such wearing activity and he had collapsed and died within minutes. He'd been dead before Dr Oaks had arrived at the house.

'Would you go and see his widow in the morning?' asked Dr Oaks. 'Just to see if she's all right. I gave her a couple of sleeping-pills to help her over last night and tonight, but she may need some more help for a few days yet.'

Mrs Renton was dressed in a simple black dress when I called. She looked pale and rather worn. I was surprised in a way because, from what I'd remembered of her husband, he wasn't a man who deserved a great deal of mourning.

'I'll miss him in a strange way,' she said. 'He was a very unhappy man, you know.'

'Tell me about him, then,' I said. A priest once told me that asking a bereaved relative to talk about their lost and loved one is perhaps the best way to help. In my very limited experience, that is perfectly true.

'He never came to terms with the fact that he was no longer a sportsman,' said Mrs Renton. 'It was as simple as that. It wasn't just the competition that he loved; it was the glory. He loved being made a fuss of, and he loved all the publicity.'

'He liked you to make a fuss of him,' I suggested.

Mrs Renton nodded. 'He liked anyone to make a fuss of him,' she told me. 'He was an awful baby really. And yet he had some good points too, you know.'

I said nothing, but simply nodded.

'He was very generous,' she said to me. 'He would always help youngsters, too; if they ever came for advice, he'd always give it. Mind you, they had to listen to some tales of his exploits, but they'd get their advice, and often a few pounds to help with their training costs.'

She talked about her husband for another half an hour or so and I said very little. Having someone to talk to seemed to help her a little, and I promised to call back at the end of the week, after the funeral.

When I got there she was out of mourning, dressed in a simple blue skirt and cardigan.

'I didn't know how long to wear black,' she said. 'But we have to live, don't we? And we don't need clothes to remind us of those we've lost.'

I agreed with her.

'My husband died intestate, you know,' said Mrs Renton.

'I'm surprised at that,' I commented. 'He seemed to me to be a most meticulous man.'

'He would never make a will,' said Mrs Renton. 'He always insisted that making wills was a morbid thing to do. He hated to have to think about dying. I don't really think he ever *did* think about dying.'

'What about the estate, then?' I asked

'Apparently it all comes to me,' said Mrs Renton. 'I don't know about such things, and I half-thought it might go to his son. But apparently this is all mine now.' She looked around, without pride or greed, at the spacious house so well filled with mementoes and trophies.

'What will you do with it?' I asked her.

'I've been thinking about it a lot yesterday and today,' said Mrs Renton. 'I can either sell the house and buy a small flat, or else I can try to make the place work for me. I can't afford to keep it going without any income. The money from the investments will hardly pay the heating bills. My husband had an income from a trust fund, but that stopped when he died.'

'Didn't he have any insurance?' I asked.

'He would never think of insurance,' said Mrs Renton. 'That reminded him of dying too.'

'So what are you going to do?' I asked.

'You'll laugh at me,' she said.

'I promise I won't!' I told her.

'I'm going to open a nursing home,' said Mrs Renton.

'A nursing home!' I repeated, quite surprised.

'There, I knew it,' she said. 'You think I'm mad.'

'No,' said I, 'that's not true. Though I do think you're a bit ambitious. There is a difference.'

'I don't mean a nursing home for people who need doctors and nurses,' explained Mrs Renton. 'I mean a home for elderly people who want somewhere to stay when they retire.'

'Are you sure you know what it entails?' I asked her.

'I think so,' she said. 'I've thought about it very carefully.'

'Old people can be very difficult,' I warned her.

' "Nursing home" probably isn't the right term,' said Mrs Renton. 'What I really mean is a home for elderly people who are fit and mobile but who can't afford to keep on homes of their own.'

'They'll live in a commune,' I suggested.

'That sort of thing,' said Mrs Renton. 'Of course, if they fall ill temporarily we'll try to keep them here, but there'll have to be an understanding that anyone who needs proper nursing care will have to go into a genuine nursing home.'

'You have thought about this, haven't you?'

'I have,' she said. 'I want to stay here and I want to do something useful. And I want to have lots of people living with me.'

'It sounds tremendous,' I agreed. 'Quite a challenge.'

'You mean you think I'm completely mad,' said Mrs Renton.

'Not at all,' I insisted.

'I shall try to ensure that we have some newly retired people here,' she went on, 'and we'll be able to do many things ourselves. We can grow our own vegetables and so on. There's plenty of land.'

'It sounds very pleasant,' I agreed. 'You'll have to take the right kind of people.'

'Oh, I will,' said Mrs Renton.

I left her then, still plotting and planning her new life. The scheme seemed to give her renewed energy.

When I got back to the surgery there was a note from the hospital on the doormat telling me that Miss Clarke was about to be allowed out of hospital. I telephoned the ward straightaway.

'Do you want a word with her?' asked the ward sister.

I said I'd very much like to.

Miss Clarke sounded very quiet.

'I don't want to go home,' she said. 'I love my parents, but my father frightens me in a way. I don't think I ought to go home.'

'Have you spoken to them about where you should go?' I asked her.

'They simply say that I should go home,' said Miss Clarke. 'But I don't think they'd stop me if I had somewhere else to go.'

Suddenly an idea flashed into my mind. I don't know what on earth made me say it, but I asked her if she'd consider doing me a favour.

'Of course,' she said. 'You've been kind to me.'

'A patient of ours died recently,' I said, 'and his widow is living alone in a very large house. She's friendly, pleasant and very quiet. I think you'd like her. Would you stay with her for a while?'

'Wouldn't she mind?' asked Miss Clarke.

'I'm sure she wouldn't,' I told her.

'Does she know about me?' she asked. 'About the pills and things?'

'No,' I said.

'Would you tell her?' she asked. 'She'd have to know.'

I put the telephone down after promising to ring back straightaway with an answer. Then I dialled Mrs Renton's number.

'I've got a patient due out of hospital,' I said, 'who was on drugs and who's just had a broken leg. She needs somewhere to live, but I'm sure she could help you with planning your new project.'

'My word!' said Mrs Renton after a moment or two's pause. 'You do believe in straight talking, don't you?'

I said nothing.

Then, after another few moments' silence, she laughed. 'How old is she?' she asked.

'In her late teens,' I answered.

'Is she still on drugs?' asked Mrs Renton. 'I have to ask.'

'No, she isn't,' I replied.

'I'd very much like to see her,' she said.

'She's at the hospital,' I said. 'On the orthopaedic ward.'

'Can I go over and see her now?' asked Mrs Renton.

'As soon as you like,' I said. 'I'll ring the hospital.'

She rang me from her home an hour and a half later.

'Miss Clarke's come home with me,' said Mrs Renton. 'I've had a word with her father, and he seems to have accepted the idea.'

After I'd put the telephone down I suddenly realized just how much I'd interfered with the lives of two of my patients. I confessed the whole affair to Dr Oaks. He was rightfully angry with me.

'It isn't your place to organize your patients' lives,' he told me. 'It's often very easy in general practice to plan people's lives for them. But it's a dangerous business. You can cause many heartaches and many extra problems and, if you do, it will be your responsibility.

In principle I knew that he was right. In practice I hoped that I might just be lucky.

thirty-six

'I see you've been asked to visit the Jacksons,' said Dr Oaks one morning as I prepared to leave the surgery.

I nodded. I had little idea how important that visit would be.

'Extraordinary family,' said Dr Oaks, leaning back against the surgery wall. 'Mr and Mrs Jackson were both killed in an aeroplane crash over Italy about four years ago. Since then the three children have lived at home with their grandmother, who happened to be looking after them at the time.'

'She just stayed on?' I asked.

Dr Oaks nodded. 'She sold up a small flat she'd got in Bournemouth, and moved in with them permanently. The oldest was then Jennie, who was about fifteen; Barry was twelve; and Michael was ten. Their granny, Mrs Jackson senior, must have been in her early eighties way back then.'

'And they've lived together since.'

'Very happily,' he said. 'The children do the shopping and most of the heavy housework. Granny, who's confined to a wheelchair, acts as a sort of foreman, making sure that everything gets done and keeping the peace when tempers fly. Jennie left school at sixteen to get some money into the household,' he went on, 'and she's now got a good job at one of the local dress shops. She has a good sense of style and colour, and I gather she's made quite an impression with the manager. The two brothers are still at school – doing very well, from all I hear.'

'I shall look forward to meeting them,' I said, picking up the list of calls I'd prepared and heading for the door. I had a numger of other visits to do, and I'd made a list which was intended to enable me to tour the town once rather than three or four times. It was lunchtime when I got to the Jacksons'.

The whole family was sitting round the kitchen table tucking into a succulent-looking steak-and-kidney pudding. The middle child, Barry, explained that the patient was Granny, who had been getting some annoying pains in her chest and also noticed some shortness of breath. Therefore, with apologies, I took Gran away from the table for a few minutes, settling her down in the front sitting-room.

I examined Mrs Jackson carefully, and eventually decided that she simply needed a few extra tablets to help keep her heart functioning effectively. I wrote out a suitable prescription and offered to help her back into the kitchen.

'That's all right, Doctor,' she said. 'I can manage, thank you.'

'She's extraordinarily stubborn,' said Michael, busy polishing his plate with a piece of bread. 'She insists on doing as much as she can by herself.'

'Have you seen the garden?' asked Barry.

'It's very impressive,' I agreed. 'Does Granny help with it?'

'Granny does the garden,' said Michael. 'She won't let any of us touch it.'

I looked out of the window again, this time more carefully. 'Granny does the garden!' I repeated. 'That's tremendous.' I really was most impressed. It was a wonderful sight, full of well-kept plants and bushes.

'We all pull our weight in this family,' Granny assured me.

'But how do you do it?' I had to ask. 'How on earth do you manage to cope with a garden when, if you'll forgive me, you're clearly confined to a wheelchair?'

'Come with me,' said Michael, pushing his now-empty plate aside, 'and I'll show you.' He stood up and led me outside. As I followed him through the back door I saw that the flower-beds and some of the vegetable-patches were raised two or three feet above the rest of the garden. Small brick walls had been built to a height of two or three feet and the areas within them had been filled with earth. The result was a series of gardening-troughs which could easily be tended by someone in a wheelchair.

'We've also got Granny a whole series of long-handled implements so that she can do pruning, hoeing and so on,' Michael told me.

'Granny always liked gardening,' said Jennie.

'We've even got a few fruit-trees which will never grow more than a few feet high,' said Michael.

'But they produce beautiful fruit,' said Jennie, pointing out the trees to me. I could see that they were quite heavy with promise.

I followed them back into the kitchen and offered my congratulations to Granny. 'You have a wonderful set of grand-children,' I told her.

'We have a wonderful grandmother,' said Jennie. 'We wouldn't have been able to stay together without her.' They all looked at one another with a deep affection which many people never know, and which is much more valuable than diamonds or gold.

'You're not by any chance going into town, are you?' asked Barry as Michael and Jennie started to move the dishes off the table.

I nodded. 'Can I give you a lift?' I asked.

'That's very good of you,' said Barry. 'Thanks.' He picked up his coat and slipped it on. 'I promised to take the small boy next door into town for his mother, to get him some new shoes.'

'Neil is four,' explained Jennie, 'and he has three brothers and a sister. If his mother goes shopping and has to take them all with her, it costs her a fortune in bus fares and ice creams.'

'So sometimes we look after the children while she goes shopping alone, and sometimes we take the children into town when they need new clothes,' explained Barry.

'Certainly, I'll take you into town,' I told him. 'I'll wait for you in the car.'

Barry came out with Neil a few minutes later and they climbed into the car. I had no more visits to do and, when I had parked outside the department store where Barry had been told to buy the shoes, I decided to go with them. I needed some toothpaste anyway.

We bought the toothpaste and the shoes on the top floor, and then fought our way into a lift ready to take us down to the ground floor. Although the lift contained no more passengers than the manufacturers had recommended on their notice inside the cabin, there wasn't much room for such activities as breathing. The manufacturers must have designed their lifts to be used by slender models and wafer-thin youths. Barry, Neil and I were crushed into one corner. Right in front of us there stood a smartly dressed middle-aged woman and an extremely shapely young woman in blue.

As people usually do when standing in lifts, we all faced the

189

front. The two women in front of us were standing quite close together. As the lift dropped past the second floor (carpets, bed linen, garden furniture and gents' outfitters) the middle-aged woman suddenly screamed. With great difficulty she lifted her hand, turned round and slapped me in the face. I could feel what seemed to be a fairly neatly defined palm-mark beginning to appear on my face as she tried to get into position for a second shot.

Everyone else in the lift turned round to stare. The attendant, obviously worried that his lift might never reach its destination, and perhaps even dreaming of being the first lift attendant to have his craft hijacked, yelled at us all to keep still. An elderly gentleman in a check jacket and a deerstalker hat winked at me and grinned broadly. He gazed at what he could see of the middle-aged woman's ample buttocks and nodded his approval. I looked away.

Barry and Neil both looked puzzled. The young girl with the blue dress and the well-filled skin turned round and looked slightly amused.

'What on earth was that for?' I demanded at last, suddenly realizing that my silence might convict me.

'You know,' cried the offended woman, her bosom heaving and rolling like a rough sea. 'You touched my bottom!'

'He'd have had a job not to in here,' muttered another woman, heavily loaded up with shopping-bags and parcels. I noticed that she was a patient I'd seen before and, after smiling my thanks at her, I tried to hide my face behind a brown-paper parcel which contained Neil's old shoes. (He had, of course, insisted on wearing his new ones straightaway.)

I quietly prayed that no other patients were in the lift – or in the store, for that matter. My prayers were unfinished when we reached the ground floor and with a great sigh of relief the attendant opened the doors.

'All wait here,' he cried.

'I'm not waiting here, I'm in a hurry,' said the man with the deerstalker hat.

'I think you have to,' said the woman who'd slapped my face. 'You're wanted as a witness.'

'He can't make me stay,' said the man with the deerstalker.

'Don't you dare leave,' snapped the woman bossily. 'A lift attendant has the same responsibilities as the captain of a ship. He can clap you in irons if he wishes.'

The man and the deerstalker left simultaneously without another word. The aggrieved woman started after him for a couple of paces and then, realizing, I suppose, that I might be tempted to escape, retraced her steps with a snort.

The lift attendant came back almost immediately with a policeman. The policeman took out his notebook, studied the woman who had made the complaint and then put it away again.

'What's the trouble, madam?' he asked.

'This man pinched my bottom,' claimed the woman.

'I deny it,' I said quickly.

'The lift was very crowded,' said the woman loaded high with parcels. 'It could have been an accident.'

'I think there's been a terrible mistake, officer,' said the luscious young thing in the blue dress. 'The young man was with me and I think he intended to pinch my bottom. He must have got the wrong bottom by mistake.'

I stared at her open-mouthed.

'Ah, well, then, that's simple enough,' said the policeman. 'Perhaps you'd be kind enough to apologize, sir.'

'Apologize?' I repeated stupidly.

'Since it was an accident I'm sure the lady would accept an apology,' said the policeman.

'Well, I don't know . . .' objected the slap-happy woman.

'Since it wasn't your bottom that was the object of the young man's attentions, I hardly think you have a case in law,' said the policeman.

'Then I suppose an apology would do,' said the woman.

I apologized quickly, took the young lady's arm and led Barry and Neil out into the sunshine.

'Thank you,' I said to the girl. 'Can I buy you dinner?'

'I shall call a policeman if you don't,' laughed the girl.

She gave me her address and I promised to pick her up the following evening. Then she told me she had to hurry off to work. As we waved goodbye to her, Neil pulled my coat. 'I like her,' he said.

'So do I,' I said.

'But I didn't like that other woman,' he said.

'Which one?' I asked.

'The one who was standing in front of us,' said Neil.

'Oh, that's all over,' I said. 'Forget it.'

'Yes, but I didn't like her,' he said, pointing to his left foot. 'She stood on my shoe.'

I bent down and rubbed the dust off his shoe. The woman's heel had left a mark on the leather. I murmured my sympathy.

'I'm glad I bit her,' said Neil, examining the damage.

'You did what?' said Barry.

'I bit her bottom,' said Neil. He looked up at us both. 'Well, she did stand on my foot,' he argued.

thirty-seven

She looked even prettier than she had when I'd met her before. I couldn't help wondering how I'd been so fortunate as to leave a lift with my reputation threatened and then end up with such a beautiful girl. Not even my mother would claim that I'm good-looking, and my gangling clumsy six-foot-three-inch frame always seems to be entwined with something inanimate.

'I've just realized that I don't know your name,' I said as I showed the girl into my car.

'And I don't know yours,' she said. I introduced myself and she told me that her name was Margaret Shore. I apologized for treading on her foot as she clambered in, and she told me to think nothing of it.

'Where shall we go?' I asked. 'What would you like to do? Do you want to go to a restaurant? Have you eaten?'

Margaret shook her head; her hair seemed light and free and appeared to float on the evening air. 'I'm not really hungry at the moment,' she said.

'Cinema?' I suggested. 'And we can eat later.'

'That would be lovely,' she said. 'What's on?'

'Well, I heard about a film on at a cinema in Yarrow Road,' I told her. 'It's about a couple of men who decide to blow up something or other.'

'Is it good?' asked Margaret.

'Well, I was told it's good,' I said, 'but I don't have that much faith in the critic.'

Margaret laughed. 'What else is on?' she asked. I liked the way she laughed.

'I really haven't the faintest idea,' I confessed.

I bought an evening paper and we decided to drive over to a a cinema a couple of miles out of town, where they were showing a film about a band of daring thieves who try to steal the Queen's personal jewels from Buckingham Palace. It didn't sound all that good but it seemed the best available.

I bought the tickets and followed the crowds shuffling out of the bitter winter cold into the warmth of the foyer, seizing the opportunity to take Margaret's hand in mine. We'd been standing in the foyer for two or three minutes before I realized that something had happened. All I could see was a small crowd of people, clearly consumed with curiosity, bending over something. For all I knew it could have been a naked midget, a hole in the floor, a couple making love or someone not feeling very well. My sense of duty and public responsibility fought momentarily with more private ambitions, and then won.

I settled Margaret down for a moment on the corner of a vacant bench-seat and excused myself. When I arrived I peered over the top of the nearest and lowest shoulders. A man, middle-aged, balding and very blue in the face, was lying flat on his back. By his side were kneeling two other men, one clearly the cinema manager and the second obviously knowing something about how to treat a sick person. Having got the patient lying on his side, he was feverishly searching for a pulse. He didn't seem to be having a great deal of success.

Forcing courage into both feet, I stepped forward and bent down.

'Are you a doctor?' I whispered.

The man shook his head and leapt back. 'Are you?' he asked. I nodded. He edged back even further. I was committed. I picked up the man's wrist and could feel absolutely nothing at all. Even his watch seemed to have stopped, smashed when he had fallen.

'Can you do mouth-to-mouth?' I asked the original first-aider, before he managed to edge back into the crowd.

He shuffled back towards me. 'Yes,' he nodded with the eagerness of someone who'd never done it before.

'Have you called an ambulance?' I asked the cinema manager. He nodedd and looked at his watch. 'Nearly five minutes ago,' he told me.

Disregarding the tiny voice inside me which warned that the man would probably get up and punch me on the nose, I ripped his coat open, unbuttoned his jacket and shirt and bared his chest. The crowd, which I had forgotten, surged forward expectantly, forgetting the big feature due to star at any moment, sensing some excitement and choosing instead to watch the live show in the foyer.

I pushed the man's case under his neck, started thumping his chest and tried to think of encouraging advice which I could give the poor first-aider, who'd got the miserable job of blowing air into those limp lungs through blue, saliva-sticky lips. The crowd was fairly buzzing with excitement. I had a horrible feeling that at any moment they would start throwing coins in our direction.

'You're doing fine. Keep at it. Don't worry. I'm a doctor,' said a voice at my elbow. I stopped for a moment and turned round. A young fellow who looked as though his qualifications were even newer and shinier than mine was crouching there and smiling encouragingly. 'You're doing all you can,' he added. I carried on thumping. Little beads of sweat formed on my forehead. I wondered what Margaret was doing.

Another five minutes passed and then a second pair of hands appeared on the man's chest across from me. I looked up. Attached to the pair of hands there was a gentleman in a neatly tied bow-tie who had a look of confidence.

'I'm a doctor,' said the newcomer, gently pushing my hands away and tapping daintily in the region of the man's heart. He looked in vain for some sign of raised jugular-venous pressure.

194

'Carry on,' he said, after a moment.

'That's so kind of you,' I murmured.

The cinema manager appeared again another minute later. 'The ambulance is here,' he said breathlessly.

I followed when they lifted the man on his stretcher down the steps and towards the ambulance standing outside.

'Can you come with us?' asked the ambulance man. There didn't seem much choice, so I got in.

'Let me in!' cried a young girl on the pavement. I opened the door. 'I'm a nurse,' she said, pulling me by the sleeve. 'Move over.'

Obediently I got out of the ambulance and hurried back inside to try to find Margaret.

'I'm sorry,' I said, when I finally managed to struggle through the crowd, back to where I'd left her. To my surprise she was still sitting there, patiently waiting.

'That's all right,' she said.

'Have I been long?' I asked.

'Only about five minutes,' she answered. 'The film hasn't started yet.'

'I had to go,' I explained. 'I'm a doctor.'

'You don't look like a doctor,' said Margaret.

'I think that's the nicest thing anyone's said to me for ages,' I told her.

'My doctor's about seventy and he smells of tobacco smoke,' said Margaret with a laugh. 'And whenever I go to see him I have to strip to the waist. Even for a sore throat.'

'I'm not seventy and I don't smoke,' I promised her.

The film was amusing enough and the manager, in recognition of my professional services, sent us both free ice creams. Afterwards we drove back into town and ate a barely palatable meal at a Chinese restaurant which had just opened. We talked easily and happily together, never once mentioning anything medical, and when I drove her home I kissed her goodnight. I could hardly believe it – the car hadn't broken down, I hadn't had my face slapped, the restaurant hadn't been closed for the night and we'd watched a film without the projectionist collapsing. It seemed as if my luck might be changing.

thirty-eight

I had been busy. It had been a week since I'd seen Margaret, and the night before had seemed endless. I'd spent a good part of it sewing up the torn perineum of a young mother who'd given birth to her second child at three in the morning. The midwife had made a small nick in the woman's skin to help ease the baby's head out, but the cut hadn't been long enough and the tear had lengthened naturally. I hadn't sewn up after childbirth since I'd been a medical student, and at first I was terrified that I would have completely forgotten what to do.

The midwife had sat her patient up, resting on a couple of pillows, and she herself sat by my side drinking a celebratory glass of whisky.

'Have you got some anaesthetic, Doctor?' she asked me, politely reminding me that it was the usual policy to numb the area I was about to start stitching. I rummaged around in my bag and found an ampoule of lignocaine.

'Do you want to borrow some gloves, Doctor?' she asked. 'Do you want the antiseptic now? I've got some cotton-wool if you'd like to borrow some.'

It was all very tactfully done, and eventually the memories filtered back. By quarter to four I was nearly finished. Crouched over the woman's damaged perineum, with a small torch jammed between my teeth, illuminating the area, I stitched away. The human body is a remarkable thing. It can recover from any minor insult – even the type of stitching I am capable of at three in the morning. I tried to ensure that the woman would still be able to cope with the normal night-time privileges of marriage, and kept poking two fingers inside to ensure that I wasn't closing up too much of the wound.

By a quarter-past four the marathon was over. I had a look at the newborn baby, congratulated both mother and father, thanked the midwife, repacked my black bag – or, rather, just threw everything into it and made a mental note remember to repack it the next day – accepted a small drink of whisky from the father, who could no longer stand, and took my leave. As I drove home it was already well and truly the next day. I love driving as dawn breaks. In fact, I could happily drive all day if the day would never quite break. There is something about the total quiet, the way the sun is beginning to filter through, and the fact that it is neither daytime nor night-time, which appeals to me.

I'd been back home just long enough to get undressed when the telephone rang. It was the desk sergeant at the local police station.

'Sorry to bother you, Doctor,' said the sergeant, 'but we have a drunk down here. I wonder if you'd be kind enough to come and have a look at him for me.'

Knowing that the alternative was to find my car festooned with tickets the next time I left it parked on double yellow lines, I agreed sleepily. The drunk turned out to be the classic Irishman who'd had so much to drink that even at that time in the morning he was still inebriated.

'You don't bother to need examining me, Doctor,' he said. 'Anyone can see I'm as pissed as a coot.'

The Law, however, doesn't work quite as simply as that, and I had to take blood samples from him before he was allowed to settle down for what was left of the night in one of the police cells.

'While you're here, Doctor,' said the sergeant as I finished filling in the inevitable forms, 'we've got a young girl who's just come in that we'd like you to have a look at.'

The girl had come to the police station and complained that she had been raped. Her alleged attacker had, so she said, taken her by surprise as she'd walked past a small patch of waste land on the way home at three that morning.

I talked to the girl and then examined her, but I could find no signs of her having been attacked.

'Tell me again exactly what happened,' I said to her.

'He followed me,' said the girl, 'and then he put his arm on my shoulder.'

'Is that all?' I asked.

'No,' she said, looking at her hands. 'I don't want to talk about it.'

197

'Look,' I said, 'I'm sorry, but I can't find any signs of your having been raped. You said that you were raped.'

'Well, he didn't actually rape me,' she said after a moment's silence. 'He didn't get what he wanted.'

'Well, what did happen?' I asked, as patiently as I could.

'He wanted to have sex with me,' said the girl. 'I'm sure of that,' she added.

'Yes, but that isn't actually an offence,' I explained to her. 'You did complain that you'd been raped. Rape is a serious offence. This man you're accusing could go to prison.'

'Well, I just wanted to frighten him,' she said sulkily.

'Who?' I asked.

'Jack,' said the girl.

'Who's Jack?' I asked.

'He's the fellow I'd been out with,' she said.

'And he's the one who you claim raped you.'

The girl nodded defiantly.

'Tell me again what happened,' I went on.

'We had a row,' she said, 'and I left him. He came after me and tried to get me to go back home with him.'

'Is that all?'

'No,' she said. 'He tried to kiss me.'

'And is that all?'

'Well, yes,' said the girl, 'but he wanted me to go back with him. He wanted to have sex with me.'

I gave up and left her with the policewoman who was standing silently by the door. Outside I explained to the sergeant what had happened. As we talked the Irishman wandered past us. He walked down the corridor, pulled a fire blanket off the wall and, before anyone could get to him, he'd pulled the release tape and was trying to blow his nose on the blanket. As the sergeant and I stared at him in astonishment a young policeman came rushing towards us. 'I'm sorry, Sarge,' he called. 'I left him for a minute and he disappeared.'

I slipped quietly away and drove slowly home to bed. It hardly seemed worthwhile getting undressed, so I just flopped down on top of the bedclothes. I'd just drifted off and was preparing to enter the wonderful world of dreams when the telephone rang again.

'Hullo, is that the doctor?' asked a bright and breezy voice.

'Yes,' I mumbled.

There was a pause. 'I just rang to see if you could tell me what time the morning surgery starts,' asked the caller.

'Nine,' I said crossly, slamming the telephone down on its rest. One of the snags with these new moulded-plastic telephones is that, however hard you slam them down, you can't break them. It just wasn't worth trying to get to sleep again, so I made myself a pot of coffee and started to read through some of the medical journals which had accumulated unopened and unread underneath the bed.

Several hours later, after surgery, I was sharing another pot of coffee with Dr Oaks, when there was a tap on the door as we talked, and it opened gingerly an inch or two.

'Excuse me, Doctor,' said a red-headed woman with an orange coat on, 'I couldn't make it to the morning surgery but I need to see you. Have you got a moment?'

I was about to ask her what the trouble was when Dr Oaks put his hand out to stop me. 'What's the trouble, Mrs Johnstone?' he asked.

'It's my hair,' said Mrs Johnstone. 'I think my dandruff is coming back again.'

'I think you'd better come along to one of the surgeries,' said Dr Oaks.

'But I'm here now,' said Mrs Johnstone.

'You're always here just after surgery,' said Dr Oaks, 'and I'm getting a little tired of it. I do eight surgeries a week or, at least *we* do eight surgeries a week' – he looked at me and winked – 'and if you can't get to one of those surgeries, then I'm afraid it's too bad.'

'Yes, Doctor,' said Mrs Johnstone, meekly. 'I'll come tonight.'

'If you're not careful,' said Dr Oaks when she had gone, 'you'll find yourself doing surgeries twenty-four hours a day, seven days a week. You have to be strict sometimes.'

'People do sometimes take advantage, don't they?' I nodded.

'Have you had Mrs Allen in yet?' he asked.

'Mrs Allen,' I repeated, and then thought for a moment. 'I don't think so.'

'You'll remember her when she does come in,' said Dr Oaks. 'She must be away if she's not been here. She usually comes along once a fortnight to fetch a prescription for something.'

'What's wrong with her, then?' I asked.

'Nothing,' he said. 'The last time she came here, she wanted me to prescribe some cotton-wool because she was making a tea-cosy for the church sale of work.'

'I don't believe you,' I laughed.

'It's true,' said Dr Oaks. 'You've hardly seen anything yet. I've had women in asking me to prescribe ordinary stockings for them, and wanting sun-tan lotion. I've been called out at night to provide people with repeat prescriptions and I've been called out to give people injections so that they could go on holiday abroad the following day. I've been called out on a Sunday to see patients with wax in their ears, to see patients with athlete's foot and to write letters for patients wanting to change their council house. I was called out one Sunday afternoon to see a patient with corns, and I was called out on Christmas night once to see a man who'd decided he wanted to have a hearing aid.'

I sat open-mouthed and listened.

I could have done so all day, but the telephone rang, and an irate woman wanted to know why I hadn't been to visit her son, who had the mumps. She complained that she'd been waiting in all morning and was anxious to go to the shops.

I left Dr Oaks shaking his head sadly at the status of the medical profession. 'Would you believe it?' he said. 'There used to be a time when people would turn the television set off when the doctor came into the room. Today they don't even turn it down.'

thirty-nine

I remember an elderly general practitioner once telling me that one of the attractions of practising medicine was that, when you press the button which sounds a bell or buzzer in the waiting-room, you never really know what you are going to get next. It may be a man with a cough, a woman with a hernia, a baby with pneumonia, a girl who is pregnant, a boy with a wart, a man with a brain tumour or a woman with marital problems.

I soon discovered that these days the general practitioner doesn't even know that the person who is waiting to come into the surgery next is actually a patient at all. For even if the waiting-room isn't full of drug-company representatives waiting to extol the virtues of their company's latest wonder product, there is a pretty good likelihood that one or two of the people sitting reading the tattered magazines will be quite healthy, with absolutely nothing at all to complain of.

Why, you may ask, would anyone want to sit in a doctor's waiting-room when he was quite fit?

Well, to begin with there are the otherwise healthy addicts who travel around the country these days, picking up prescriptions wherever they can. These people register with general practitioners as temporary residents and tell them some hard-luck story about having run out of their pills. Once the unsuspecting doctor has written out his prescription, the patient moves on to another area and another doctor, doing the same thing again, perhaps under a different name.

I had always thought that it must be fairly simple to spot an addict trying to get a supply of his drug. But it isn't really half as easy as it might sound. To begin with, there is no strict list of drugs to which patients get addicted. People can get addicted to just about anything. Even drugs usually prescribed for patients with arthritis have their fans.

Within a week of my starting work as a general practitioner, I found myself sharing the surgery with a young man spinning me a story about being away from home and having lost his bottle of pills. The pills he told me that he was taking were sleeping-tablets, and I asked him why he needed them. His answers were evasive and inconclusive and eventually, to save time, I gave him a prescription. However, I gave him a prescription for two tablets and wrote on the prescription form in such a way that it could not possibly be altered. I worked out that, with the cost of the prescription at twenty pence, the young man would be paying slightly over the black-market price for his drugs. I was happy that I would not be depriving a patient in genuine need, and also that I had not provided an addict or pusher with a saleable supply. I never did know whether or not that young man's plea was a genuine one.

Then there are the people who want time off work to watch a football match or to go to the seaside. These people give themselves away by turning up at surgery on the day of the big match or on a Friday morning already dressed in their holiday clothes.

There are some illnesses, of course, which it is impossible to diagnose without extensive tests. For example, if a patient comes into surgery and complains that he has a backache, it is almost impossible for any doctor to tell him that he does not have a backache. To some extent the doctor can only guess.

During my first fortnight with Dr Oaks I noticed that, every day there was any sunshine, one particular man would come to the surgery complaining of a pain in his leg and asking for a day off work. I gave him his day off for the first few times and then I got suspicious. I hadn't been able to find anything wrong with him, so I told him that the time had come to do some hospital tests. I gave him a form for some blood tests and warned him that if the condition didn't improve we would have to do some more. I told him he'd have to attend hospital at three in the afternoon, rang up the hospital and arranged for them to keep him waiting until about half-past four, and then waited to see what happened.

The result was a negative blood test and a patient whose pain miraculously disappeared. It's no more fun sitting in a hospital waiting to have a blood test done than it is sitting at work.

Then there are the district nurses, health visitors, social workers, administrators from the Family Practitioner Committee, psychologists studying doctors, voluntary workers, regional medical officers, and so on. All these people want time with the doctor; they all seem to have all the time in the world, and they all want to talk and talk and talk. It would be quite easy to work as a general practitioner and to keep perfectly busy without ever actually seeing a patient. I have it on good authority that there are family doctors who do just that.

But the visitors most frequently found lurking in doctors' waiting-rooms, as I hinted earlier, are the drug-company representatives. There are several thousand working in the United Kingdom alone. Some call themselves 'detail men', others like to be known as 'marketing advisors', a few are called 'medical information executives', and others have even grander names, but it is their job to sell their company's products just like any other salesman.

I remember well one particular visitor from a major international company. When he came into the surgery he was obviously suffering from a pretty severe cough. He could hardly speak in between fits of coughing, and I felt quite sorry for him.

'Why don't you go home?' I asked.

'That's just where I'm going next,' the poor man replied. 'I think it's sitting in waiting-rooms that's given me this cold.'

'Have you had any pains in your chest?' I asked him.

He nodded.

'Been breathless?' I asked.

He nodded again.

'You'd better let me have a listen to your chest,' I suggested.

The representative peeled off his jackt, pullover and shirt, and I listened carefully. He had quite a severe chest infection.

'You'd better have an antibiotic,' I said. 'I'll prescribe something.'

'You haven't got anything I could have, have you?' he asked. 'I haven't got any money for the prescription charge.'

'Certainly,' I agreed. 'I'll give you something from the stock.'

I soon found him something suitable from Dr Oaks' remarkable store of drugs and handed it to him. 'It's from a competitor, I'm afraid,' I said.

He shrugged. 'I left my wallet at home again,' he explained, 'and we live miles from the nearest chemist.'

'That's all right,' I told him. 'That's what the stock's for.'

'How do I take them?' the man asked.

'You take the tablets four times a day, every six hours or so, and the medicine you take two teaspoonfuls at a time every four hours during the daytime,' I said.

'Do you have a piece of paper?' he asked me. 'I'll forget that. I really feel awful.'

'Take this,' I told him, pushing a notepad across the desk to him. 'You'd better write it – you'll not be able to read my writing.'

'Have you a pen I could borrow?' asked the representative.

I handed him a ballpoint pen which I'd been given less than an hour before by one of his rivals. He wrote out the instructions I'd given him and then put the pad and pen into his pocket. I didn't like to object.

In addition to these callers, in the course of his daily work every general practitioner sees a number of perfectly healthy people who visit him to obtain official assurances about their health status. A number of people come along for medicals required by insurance companies unwilling to provide insurance cover for untested apparatus. These medicals are usually easy to do and, since the pay is good and the clients financially reliable, most doctors are keen to do as many medicals as they can.

After I'd been assistant to Dr Oaks for several months, the manager of one of the local life assurance offices telephoned me to ask whether I'd be willing to see a client for them. We fixed an appointment up, and a few days later I found myself asking a perfect stranger a whole series of what seemed to me to be totally impertinent and even irrelevant questions about his own medical and social history, and about the medical and social history of all his relatives.

The client, a fit football-playing sales representative, did not seem to mind the questions; he answered them briskly and without objection. The medical examination itself was little more than a formality, since it was patently clear to anyone that there was nothing physically wrong with him.

When I received a second call a little later asking me to do another medical, I agreed immediately. I even agreed to do it at eleven o'clock in the morning, the time I normally got to the end of the morning surgery, since that was the time the client found most suitable.

I had a suspicion that this fee might not be so easy to earn when I asked the client his name, just to make sure that I'd got the correct set of forms in front of me. I didn't want to fill in his answers to the questions on another man's form.

'Pardon?' he asked, rather gruffly.

'Your name?' I asked, politely.

The man thought for a moment before replying. Eventually inspiration hit him. 'Jones,' he said. 'William Jones.'

I checked with the form. The names matched.

'How old are you?' I asked.

'How old am I?' he asked.

'How old are you?' I asked again.

'Twenty, er, twenty, er . . .' stutttered the client.

'Thirty-three?' I suggested, studying the form which already had some basic facts neatly printed on it.

'That's right,' he smiled contentedly. 'Thirty-three.' He nodded happily.

'Is your father still alive?' I asked.

'I don't know,' the client eventually answered.

'Your mother?' I asked.

'She doesn't know either,' replied the man.

'Is she alive?' I asked.

'Oh, yes,' came the answer.

'Is she well?' I asked. On reflection, I thought I could have phrased the question better, but at the time it seemed suitable.

'She isn't well,' said the client, sadly shaking his head. 'She has a lot of trouble. Her legs, you know. They swell occasionally. And she gets a bad back, and last week she had a cold.'

And so it went on. Things got worse rather than better as we continued down the list of questions.

'Have you ever had any mental disorder?' I asked.

'Any what?'

'Have you ever been mentally ill?' I tried.

'Mental?' asked the client.

'Have you ever had any trouble with your brain?' I asked hopefully.

'Oh, my brain,' said the client, pointing to his head. He grinned at me. 'It hurts sometimes,' he said.

'When does it hurt?' I asked.

'When I get hit,' replied the man.

'Do you get hit often?' was my next question.

'Only at the weekends,' the man assured me happily. 'Usually on Saturdays.'

'Have you ever been in hospital?' I asked, trying another line of attack.

'Oh, yes,' Mr Jones replied straightaway. 'I've been in lots of hospitals.'

'Ah ha,' I said, pen poised. 'Tell me about these hospitals.'

'Well, I went in a hospital at Southport to see my Uncle Harry,' said Mr Jones. 'He had a hernia. And I went into a hospital in London to see my sister. She was having a baby . . .' He seemed ready to go on for the rest of the morning, so I stopped him.

'Have you ever been in a hospital bed?' I asked.

'No,' said Mr Jones indignantly. He seemed offended, so I smiled at him and pointed at the form, blaming the insurance company who'd set the questions.

It took an hour and a half to complete that form. I didn't start my morning visits until one o'clock and I didn't finish them until the evening surgery was about to start. I had at least learnt that insurance medicals are not always money for old rope.

As well as insurance medicals, I also found out that doctors in general practice are expected to do medical examinations for people preparing to emigrate. The first such examination I did was a tremendous event, for a family of six turned up. They all insisted that they wanted to be dealt with together, so I took some chairs from the waiting-room into the surgery, sat the intending travellers down and began to question them.

'Have any of you ever had any chest diseases?' I asked.

'No,' they chorused. Two of them shook their heads as additional evidence.

'Have any of you ever had eczema?' I asked.

'No,' they chorused.

'Have any of you ever had any mental disorder?' I asked.

'Him!' they all laughed, instinctively pointing to the youngest and most mischievous member of the family.

I hammered their knees lightly with the careless grace of a musician playing the xylophone. They all put their tongues out together, and the noise they made when requested to say 'Ahh' would have won them places in any choir. We turned the eye-test chart into a party game by requiring each of the six to read a letter in turn. It was all extraordinary fun, and the next emigration medical I did seemed very flat by comparison.

Dr Oaks had a number of medical appointments outside his practice, which earned him extra money and provided some variation from the usual routine. One of them was as medical officer to one of the largest hotels in the town. It was his job to conduct the medicals on potential employees, checking up to make sure that waiters didn't have wooden legs and that housemaids had durable knees.

I'd been in touch with the hotel management several times when they'd needed medicals doing on youngsters starting work there, and once when they'd had an elderly lady fall ill in the dining-room and had wanted her removal, without too much public fuss, to a local hospital or nursing home. And then, one midwinter afternoon, I received a call asking me to pop into the hotel to see one of the waiters, who had been taken ill the night before.

I parked my car outside the front of the hotel and marched in through the impressive swing doors, rather as I imagined a Harley Street specialist might march in through the doors of the Savoy. Admittedly few Harley Street specialists arrive in rust-coloured motor-cars, but, then, I doubt if many of them are accustomed to having to wait for ten minutes in the lobby while the only receptionist on duty carefully makes out a bill for a departing guest. Such are the trials and tribulations of the young doctor on the first few broken rungs of the professional ladder.

At last one of the under-managers appeared and greeted me haughtily. He clearly felt insulted that his hotel should have been expected even to acknowledge the presence of such a disreputable-looking guest.

The man I'd been called to see, a waiter, was not an important member of the staff; his quarters were at the back of the hotel and could only be reached by passing through the kitchens, and up a set of rickety wooden stairs. The tiny room was, I suppose, a part of the building which had once housed horses rather than human beings. It was decorated with whitewash, and freezing cold, and as I climbed the stairs I heard the scurrying and bustling of small-footed creatures anxiously evacuating the immediate area.

The waiter was lying on top of his bed covered in a thin blanket and an overcoat. He looked pale and very, very miserable. He told me that he had been sick several times, that he had also had diarrhoea and that he felt quite cold and miserable.

'What have you been eating?' I asked.

'The staff eat the same as the guests,' said the under-manager stuffily.

'Well, I think he's got food poisoning,' I said.

'Well, they don't always eat exactly the same as the guests,' said the under-manager quickly. 'Sometimes the staff eat the food that was left over from the guests' meals.'

I looked at him quizzically.

'Not off the plates,' the under-manager explained hastily, 'but left over in the kitchens.'

'It's heated up again, I suppose,' I said.

The under-manager nodded. 'We always like the staff to have hot food,' he smiled at me.

'That's why he's got food poisoning,' I explained.

'Well, what do we do with him?' asked the under-manager. 'Shall I ring for an ambulance?'

'He doesn't need a hospital bed,' I pointed out. 'He just needs looking after.'

The unfortunate waiter groaned and heaved himself up on to one elbow and, before anyone could move, he was sick all over the under-manager's shoes.

'Oh dear, oh dear,' sighed the under-manager. 'I don't know what the manager will say about this.' He headed for the door. 'I really think he'll want to have a word with Dr Oaks.'

'I'm Dr Oaks' assistant,' I told him. 'I'm afraid Dr Oaks isn't available at the moment.

'I'm sure Dr Oaks would have wanted him to go into hospital,' maintained the under-manager. 'We can't keep running across here to keep an eye on him.'

'He hasn't got any relatives living around here?'

'None,' replied the under-manager. 'His family are in Spain. Do you think we should get in touch with them?'

'That's not necessary,' I told him. 'He'll be better in twenty-four hours.'

'Well, who's going to look after him?' asked the under-manager.

'How many staff have you got?' I asked.

'Thirty-six,' replied the under-manager.

'Then I should think you could spare a couple of people to keep an eye on him, provide him with cold drinks, keep him clean and so on,' I pointed out.

'Well, really,' was all the under-manager could say. He set off down the stairs and I followed closely behind. We didn't speak as we crossed the courtyard but, as we entered the kitchens, I tapped him on the shoulder.

'I think you should move him into the hotel,' I suggested. 'He'll be far more comfortable there.'

'We can't possibly do that,' said the under-manager without hesitation.

'Have you got a telephone I could use?' I asked.

'A telephone?' asked the under-manager. 'You're going to ring for an ambulance?'

'No,' I told him. 'I'm going to ring the public health department. I think I may have to recommend that the hotel be closed since there is a case of food poisoning on the premises.

The under-manager paled until his facial colour nicely matched that of his shirt collar.

I waited in the lobby while he telephoned the manager and obtained permission to move the waiter across into a spare room, and to get one of the housemaids freed from her other duties so that she could sit with him.

As I left the hotel I felt quite pleased with myself.

forty

'It's Peter's tonsils again, Doctor,' said Mrs Wilson. 'He gets this every month now.'

Peter looked pale and drawn and rather fed-up. He followed behind his mother, hugging a rather threadbare teddy bear, a small and rather battered motor-car and a comic annual.

I peered down his throat but could see nothing very much except a half-sucked sweet which bobbed around like a small boat on a rough sea.

'He usually needs penicillin,' said Mrs Wilson. 'It's the only thing that gets rid of it.'

'Ah,' I said. I wondered why Dr Oaks had given in so easily. The poor boy must have had pints of penicillin mixture if he'd been having it once a month. I couldn't help thinking that Dr Oaks wasn't such a good doctor as I thought he was.

'Don't you think it's time he had his tonsils out, Doctor?' she asked.

'Oh, I don't think so,' I replied. 'Peter's tonsils aren't any bigger than they should be.'

'But everybody should have a tonsils operation at some time or other, shouldn't they?' argued Mrs Wilson.

'Should they?' I asked.

'I always thought they should,' she said.

'I didn't,' I said.

'Well, why can't he have his tonsils out?' asked Mrs Wilson.

'He doesn't need to have them removed,' I told her, 'and since any operation is dangerous it would seem silly to subject Peter to one he doesn't need.'

'Oh, well, if you put it that way, Doctor,' she said, 'then I'm sure you're right.'

I gave her a prescription for some cough medicine which I told her to give Peter four times a day.

'Is it penicillin?' asked Mrs Wilson.

'It's something new,' I told her. 'It's really very good. It isn't actually called penicillin, but it will help clear Peter's throat up.'

'Oh, it's new, is it?' she said with enthusiasm. 'Well, that's good.'

I made a mental note to tell everyone that everything I prescribed was 'new'.

I used to think that it was only fashion designers who catered for and got rich on the public's varying tastes. I used to imagine that it was only dress-conscious women who followed outrageous fashion trends. I only learnt just how wrong I had been when I started work as a general practitioner. Then I realized that for centuries doctors have been aware that diseases and their necessary and recommended treatments can become fashionable and that, as a direct consequence, many doctors have made their reputations and their fortunes by performing the right operations at the right time on the right people, or by convincing the ever-gullible public that they have found a new disease well worth avoiding.

In seventeenth-century France, Louis XIII had 212 enemas in the space of one year alone. During the same twelve months he also had 215 purges and was bled 47 times. Another eminent Frenchman, the Canon of Troyes, is reputed to have had no less than 2,190 enemas in the space of a two-year period and, if my pocket calculator is working properly, that means that he had three enemas a day. Needless to say, these fashionable men led the public, and demands for enemas and purges were tremendous.

Edward VII's appendectomy was one of the first to be performed but, within weeks, the operation was being done up and down the country as fast as surgeons could operate. Because of the publicity from the delay to the Coronation, it was suddenly very, very fashionable, and anyone worth knowing had his appendix removed without further delay. The appendix could at that time have been described as the most unwanted organ in Europe.

Other operations have also been made popular. A surgeon called Sir Arbuthnot Lane made his name and his fortune by removing people's bowels. He did this on the rather strange grounds that if the bowels were removed there would be no more constipation to worry about. He was right – his patients all had fierce, uncontrollable but fashionable diarrhoea – but perhaps it's a good job he wasn't an eye surgeon for, if he had been, he might have argued that taking eyes out made it unlikely that patients would ever have to worry about getting grit in them.

In the middle of this century tonsillectomy suddenly became fashionable. In the 1930s half to three-quarters of all children had their tonsils out. Since no one really knows whether or not these children really needed to lose their tonsils, the American Child Health Association conducted an unusual (and, to some establishment figures, probably unethical) survey. They studied 1,000 eleven-year-old New York children. They found that 61 per cent had had their tonsils out; the other 39 per cent were then referred to physicians, who recommended that half of these needed to have their tonsils removed. Of the ones left whose tonsils hadn't been condemned, another set of physicians recommended that about half should have tonsillectomies. And so it went on, until only sixty-five children of eleven years old remained with their tonsils uncondemned. These sixty-five escaped only because the American Child Health Association ran out of physicians to whom they could refer the children.

Our tonsils are there for a very good reason – to catch infections which would otherwise penetrate deeper into the body. People who lose their tonsils lose a potentially valuable defence mechanism, and it is only reasonable to recommend the removal of a pair of tonsils if they are proving genuinely troublesome. Tonsillectomy does not reduce the frequency of colds, and there is little chance of the operation's making any great difference to the health of many of the patients who do undergo it.

In America, tonsillectomy is said to cause more deaths than diphtheria, rubella, scarlet fever, chicken-pox and whooping cough combined. American parents spend 150 million dollars a year on having their children's tonsils removed, and yet there are 300 deaths a year from the operation and very few from enlarged tonsils.

There are today, of course, many other fashionable operations and treatments. Many patients happily munch vitamins which they hope will do them good. There are many people who, like Mrs Wilson, demand antibiotic therapy for any infection. The latest drugs are discussed knowledgeably in waiting-rooms up and down the country. If doctors are the equivalent of fashion designers, then patients are most certainly the eqivalent of the fashion-house customers.

The rest of that day was very busy, and I did not see Dr Oaks till the next. He was getting into his car, and I hurried out to catch him. I wanted to have a word with him about young Peter Wilson and to try to warn him – politely, of course – about the dangers of prescribing antibiotics unnecessarily.

'I saw Peter Wilson yesterday,' I told him, wondering if he'd remember the name.

'Nice little chap,' said Dr Oaks. 'Mother's always bringing him up with a bad throat.'

'That's the one,' I confirmed, quite impressed.

'Hope you didn't fall for that business about an antibiotic?' said Dr Oaks.

I looked at him, puzzled.

'She always takes an antibiotic,' said Dr Oaks, 'or at least likes to think she's getting one. I usually give the little fellow a bottle of cough medicine and tell her it's a type of penicillin. Keeps her happy and doesn't do the little fellow any harm.'

'Exactly what I did,' I told him.

'Splendid,' said Dr Oaks. 'Knew you would. Now I must rush. Off to play some golf.'

He slammed his car door and disappeared off up the road, anxious to get away before anyone stopped him for advice.

I had dinner again with Margaret that evening. We went to a restaurant at a hotel in a nearby village, and I spent the first hour of the evening trying to avoid the eyes of a couple whom I'd met in surgery, and who I felt sure would want to join us and discuss their ailments at length if they got the chance. By feigning a stiff neck I managed to keep my eyes averted. By the time they'd gone I really had got a stiff neck.

In my first few months as a general practitioner I'd frequently given advice to patients wanting to know how to lose weight. I'd found the problem so common that I'd programmed myself to slip into gear, produce a diet sheet, advise about calorie-controlled dieting and talk about the uselessness of patented preparations advertised in magazines and newspapers, without any mental effort at all.

213

The real truth about dieting came home to me, however, when I realized that Margaret was dieting.

'What on earth do you want to diet for?' I demanded. 'Your figure is perfect!'

'How do you know?' she asked mischievously.

'Well, it looks perfect from here,' I corrected myself.

'I've bought a book on dieting and it's full of good advice,' said Margaret. 'The author promises that if you follow it you can lose a stone in a week.'

'What do you have to do?' I asked. 'Get yourself locked up in a dungeon or run twice across the Sahara in a plastic mackintosh?'

'You have to eat a hard-boiled egg every other hour, a glass of water every hour and very little else,' she said. 'I'm having a bit of a night off tonight,' she added quickly.

'How seriously do you take all this?' I asked, worried.

'Very,' said Margaret earnestly. 'When I weigh myself I always take my hair-grips out, pluck my eyebrows and cut my toe- and finger-nails. It can make all the difference.'

'You don't wear false teeth, do you?'

'No,' she said quickly, looking offended. 'Why?'

'You could take them out as well,' I pointed out.

'I think you're making fun of me,' said Margaret, concentrating on her meringue.

'Have another glass of wine,' I suggested.

'Right,' she said. 'Do you like fat women?'

'Love them,' I promised.

forty-one

The British general practitioner is responsible for the medical care of his patients twenty-four hours a day for 365 days a year. When people go on to a doctor's list, that doctor is legally responsible for them, even though he may be off duty, away on holiday or lying sick in a hospital bed. Any other doctor who temporarily takes over the responsibility, either as a member of a duty rota or, as in my case, as an assistant is merely responsible in a purely practical way. It is the doctor named on the patient's medical card who permanently carries the legal responsibility for that patient.

In order to reduce the weight of this responsibility, general practitioners are, of course, entitled to call for specialist help when they feel that a particular problem is defeating them. The doctor in general practice can then either send his patient along to a hospital out-patients' department to be seen by a specialist or else he can, if the patient is unable to move, arrange for the specialist to visit the patient at home.

Most patients can travel to hospital, of course, but occasionally it is necessary for them to be seen by a consultant at home. The first time I had to take advantage of this facility was when Mr Symonds was having trouble with his heart. His pulse was irregular and he was bothered by occasional flutterings in his chest. I could find nothing of any real significance when I examined him, but I felt that he ought to be seen by one of the consultant physicians. Since Mr Symonds was paralysed from the waist down I felt that a visit at home would be much easier for everyone concerned, so I telephoned Dr White at the hospital and explained the situation to him. I did try to get hold of Dr Eastwood, the other consultant physician, but he had apparently flown off to Geneva to attend an international conference on liver disease. All successful doctors these days belong to the international jet-set and, even in out-of-the-way centres, leading specialists disappear abroad at regular intervals.

I arranged to meet Dr White at the Symondses' bungalow after evening surgery one day. To ensure that I would be there before the great man, I fixed a time giving me plenty of room to cope with a lengthy surgery. As luck would have it, of course, business was slack that evening. As one regular attender put it, it looked as if I'd either cured or killed everyone. One of the advantages, or disadvantages, of running an open surgery, which means that anyone who turns up at the right time can see the doctor, is that occasionally things are ridiculously busy and occasionally they are delightfully quiet.

I had half an hour to wait before Dr White was due to turn up, and it didn't really seem long enough to do anything worthwhile elsewhere, so I simply drove round to the Symondses' to wait for him there. As usual Mr Symonds was sitting in his armchair by the fire with a newspaper on his lap but with his eyelids closed. Although he had a newspaper delivered daily, I don't think he ever read any more than the front page.

'Good evening, Doctor,' said Mrs Symonds with a happy smile. 'Nice to see you. Would you like a cup of tea?'

'Not just now, thank you,' I replied, smiling back at her. I was always suspicious of food and drink offered me in the Symonds household. My first visit there had taken me into the kitchen to try to find some old tablets that Mr Symonds insisted he'd put into a cupboard above the sink. Mrs Symonds had been in there making mince pies and she'd been using her false teeth to crimp the pastry around the edges. The result was aesthetically pleasing, I suppose, but I found it rather disturbing nevertheless. I like my own teeth to be the first to leave their imprint on the mince pies I eat.

I tapped her husband lightly on the shoulder to waken him.

'Ah, hello, Doctor,' said Mr Symonds, rustling the newspaper 'I was just taking a look at the paper.' He held the paper out to me, opening it to the first inside page as he did so. 'Have you read this?' he asked me.

The page was entirely taken up with two photographs of a well-built young woman who had no clothes available when the photographer had arrived. I admired the shape of the model, refolded the newspaper and handed it back to Mr Symonds.

'Fascinating,' I agreed, not quite certain whether or not he knew what he'd shown me. When he winked at me I guessed that he might well have been aware of what was on page three.

'Have you got that urine sample for me?' I asked him. I'd visited Mr Symonds the previous day and asked him to make sure he had a urine sample ready. I suspected that Dr White might want a sample to test as part of his examination and I wanted to be prepared.

'It's in the kitchen,' said Mr Symonds, 'by the sink.'

'Splendid,' I said.

'Nice day, isn't it, Doctor,' said Mrs Symonds, suddenly appearing in front of me and beaming broadly.

'Lovely,' I agreed. I had discovered on my second visit to the household that Mrs Symonds seemed very friendly, but in fact she was suffering from narrowing of the cerebral arteries. She was quite incapable of a sensible conversation, although she could get by with superficial chatter which fooled many casual callers. If you asked her serious questions such as 'What day is it?' or 'What is your name?' she would be quickly confused. In my presence she had once come into the room and begun to punch her husband on the arm, asking him who he was and what he was doing in her house. Fortunately she was a lightly built lady whose punches carried litttle weight.

'Shall we put the light on?' I asked Mrs Symonds. I pointed up at the gas-mantle over the fireplace. She nodded happily, so I picked up a box of matches, switched on the gas and lit the lamp. The Symondses had no electricity in their household, for reasons which I had never properly understood. I think the truth of the matter was simply the fact that neither of them liked the thought of it. I think that, like James Thurber's aunt, they suspected that empty sockets would allow dangerous electricity to drip out on to the floor.

As the gas-flame gradually increased in intensity the light flickered around the room. More than a yard or so from the lamp it was difficult to read during the later evening hours, but the Symondses seemed to manage quite well.

I sat and talked to Mr Symonds in the shadowy light until Dr White turned up twenty minutes later. I answered the door to him myself and helped him in with his several bags and boxes of medical equipment. He looked as if he'd come to stay for a week, or at least to perform a heart transplant operation.

'This is Dr White,' I said to Mr and Mrs Symonds, before Mrs Symonds could start throwing any of her punches. 'He's a specialist from the hospital.'

'Would you like a cup of tea?' asked Mrs Symonds automatically.

'That would be very nice,' said Dr White quickly, with a condescending smile.

'A chocolate cake?' asked Mrs Symonds.

'Thank you,' said Dr White. 'That would be very nice.' He unpacked his equipment and placed an expensive-looking electrocardiograph machine on the table in the centre of the room.

'Where can we plug it in?' he asked me.

'There we have a problem,' I admitted. I'd forgotten that he'd bring an electrocardiograph with him. 'There isn't anywhere.'

'Never mind,' said Dr White. 'I've brought my extension lead.' He uncoiled a long black lead and placed it on the table-top beside the electrocardiograph. 'We can plug in the end of this in the front room. It'll even reach upstairs,' he said proudly.

'I'm afraid there aren't any sockets anywhere,' I had to tell him. 'Mr and Mrs Symonds aren't connected to the electricity supply.'

'Not connected to the electricity supply?' asked Dr White in astonishment.

I confirmed that he'd heard right, and pointed to the gas-mantle.

'Well, that's amazing,' he said. 'Quite extraordinary.' He carefully refolded his long black lead and put it back into the box with the electrocardiograph machine. Shaking his head sadly, he then put the machine itself back into its carrying-case.

'Here's your cup of tea, Doctor,' said Mrs Symonds, handing Dr White a china cup brimming with strong-looking tea, In her other hand she carried a plate upon which there rested a choco-late cake, neatly decorated around the edge with the same sort of marks which one normally sees on mince pies. I didn't think it would be tactful to say anything to Dr White.

'Let's have a look at you,' said Dr White to my patient. Mr Symonds unfastened his second shirt-button and revealed a small triangular patch of white vest.

'I'll need more than that,' said Dr White rather haughtily.

Mr Symonds undid another button and revealed a rather lar-ger triangle of white vest.

'Would you take off your shirt and vest?' asked Dr White coldly. He scowled at me disapprovingly.

The examination seemed to go on for ever. First of all there was the chest to be examined, then the blood pressure to be taken, then the nervous system to be tested. Dr White produced an apparently endless supply of tiny instruments from his bag with which to test and assess Mr Symonds' nervous system. He could apparently find nothing wrong.

Eventually he put his patella hammer down on the table and took a gulp of his tea. He pulled an unhappy face which told me quite clearly that I'd been wise to reject Mrs Symonds' kindly offer. To counter the taste of the tea he took a bite out of the chocolate cake. That seemed to satisfy him, for he nodded his approval. Teeth-marks don't taste.

'Well, I don't think there's much more we can do here,' said Dr White eventually. 'There doesn't seem to be much wrong with him.' He paused for a moment as he put his instruments away in his bag. 'I don't suppose you could produce a urine specimen, could you?' he asked Mr Symonds.

'There's one in the kitchen,' I said smartly, feeling quite pleased with myself.

'In a milk bottle,' added Mr Symonds.

Dr White and I trooped into the kitchen where Mrs Symonds was standing in front of the cooker. We both examined the shelf above the sink quite carefully. There was no sign of any urine specimen, although two milk-bottles lay in the sink, quite empty

It was only when I saw the teapot on the draining-board that the awful truth hit me.

'It must have been thrown away by accident,' I said hastily. 'Would you like me to get another specimen for you?'

'No, never mind,' said Dr White rather crossly. 'I'll leave that to you.' He marched back into the other room, picked up his bags and cases and struggled to the front door. I heard him cry out in anguish as he stumbled against an umbrella-stand in the darkness. One way and another, it really hadn't been Dr White's evening.

forty-two

Most large factories employ their own medical officers to take care of minor injuries sustained at work, to look after major accident victims until an ambulance can arrive, and to try to ensure that the factory is kept as safe as possible for all employees.

Smaller factories, however, cannot afford to employ a full-time medical officer and instead they hire local general practitioners on an hourly basis. One of Dr Oaks' local colleagues had a job as medcial officer to a factory making cardboard boxes. It was his allotted task to visit the factory once a week and hold a surgery which workers could attend. The idea was to enable the personnel department to keep a check on the health of new employees, and to check on personnel returning from sick-leave to make sure that they were fit for employment.

Dr Williamson, who had the job of visiting Bulk Box Boards Ltd, telephoned me one Tuesday and asked if I would go to the factory for him.

'I've got to go on a course,' he added dryly.

'Golf?' I inquired, remembering Dr Oaks.

'Naturally,' agreed Dr Williamson. He promised to see that the fee for the session was redirected, and I happily consented to attend in his place.

I knew the factory from the outside quite well, having many times sat in my car fuming while large lorries carrying raw materials struggled to turn into its gates, or while equally large lorries carrying finished cardboard boxes struggled to make their way out. The road outside the factory was far too narrow for heavy lorries, and each entry and exit resulted in great delays and inconvenience for all other motorists.

I was met at the gates by a dapper little man in a light-grey suit. The breast pocket of his jacket was filled with pens and pencils and his pockets bulged pregnantly.

'Where have you left your car?' he asked me.

I pointed to my Mini, which I'd left in the road.

'Oh, I should bring it into the factory,' he suggested. 'You can park it by the canteen, which is where we hold the surgeries.'

'That's very nice of you,' I acknowledged.

'Not at all,' said the man kindly. Then he rather spoilt it. 'If you leave it there,' he said, 'the lorries won't be able to get in and out.'

I moved the car and followed him into the canteen. The walls were covered with brightly coloured posters, most of them carrying industrial safety hints. There were posters promoting safety boots, safety helmets and goggles. Twenty or thirty men in smart blue overalls stood around waiting. A chair and a table had been arranged at one end of the canteen and a temporary screen put up around them. The screen was made of sheets of cardboard resting against stacking chairs.

'If you'll sit down here, Doctor,' said the man with the pens, 'I'll get the first victim.' He disappeared and then reappeared almost at once with a tall distinguished-looking Indian who wore a beautiful white turban in addition to his blue overalls.

'Good afternoon,' I began cheerfully.

'He doesn't speak any English, Doctor,' said the man with the pens.

'What's wrong with him?' I asked.

'He's been offered a job as a machine operator,' said my guide.

'Take off your clothes,' I said to the Indian.

The man grinned at me and nodded furiously.

'Do this,' ordered the man with the pens, standing right in front of the Indian and unbuttoning his shirt. The Indian just stared at him.

'Dr Williamson usually just has a listen to their chests,' confided my guide, rebuttoning his shirt. I noticed that he wore a small plastic name-badge which announced him as Mr Peyton, Assistant Personnel Manager.

I poked the end of my stethoscope through the gap between the third and fourth buttons of the Indian's overalls. Then I listened to his hear. I could hear nothing abnormal.

'All right, Doctor?' asked Mr Peyton.

'All right,' I nodded with my fingers crossed.

'I'll get the next,' said the man with the pens, disappearing with the Indian and reappearing a moment later with a corpulent man who threatened to burst out of his overalls and spill all over the canteen.

'Jones,' said the fat man. 'Tool room.'

'Good afternoon, Mr Jones,' I said politely. 'What can we do for you?'

'Back,' said Mr Jones.

'Bad?' I asked.

Mr Jones, a man of the few words, nodded.

'Have you been off work?' I asked him.

'I want a job with no bending or lifting,' said Mr Jones firmly.

'You need to lose a little weight,' I said. 'That would help you.'

Mr Jones said nothing but turned a rather unhealthy colour.

'We don't have anything for him without lifting or bending,' whispered Mr Peyton.

'They don't seem to have anything for you without lifting or bending,' I told Mr Jones.

'Then I'll need a note,' said Mr Jones with a satisfied look on his face.

'I'm not sure what to do about that,' I said, uncertain about whether or not to refer the man back to his own doctor.

'That's how it is, is it?' said Mr Jones, filling himself up with air and glowering at me. 'We'll see about that.' He stormed away, and a moment later I heard the canteen doors being pushed open. When I looked out from behind the screens the canteen was deserted.

Mr Peyton sighed unhappily.

'Where have they all gone?' I asked.

'Strike,' said Mr Peyton, resignedly.

'Strike?'

'They've been looking for an excuse all week,' said Mr Peyton. 'They want an extra week's holiday next year.'

'I'm not sure what that has to do with Mr Jones' bad back,' I had to admit.

'Just an excuse,' said Mr Peyton.

'What do we do now?' I asked.

'You can wait or you can go home,' said Mr Peyton.

I decided to wait a while, and sat down. I picked up an old copy of one of the tabloid newspapers abandoned on a chair and then, remembering that I had my diary with me, sat back instead to read the fascinating pages of miscellaneous information with which diary publishers pack their publications. I always find it amusing to see how far it is from Exeter to Leeds, and how many rods there are in a perch.

I waited for nearly an hour and eventually the men came back. Again Mr Peyton brought one of them behind the screens to be examined.

'What happened to the last fellow?' I asked Mr Peyton, as I prepared to listen to the new fellow's chest. 'The one with the back.'

'He's gone home,' said Mr Peyton. 'He said he was going to call his own doctor out.'

The new fellow had been given a job as a welder and needed a physical check-up. He seemed perfectly fit and obviously had no artificial parts or missing items. I signed him fit to begin work.

As soon as I'd done that, a distant hooter sounded and the canteen emptied again.

'Now what have I done?' I asked.

'Not you this time,' said Mr Peyton. 'That was the tea-break hooter. They have to have twenty minutes' break.' I looked out of the window and noticed that the men who had been standing chatting in the canteen were now standing chatting outside the canteen. One or two of them were swigging tea from vacuum-flasks.

The problems of being an industrial medical officer were becoming more and more apparent as the afternoon went by. By the time the men had finished their tea-break it was four o'clock.

'What time do we finish?' I asked Mr Peyton.

'The men go home at four-thirty,' came the answer.

'So we've got to see all these men in half an hour?' asked, horrified.

Mr Peyton nodded, sighed and moved around the screens. I pushed them back to get out of my makeshift surgery. As I did so, the chair holding up one screen tipped over. The resulting crash was deafening. It did at least have the effect of silencing the chatter.

'Ask them to undo their buttons,' whispered Mr Peyton.

'Undo your buttons, please,' I said.

The men looked at one another and then slowly unfastened the buttons of their overalls.

'Ask them to pull up their vests,' whispered Mr Peyton.

I asked the men to pull up their vests.

'Get in line,' shouted the little man with the pens. The over-alled workers shuffled uneasily but surely into a line.

'Just walk along the line and have a listen,' whispered Mr Peyton.

I put my stethoscope in place and walked along the line, giving each heart and each pair of lungs ten seconds to prove their healthiness.

'Now touch your toes,' directed Mr Peyton.

'Can I let go of my vest?' asked a particularly stupid man with red hair and tattoos on his face and arms.

Mr Peyton ignored him and repeated the instructions. They all bent forward and reached for their toes.

'You're all fit,' I told them. Mr Peyton looked at me and smiled happily. His top set of false teeth slipped forward dangerously, and he stopped the grin skilfully. Most of the men seemed happy, but four began to protest furiously.

'You're not as fit as you might be, however,' I said to them. 'You can all have a week off. Go and see your own doctors in the morning.'

The four men smiled and then shuffled out of the canteen behind their colleagues. Mr Peyton clapped me on the back.

'Splendid stuff, Doctor,' he said.

I left very much wiser than I had been when I had arrived. Industrial medicine seemed to me a very special branch of the profession.

forty-three

'Doctor, I don't like the look of my husband,' said Mrs Wright, wheezing into the telephone. It was four in the morning and at that time of night I am never at my best. I could not understand why Mrs Wright was ringing me to complain about her husband.

'I'm sorry,' I said, stalling for time and hoping for more information. 'Could you say that again?'

'I don't like the look of my husband,' she repeated conscientiously.

'How does he feel?' I asked, hoping to hear something more specific about the patient's complaint.

'A bit clammy,' came back the reply without a pause. 'A bit clammy but warm.'

'Is he breathing all right?' I asked uncertainly, getting worried.

'Oh, yes,' said Mrs Wright, 'he's definitely breathing.'

'Do you want me to come and look at him?' I asked her, accepting defeat and a ride through the early-morning rain as inevitable.

'If you would, Doctor,' she said.

Mr and Mrs Wright were both in their seventies and they lived in a second-floor council flat. Mrs Wright had been a shop assistant until her sharp tongue had savaged the shop manager once too often. I wasn't that she was over malicious, but she had always had an unfortunate ability to say the wrong thing at the wrong moment with precision timing. She was, however, better endowed with tongue than with teeth, and her comments were never, to my knowledge, meant to be hurtful or damaging.

For the last twenty years of his life her husband had been a determined and assiduous drinker. His earlier years had been spent working on the railways, but his true life's work had become apparent only in the autumn of his life.

The front door to the flat was open when I arrived at Romney Flats, an austere and chilly building composed largely of concrete and bearing an uncanny resemblance to a film-set for a movie about the brave new world to which we can all look forward. I walked in after knocking and called out to Mr and Mrs Wright.

'In the bedroom, Doctor,' cried Mrs Wright breezily.

I squeezed down the narrow hallway, hunching my shoulders to avoid brushing reproductions of great masterpieces of art from the walls. The reproductions, mostly made out of plaster and given an original three-dimensional effect by an artist reared on interminable feasts of flying ducks in threes, rubbed frames with highly coloured photographs of young children in their school uniforms, all with their hair well watered and brushed, and all with fixed grins showing their teeth.

Mr and Mrs Wright were both lying in bed. He wore a bright-red knitted balaclava helmet and a pair of highly coloured striped pyjamas which bore the stains of a hundred night-time drinks, and she wore a hair-net, a score of yellow plastic hair-rollers and a pale-blue quilted dressing-gown buttoned to the neck.

'Nice to see you, Doctor,' said Mr Wright with a toothless grin. His teeth smiled at me on their own, from within a water-filled tumbler on the bedside table.

I smiled back at him and said good morning.

'Sorry to bother you, Doctor,' said Mrs Wright. 'We know how busy you are.'

'Our niece is an optician's receptionist,' said Mr Wright confidentialy, 'so we know how busy you medical people are.'

'The problem is our conjugated rights,' said Mrs Wright firmly.

'I think I need some legover pills,' said Mr Wright.

'We meant to go down to the surgery,' confided Mrs Wright.

'This has happened before, you know,' Mr Wright assured me.

'But it's the waiting,' said Mrs Wright, 'with you not having a disappointment system and George having a weak bladder.'

I began to feel superfluous. The conversation didn't seem to need me at all.

'I think he's got loss of yarnings,' said Mrs Wright, nodding in her husband's direction. A yellow roller slipped out from underneath the hair-net and escaped. It rolled down the pillow and disappeared under the bedclothes.

Mrs Wright reached for a cold cup of coffee which was standing on a wooden chair beside the bed. She picked up the saucer with her left hand and the cup wobbled dangerously.

'I'd give my right arm to be ambidextrous,' she said, skilfully lifting the skin off the top of the coffee.

'What exactly is the problem?' I asked, stifling a yawn and scratching the top of my head with my pen.

'Relations,' said Mr Wright. 'Relations!' He breathed out as he spoke, and I was enveloped in a sweet-smelling haze of alcohol fumes.

It eventually transpired that their problem was a simple one. They had attempted to have intercourse but, despite the most strenuous efforts, had failed. The problem, as Mrs Wright had pointed out, had been entirely her husband's fault.

'It's all limp and looks as if all the stuffing's been knocked out of it,' she complained.

I moved closer to the bed, pushing aside a quantity of empty beer-bottles with my feet. 'Let me have a look, then,' I said.

Mrs Wright threw back the bedclothes and untied her husband's pyjama cord. Mr Wright contented himself with a passive role, staring down at the wounded warrior on the battlefield bared.

'There it is, Doctor,' said Mrs Wright, disdainfully. 'No use to man or beast.'

I bent forward to take a closer look and slipped on a beer-bottle. I just managed to stop myself from falling on to the bed.

'Why don't you throw out some of these beer-bottles?' I asked them both exasperately. 'Someone's going to break his neck!'

'I never have the time, Doctor,' said Mr Wright.

'It's my back, Doctor,' said Mrs Wright inconsequentially.

'I'll take them,' I sighed, picking up half a dozen bottles and moving towards the door. 'Where shall I take them?'

'Down the stairs and out the back,' said Mrs Wright. 'There's a big bin there.'

I trotted off down the stairs, found the dustbins and deposited my botles. Then I trotted back upstairs.

'I've found some more for you, Doctor,' said Mrs Wright, pushing another half-dozen bottles into my arms.

'How did I start doing this?' I asked rhetorically.

'You nearly broke your neck,' said Mrs Wright.

I refused a third load and went back into the bedroom. Mr Wright was still lying in bed with the sheets thrown back and his pyjamas opened wide. The centrepiece of the show remained dormant.

'I think I need a health surveyor,' said Mr Wright.

'You need an undertaker,' commented his wife.

'Turn on your side,' I told him, taking out my keys and opening my drug bag. I took out a rubber glove as he moved on to his side.

'Pull up your knees,' I told him, pulling on the glove.

When he was curled up in that position in which he had lain in his mother's womb, I stabbed my forefinger into his back passage.

'Elsie!' screamed Mr Wright furiously. 'The doctor's gone mad!'

'It's prostate trouble,' I told him, ignoring his outburst.

'I know it is,' said Mrs Wright. 'I could have told you that.'

I looked at her questioningly.

'It's been prostrate all night,' she said, pointing to the offending member as Mr Wright rolled over on to his back.

'There are two reasons why your lovemaking has been unsuccessful,' I told them both. 'First, you drink too much beforehand, and secondly you have an enlarged prostate gland.'

'Drink too much!' said Mr Wright.

'As Shakespeare said,' said I, ' "alcohol heightens the desire but diminishes the ability".'

'Did he really say that?' asked Mrs Wright.

'I haven't the faintest,' I confessed.

'I don't believe he'd say a thing like that,' said Mr Wright.

'Nor me,' said Mrs. Wright.

'And you need to have your prostate out,' I shouted at them both.

'Me?' asked Mrs Wright, stabbing her chest with a podgy finger.

'You!' I shouted, pointing at Mr Wright.

'Now see what you've done,' said Mrs Wright, 'calling the

doctor out at night.' Mr Wright sat up and fastened his trousers.

'I'll give you both some medicine to get you to sleep,' I said, rummaging around in my bag.

'I'm not bothered about going to sleep,' said Mrs Wright.

'I want you to go to sleep,' I told her, savouring the word with envy.

'Aaaaaaaaaaaaaaaah!' screamed Mr Wright suddenly, clutching his back, obviously in pain.

'He's dying!' screamed Mrs Wright. 'He's dying, for sure!'

'What's the trouble?' I asked, feeling Mr Wright's pulse. It seemed perfectly all right to me.

'Pain,' gasped Mr Wright. 'I've got a pain in my back.'

'Lucky you're here, Doctor,' said Mrs Wright.

I said nothing at all.

'It's awful,' said Mr Wright. 'Do something, Doctor.'

I lifted him up a few inches. 'Show me where the pain is,' I said.

'Here,' said Mr Wright, rubbing the lower part of his back. I peered down between his back and the bedclothes.

'Ah,' said I. 'I know what the trouble is.'

'I always said he was a good doctor,' said Mrs Wright with a smug smile. 'I never believed what other people said.'

I looked at her for a moment, but stopped myself saying anything.

'What is it, Doctor?' asked Mr Wright. 'Do I have to go into hospital?'

'I can cure the problem myself, here and now,' I promised.

'Wonderful,' said Mr Wright. 'Do something quickly.' He rolled around in agony again.

I reached in underneath his back and then stood up.

'There it is!' I said triumphantly, holding a bright yellow hair-roller on my outstretched hand.

'Well, I never! Is that what it was?' asked Mr Wright.

'That's it,' I confirmed.

'I thought it was something serious,' said Mrs Wright, clearly disappointed.

'Take two teaspoonfuls of this medicine,' I told them both, taking a small bottle of sedative medicine out of the bag. I handed the bottle to Mrs. Wright, who read the label carefully.

'It says here to take one teaspoonful,' said Mrs Wright.

'Read on,' I told her.

'Except under medical supervision,' she said.

'That's right,' I said triumphantly.

'But it says it's dangerous to exceed the stated dose,' said Mrs Wright, still unhappy.

'Well, take one dose of one teaspoonful,' I told her, 'and then take another dose of another teaspoonful.'

'Right you are,' said Mrs Wright, satisfied.

I left them both hunting for a teaspoon. On my way down the stairs I looked at my watch. It was ten past five. Another day was about to begin.

The day seemed to go on as it had begun. When I got back to bed I was far too awake to sleep again. I lay between the sheets, my mind in a whirl. I thought of Margaret and the future and of stile-climbing sheep, I thought of the practice, of Mr Wright and the day ahead; but I mostly thought of Margaret.

Eventually I did fall asleep. I slept too long, of course, and woke up with minutes to spare before surgery was due to start. I threw back the curtains to see what sort of weather we were to enjoy or endure, and very nearly fainted in shock. Outside the surgery there stood a huge eight-wheeled coach. I had grown accustomed to dealing with large surgeries on occasion, but never had I been so popular as to attract patients by the coachload.

Not until the surgery started did I discover that the coach had brought a single patient – a coach-driver. He came in complaining of a rash underneath his arms. When he walked he looked like a tin soldier, holding his arms well away from his chest.

'Have you bought any new sprays recently?' I asked, as soon as I'd inspected his armpits. They were red and raw.

'Funny you should ask,' said the driver. 'I have a bit of a problem with sweating and in my job it's embarrassing if you have to share a coach all day with a lot of other people.'

'So you bought a deodorant,' I said.

'My wife got me some stuff that kills off all the bugs that live on the skin,' he said. 'Do you think I'm allergic to it?'

'No,' I told him. 'Your problem is that you've killed off the bugs that normally live on your skin and you've been invaded by hordes of new bugs which make you itch.'

The coach-driver turned up his nose and tried to get away from his own armpits. Needless to say, his attempts were singularly unsuccessful.

'How do I get my own bugs back?'

'Just stop using the spray,' I told him. 'They'll come back.'

The next patient was a boy of seven complaining of an itchy tummy. When I examined him I could clearly see the tell-tale marks left by the human flea.

'Ah, it's fleas,' I said, thoughtlessly. My night-time conversation with Mrs Wright had left me with her limited skills in diplomacy.

'Fleas!' cried his mother. 'How dare you!'

I stared at her in astonishment.

'We're a clean family!' she said furiously, going red with anger.

'But—' I began, trying to point out to her that I had intended no slight on her or her family.

'Nigel is bathed every day and he has fresh clothes twice a week,' she insisted. 'Our house is spotless!'

'I'm sorry,' I said. 'I believe you.'

'Hmm,' sniffed Nigel's indignant mother.

'Does Nigel ever go out of doors?' I asked her.

'Well, of course he does,' said his mother. 'What a silly question.'

'Well, I'm afraid the human flea is an excellent jumper,' I told her. 'And it changes hosts quite regularly.'

'But we don't have any dirty friends,' said the unhappy lady, wrinkling up her nose. 'My husband is an accountant.'

'Do you travel on buses or trains or walk in the street?' I asked.

'Of course,' said the woman, less indignantly.

'Well, I'm afraid it isn't always possible to choose the passengers and pedestrians with whom one comes into contact,' I said.

Eventually she calmed down and led Nigel away, undoubtedly to be disinfected and scrubbed. I did not dare tell her that within days of arriving in practice I had been hunting my own fleas.

Every patient that day seemed to have a fetish about cleanliness. However, the rest of the surgery was pleasantly uneventful. The main problem was that I kept finding myself falling asleep. Several times I only just managed to prevent myself falling off the chair.

While interviewing a woman who wanted to start taking the contraceptive pill, I completely forgot what questions I had asked and what questions I had not asked. I even forgot the problem which had brought her into the surgery.

'What would you say was your main problem?' I asked, hoping to re-establish the purpose of the conversation.

'My major problem?' repeated the woman uncertainly.

'Your major problem,' I confirmed.

'Personally?' she asked.

'That's it,' I said.

'My weight, I suppose,' said the woman. She seemed puzzled and that puzzled me.

'You want to lose weight?' I asked her.

'A few pounds,' she said. 'I want to get a bit off my hips and put a bit on my bust.'

'Ah,' said I with my understanding nod. I drifted off again and found my eyes closing once more. Mr Wright's beer-bottles drifted across my field of vision.

'I'll give you some tablets,' I promised, drifting back into reality for a moment. I remembered something about weight being the problem.

'I read somewhere that if you hold them in warm water they get bigger,' said the woman. 'Is that true?'

'Oh, no,' I said. 'They dissolve sometimes, but I don't think they get bigger.'

'Dissolve?' she said.

'Oh, yes,' I said.

The woman seemed to go pale.

'Are you all right?' I asked.

She nodded.

'Would you like a glass of water?' I asked her.

She shook her head vigorously.

'I'll give you something that will help you,' I promised. 'If you take these three times a day you'll go right off your food.'

'Thank you,' said the woman, almost inaudibly.

'Pleasure,' I murmured.

'Do they really disappear?' she asked.

'Oh, yes, completely,' I said. 'You can get some from the chemist's that disappear completely. But cold water tastes better, don't you think?'

'They also say that they get bigger if you stand up a lot,' said the woman. 'What do you think of that?'

'I don't understand that,' I had to confess. I thought about it for a moment. 'That's got me beat,' I agreed.

'Can I have some contraceptive pills, then, Doctor?' she asked.

I remembered then what she had originally come to see me for.

By lunchtime I was prepared to abandon the rest of the day to Fate, but I was pleasantly surprised and encouraged when I met Dr Oaks in the hallway – as I was on my way out to see a child with a sore throat.

'I saw Mrs Renton yesterday,' he said. 'Widow of our high-jumper.'

'Oh, yes,' I said. 'I remember her well. How is she?'

'Splendid,' said Dr Oaks. 'You remember she was going to turn the house into an old people's home?'

'I remember,' I said.

'It's going very well,' he told me, 'and that girl she's got there with her seems to be doing a good job.'

'Miss Clarke,' I reminded.

'Miss Clarke,' he agreed. 'She's quite a find, Mrs Renton insists.'

'I'm very relieved to hear that,' I commented. 'If you remember, I partially threw them together.'

'I remember,' Dr Oaks nodded. 'That's why I told you.' He paused. 'But you can thank your lucky stars that this has worked out. And don't ever try running your patients' lives again. That's not your job.'

I accepted his admonition and set off for the front door.

'Were you up a lot in the night?' he asked as I struggled to open the grandfather clock in the hallway.

'Yes.'

'Well, for heaven's sake go to bed,' said Dr Oaks. 'I'll look after the calls this afternoon. You get some sleep.'

I thanked him and went up to bed, where I slept soundly until the time for evening surgery.

forty-four

'How on earth can you be shy?' asked Margaret. 'You're a doctor, aren't you?'

'That doesn't stop me being shy,' I told her, 'any more than it stops me sneezing, laughing or worrying about my overdraft.'

'Mother is dying to meet you,' insisted Margaret, 'and I'm sure you'll both get on well together.' She opened the car door and started to clamber out. Unexpectedly, she turned back and kissed me on the cheek.

I can't remember how she managed to do it, but she'd succeeded in persuading me to go home with her for tea. I don't know exactly why, but I'd always found in the past that my girlfriends had daunting mothers. As I sat sipping my tea and chewing daintily on chocolate cake I always felt that I was under close scrutiny and proving to be full of flaws.

Her parents lived in a tiny cottage in a village about ten miles out of town. Her father managed a small shoe-store, and her mother, according to what Margaret had told me, managed her father. Since her father's shop was open on Saturdays, our visit had been planned for Sunday afternoon and, in honour of the occasion, I'd taken my best white shirt along to the local laundry instead of washing it in the bathroom myself. The laundry had done a marvellous job at removing the variegated stains which had been a part of the shirt for so long, but in their enthusiasm they'd put two razor-sharp creases down the front, which gave me an uncharacteristic military air.

With the introductory formalities over, Margaret and I sat down together in the front room while Mr and Mrs Shore fussed around in the background. Mrs Shore busied herself with the tea-tray while her husband brought in first the tea-pot, then the tea-cosy, then the tea-pot stand, then the tea-strainer. After a short delay he returned with the best tea-cosy, out of which he first shook two mothballs, before using it to replace the everyday cosy.

'That's a splendid picture,' I commented, desperately anxious to break the silence which threaened to drown us all. I nodded towards a print of a Constable landscape which decorated the chimney-breast.

Margaret played with her watch-strap, and her father turned the tea-cosy round so that the spout poked through the hole through which the handle had been visible.

'I stayed in Willy Lott's cottage once,' I went on. 'It's beautiful countryside around there.'

'I'll just fetch the cake-stand,' said Mr Shore, giving the tea-cosy a final pat before hurrying off back into the kitchen.

'What's the matter?' I whispered. 'Have I done something?'

'He's just shy,' explained Margaret, squeezing my arm. 'He left school at fourteen, and you've been to university.'

'I like your tea-cosy,' I murmured. Margaret burst into a fit of giggles. She was still giggling when her mother pushed open the door and came into the room carrying a tray which was piled high with sandwiches, cakes, cups, saucers, plates and cutlery.

'Let me help you,' I said, clambering to my feet and moving towards Margaret's mother with outstretched arms, ready to take the tray from her.

'It's quite all right. I can manage,' she smiled. 'But thank you.'

'Oh, no, that's much too heavy for you,' I laughed. 'Let me take it for you.' I took hold of my end of the tray.

'It's really all right,' said Mrs Shore. 'It isn't heavy.'

Both anxious to please, both holding the tray, we both let go at once. The sounds of smashing crockery brought Mr Shore rushing out of the kitchen and arrested Margaret's giggles instantaneously. Mrs Shore and I stared at each other quite horrified. For a few seconds no one moved. And then, without any warning, we were all laughing. The tension had evaporated as the cups and saucers had smashed.

'You two sit down,' said Margaret, standing up at last. 'I'll clear up the mess.'

'I really don't know what to say,' I said. 'It was all my fault. You must let me know how much it costs to buy a replacement tea-set so that I can pay for it.'

'You'll do nothing of the kind,' said Mr Shore. 'It was an accident, a pure accident.'

'No, it wasn't,' said Mrs Shore. We both looked at her quickly. 'It was entirely my fault,' she said. 'I don't break much in the kitchen, but when I do break something I like to do it properly.' She stopped to wipe a few ears from her eyes. 'I haven't laughed so much for years,' she said.

'Would you like a piece of chocolate and cucumber cake?' asked Margaret, offering me a badly damaged piece of cake which had been involved in a tumble with a number of cucumber sandwiches and which had undoubtedly come off worst.

'Oh, you'll have to throw it away,' said Mrs Shore. 'We can't eat that.'

'You can't throw all that food away!' I told her. 'Most of it's just bruised.'

'I don't think this is bruised,' said Margaret, holding up half a tea-cup. 'It looks pretty fractured to me.' She started to giggle again.

'Move all the decent sandwiches and cake out of the way and pick up the larger bits of crockery, and then I'll get the vacuum-cleaner out and tidy up the rest,' said Mrs Shore.

To our surprise, when the damage was eventually studied properly we found that several of the plates, saucers and cups were undamaged and that the majority of the cakes and sandwiches were still perfectly edible. Mr and Mrs Shore and Margaret cleared up the mess while I kept out of the way.

We'd just finished tea when the door-bell rang. Mrs Shore answered it and had a lengthy whispered conversation with the caller before coming into the front room and whispering in Margaret's ear. I tried to remain totally uninterested and appear unaware that anything unusual was going on, but it isn't easy to ignore the fact that two women are carrying on a secret conversation no more than two feet from your ears. Eventually Mrs Shore disappeared again, dragging her husband off with her.

'It's Mrs Meredith,' explained Margaret in a whisper. We seemed to have been whispering all afternoon. 'She lives next door and she gets bronchitis. She says she's got one of her attacks on and wants to know if you'd have a look at her. Mum told her that you were coming, you see.'

'Is that what all the fuss was about?' I asked.

Margaret nodded.

'I'll have a look at her,' I said. 'Shall I see her in here?'

'Thank you,' said Margaret. 'I'll go and tell Mum.' She leant across and gave me a kiss on the cheek again before rushing off into the hallway where her mother and Mrs Meredith were in conference.

'This is Mrs Meredith,' said Mrs Shore, ushering in a sunburnt slender woman in her late fifties or early sixties who seemed to have a slight wheeze.

'It's my chest, Doctor,' said Mrs Meredith. 'It seems to have tightened up.'

'What do you normally use?' I asked her. 'Do you take any medicines?'

'I have a spray,' said Mrs Meredith, 'but I've used it all up.' She produced a battered aerosol spray can from her pinafore pocket and handed it to me.

I talked to her for a while longer, but it seemed that all she wanted was a repeat prescription for another aerosol spray. Fortunately I'd learnt always to carry a prescription pad in my pocket, and I quickly wrote out the order for the chemist.

Mr and Mrs Shore and Margaret and I were having another cup of tea when the door-bell rang again. Again Mrs Shore went to answer the bell, but this time she came back and whispered in my ear. She told me that another neighbour, a lady in her seventies, had come to ask if I could do anything about her gout.

During the course of the next hour and a half I dealt with a small boy with abdominal pains, an elderly man who had trouble with his waterworks and a middle-aged woman who wanted to know if I could arrange for her grandmother to be given a smaller flat. I'd even seen a small boy from a house across the village green, who had brought with him his budgie which needed to have its claws cut. I'd chickened out of that one and recommended a visit to the vet.

'It's been very nice having you,' said Mr Shore eventually, as we prepared to leave.

'Thank you for coming,' said Mrs Shore.

'I enjoyed it very much,' I said. 'Thank you for asking me.'

We all shook hands several times and Margaret kissed her mother.

forty-five

Dr Oaks cornered me just as I was about to leave the surgery to start my visiting round one morning. He looked unusually serious, and I desperately racked my brain trying to remember whether I'd done anything to feel guilty about; even before he spoke I could feel the butterflies beginning to stamp into position in my stomach.

'I saw an old friend of mine yesterday,' said Dr Oaks, 'a chap who used to be a medical school with me.' He smiled, and some of the less malicious butterflies abandoned their callisthenics for the time being. 'He joined the Army as soon as he qualified and now he's a lieutenant-colonel at an army base near here.'

I couldn't think what was coming. I couldn't imagine that the Army had requested the loan of my services. I was sure they had enough troubles of their own.

'He's also the Area Disaster Commandant,' said Dr Oaks, rather embarrassed. He scratched the tip of his nose and pulled at his moustache. 'That means that, if we get involved in a nuclear war, he's in command of what is left of the medical facilities in the area.'

I didn't really understand what Dr Oaks was getting at, but I had a lengthy visiting- list I wanted to get on with, so I simply nodded by understanding.

'For some time he's been toying with the idea of having an exercise in the area,' said Dr Oaks. 'You know the sort of thing. We all pretend that the Third World War has started.' He looked at me carefully to make sure that I was still taking him seriously.

'Colonel Rathbone wants to have someone in a civilian capacity to act as liaison officer between the armed forces and the local medical services,' explained Dr Oaks. 'I suggested that you might be the man for the job.'

'Me?' I cried in horror. 'You don't really mean that, do you?'

'Why not?' asked Dr Oaks. 'It'll be good experience for you.'

'You can't be serious!' I said, genuinely terrified. 'I was in the cadet force at school, but I never rose above the rank of private, and if it had been possible to have a lower rank I'd have had it.'

'But you won't actually need to be in the Army,' pointed out Dr Oaks patiently. 'You'll be liaison officer between the army medical officers on the one side and the hospital staff and general practitions on the other side.'

'There must be someone else who can do the job,' I suggested, 'someone with more experience and better knowledge of the area.'

'Well, we'd both be very honoured if you'd take it,' said Dr Oaks, 'but, if you won't, then I suppose we'll have to look elsewhere.' In my heart I knew they were offering me the job because no one else wanted it, but somehow I just didn't have the courage to turn it down and offend my employer. Dr Oaks looked at me and waited for me to reply. The silence was unbearable.

'Oh, well,' I agreed, 'since you put it like that.'

'Good fellow,' said Dr Oaks, patting me on the back. 'The disaster is planned for next Monday. Give old Rathbone a ring when you've got a minute, will you?' He pushed a piece of paper, with a telephone number scrawled on it, into my hand and disappeared into the sitting-room.

I telephoned Colonel Rathbone that evening and explained to him that Dr Oaks had convinced me I was needed.

'It's all fixed for next Monday,' said the Colonel. 'I've had a word with the police and the fire service, and they're going to stage a mock railway accident in a disused siding. What I want you to do is to contact the hospital, have a word quietly with a few of the doctors and prepare them. Then I'd like to ring round a few general practitioners and warn them that we might need their help.

'But isn't this supposed to be a surprise?' I asked. 'If I tell everyone, they'll all be expecting it, won't they?'

'Well, it's supposed to be a surprise to some of the people,' admitted Colonel Rathbone. 'If it's a surprise to everyone things will be quite chaotic, won't they?'

I agreed with him that things would be quite chaotic if a warning wasn't given, and resisted the temptation to ask him the purpose of the exercise.

'The most important thing is that the casualty officers at the hospital are prepared,' he said. 'I want them to be ready to deal with a couple of hundred injured people.'

'Good heavens!' I said. 'A couple of hundred!'

'We may as well do it properly,' explained Colonel Rathbone. 'Some of my men will be acting the parts of casualties. They'll be dressed in bandages by my medical officers. You'll have to warn the telephone operator at the hospital that the code word is "Purple Paterns",' he said. 'My aide will ring you at some time on Monday with that message. You will then pass the code word on to the telephone operator at the hospital, to the clinic in Clothier Street, to the health centres in town and to the surgeries of your colleagues in general practice.'

'It's rather like one of these chain letters, isn't it?' I suggested.

'I beg your pardon?' snapped the Colonel.

'It's rather like one of these chain letters – you ring me and I ring the hospital telephone operator and he rings the hospital staff,' I explained.

'Well,' admitted Colonel Rathbone gruffly, 'it's not the way I'd have put it myself, but I suppose your comparison is not totally without sense.'

After he'd put the telephone down, I rang the hospital and spoke to the surgical registrar, asking him to pass the message on to his colleagues. Then I rang two or three other general practitioners and warned them that at some time on the folowing Monday they might expect to see soldiers dressed up in white bandages and red tomato ketchup. None of the people I spoke to seemed very excited by the plan.

I then forgot about the whole business. With the winter in full swing, surgeries were busy and visiting-lists lengthy. I had hardly a moment to myself for the rest of that week. One particular problem kept me especially busy. The patient concerned was a man in his late sixties, a gentle old fellow who had consulted me for advice about his rheumatism. I'd prescribed some tablets for him, given him advice about keeping warm and told him to walk about the town and the parks as much as he could. I'd told him that exercise is one way to keep fit and mobile, and that too much bed-rest is bad for any of us.

'I did what you told me, Doctor,' said the old man when I saw him for the second time. Tears were visible in his eyes.

'Good,' I said. 'Didn't it help?'

'It helped the rheumatism,' he agreed, 'but it's got me into trouble.' A single tear trickled down his cheek and was wiped away on a threadbare sleeve.

'What sort of trouble?' I asked, puzzled.

'I got into the habit of walking through the park every afternoon,' explained the old man. 'I'd get there about three, feed the ducks on the lake with a few scraps of bread, take a look at the birds in the aviary and then slowly make my way home.'

'Sounds good,' I commented.

'The trouble was,' he said, 'that as I was coming home the children were coming out of school.'

'Don't tell me they caused you any trouble!' I said.

'No, nothing like that,' said the old man. Another tear started its journey but was wiped away quickly before it could travel more than an inch or so. 'I enjoyed seeing them in the park. They always seemed to be so full of life.'

I waited for him to tell me the rest of the trouble. He blew enthusiastically into an ancient handkerchief before continuing with his story.

'I started to buy a few sweets for them,' he went on at last. 'Nothing expensive, just ordinary boiled sweets and jelly babies. Things like that. I like children,' he said simply, after a short pause.

'So what caused the problem?' I asked the old man. 'What's worrying you?'

'It was all very pleasant,' he told me, 'until one day a young policeman saw me handing out the sweets. He came across and told the children to get off home.'

'What on earth did he do that for?' I asked.

'He said they shouldn't ever stop to take sweets from strangers,' said the old man. 'He told them it was dangerous. And then when they'd gone he threatened to have me locked up if he saw me giving them sweets again.'

'I suppose he thought he was just being careful,' I said, trying to comfort the old man. 'Young children do sometimes get tempted away by adults offering them sweets.'

'He didn't have to warn the children about me,' he said. Tears were coursing down both cheeks, unnoticed. 'I don't go near the park now. I dread to think what the children say about me.'

I had to talk to him for twenty-five minutes and promise to see him again the following day before I managed to quieten the old man down. He came to see me the following day, and he was still full of tears.

With a flash of inspiration I telephoned the police station when he had gone. I explained the situation and asked the station sergeant if there was any chance of the young policeman calling round on the old man, just to reassure him and explain to him why he'd been cautioned. The sergeant thought for a moment and then said he thought he might be able to do better than that.

'You say this old fellow of yours likes children?' asked the sergeant. 'And he likes to get about a bit?'

242

'That's right,' I agreed.

'Well, one of our lollipop men retired last month, and we've been a man short since then,' said the police sergeant. 'The money is awful but the job might suit him.'

'You mean helping the children across the road after school?' I asked.

'That's it,' said the policeman.

'Sounds just the ticket,' I confirmed. I went straight round to the old man's house and found him on the doorstep just about to put his key into the lock. When I told him about the job he was tearful with joy. He told he'd go straight down to the police station and apply for the job.

What with that and all the routine work, I had literally forgotten all about the Colonel's planned disaster. I was puzzled, therefore, when Miss Williams told me on Monday morning at about eleven that she had a colonel on the line for me. It took me a few seconds to remember just who Colonel Rathbone was.

'Hello!' I said. 'How is it all going?'

'You may well ask!' stormed the Colonel. 'It's been an absolute fiasco.'

'Oh dear,' said I. 'You mean it's cancelled?'

'Aborted is a better word,' said Colonel Rathbone. I could hear his blood pressure rising from where I was sitting. 'Thirty-five of my men have just been turned away from the hospital by some clerk in the casualty department.'

'But—' I began.

'Some woman at the clinic told a lorry-load of my men to go and play elsewhere!' roared the Colonel, now completely out of control.

'Well—' I began again.

'I really do think you might have done a little better,' said the Colonel finally. Then he slammed the phone down before I could point out to him that I hadn't received the code word, so I could hardly be blamed for not warning the hospital, the clinic and so on.

'He sounded in a bit of a tizzy,' said Miss Williams as I replaced the receiver and rubbed my ear.

'He is,' I agreed.

'It's obviously going to be one of those days,' she said. 'I had a strange call an hour and a half ago. Some fellow rang up, yelled "Purple something-or-other" at me and then slammed the phone down.' She shrugged her shoulders and walked out of the surgery. 'There are some funny people about,' she complained to no one in particular.

forty-six

I very nearly succumbed to the temptation to give old Arthur a bottle of cough medicine when he first came into the surgery. He looked just like the classic English tramp, his navy blue raincoat tied around the waist with a piece of parcel-string and his straggly, greasy hair long and out of control. He had a well-developed beard, and a pair of shoes designed to keep the wearer's feet cool in summer and wet in winter.

Arthur complained of a cough and a bit of pain in his chest. I told him to sit down and asked him a few questions about his medical history. As a wanderer Arthur had no medical records to which I could refer. He told me that he was in his late fifties, that he usually slept out of doors and that he had been perfectly fit and healthy for most of his life. He admitted that he smoked twenty or thirty cigarette stubs a day, but insisted that most of the cigarettes he picked up were tipped.

The smell from the other side of the desk was not encouraging, and I had no real desire to explore beneath the raincoat, but I felt duty bound to do so.

'What?' demanded Arthur. 'You want me to undress?'

'That's right,' I said.

'I haven't taken my clothes off for years,' he insisted. 'I can't even remember what I've got on.'

'Well, if you want me to try to get rid of that cough,' I told him, 'you'll have to let me examine you.'

Eventually, with great reluctance, Arthur started to strip off.

It reminded me of those games we used to play when children. Someone wraps up a small toy in endless sheets of newspaper and the resulting parcel is passed around, each child removing a piece of paper whenever the music stops. Arthur took off the blue raincoat and, underneath that, he had a plastic mackintosh. When that was removed I could see that he had an overcoat on as well. Underneath that he wore a light-blue ladies' anorak. With his thick layer of wrappings in place, Arthur had looked well fed and comparatively healthy. Without the wrappings he looked cadaverous.

'Everything?' he asked, halting at the zipper on his anorak.

'Everything,' I nodded.

'We're getting into unexplored country,' grinned Arthur, showing a mouthful of healthy red gums decorated with stumps of two or three well-worn teeth.

Beneath the anorak there were several thick wads of newspaper. As Arthur carefully laid these on the floor, I examined the dates, and found that most of them were eighteen months old. After these newspapers there came a couple of holey sweaters and a few more newspapers, and then, finally, a grey woollen shirt came into view. That concealed nothing more than an ageing yellow vest which, judging by the monogram on the breast, had probably once warmed the chest of an aristocratic gentleman.

'Can I keep my trousers on?' asked Arthur, now beginning to shiver despite the fact that the temperature in the surgery was comfortably warm.

I nodded.

'Enough is enough, eh, Doctor?' he grinned.

I smiled at him and nodded again.

I listened to his chest carefully and could find nothing more than evidence of a mild infection.

'I'd like you to have a chest X-ray,' I told him as he began to dress himself again.

'Do I have to go to the hospital for that?' asked Arthur.

'Yes,' I told him, 'but they won't keep you. It's only for a few minutes.'

'Do you promise?' asked Arthur. 'I don't want to go into hospital.'

245

'I promise,' I agreed. 'They won't keep you in.'

I wrote out the X-ray form and then helped the poor old tramp to get dressed. It was not as difficult as it might sound, since the newspapers were all shaped to fit against the curves of Arthur's bony chest. At last the raincoat was on and he was dressed again.

'You come back and see me in three days,' I told him, 'and I'll have the X-ray report back by then.'

'I'll go there now,' promised Arthur. 'They won't keep me in, will they? I don't want to go into hospital.'

'They won't keep you in,' I assured him. 'And here's a prescription for some medicine which will help you.'

'Thank you, Doctor,' said Arthur quietly, putting the prescription in his pocket. As he did so I could have kicked myself. How was an old tramp like him going to find the money for the prescription charge?

'Wait a minute,' I said quickly. 'I might have some medicine in the drugs cupboard. It'll save you a visit to the chemist.'

'That would be very good of you, Doctor,' said Arthur.

I scrabbled around in the huge cardboard box underneath the desk where Dr Oaks kept his stores of cough medicines and antibiotics, and eventually found something suitable.

'Don't forget,' I told him as he left. 'I'll see you in three days.'

'I'll be here,' promised Arthur, waving me a cheery goodbye.

The chest X-ray report came back from the hospital right on time. When I saw it I felt almost angry with myself for having ordered it. Why, I asked myself, couldn't I have just given Arthur a bottle of cough medicine and left him alone? The X-ray report was unequivocal. Arthur had an enormous cancer of the bronchus. Even with miracle surgery his time on this earth would be strictly limited.

I dreaded his reappearance in the surgery, and even half-hoped that he wouldn't come back. I knew that if he did come I would have to try to persuade him to go into hospital. And somehow I knew that not even a hospital could help him. As patient after patient came in and left, I began to hope that perhaps Arthur had moved on and forgotten his promise. But he hadn't. He turned up right at the end of surgery, and the change in him even in those few days had been quite horrifying. His eyes seemed darker, his cheeks seemed hollower and his cough was no better at all.

He sat down on the other side of the desk and reached into his raincoat pocket.

'You've been very good to me, Doctor,' he said. 'I've brought you a present.' He pulled out a dead pigeon which he placed carefully on the desk in front of me. 'They make good eating,' he assured me.

'Thank you,' I managed to murmur. 'Thank you very much.'

'You've been very good,' he repeated. 'I got it in the park. Pigeons are stupid. You can catch them if you have the patience.'

I left the pigeon where it was and opened out the X-ray report.

'I've had the report about your X-ray,' I told him.

'I just use a handful of breadcrumbs,' said Arthur. 'I stand in one spot and sprinkle a few crumbs on the ground. Then I hold the crumbs in my hand. Eventualy one of the greediest devils will land on my palm, and then it's easy. They're really stupid birds. They never learn.'

'I want to have another look at you,' I told him.

'You want me to take my clothes off again?' asked Arthur. He didn't seem surprised.

'That's right,' I agreed. 'It won't take a minute.'

He stood up, and was unfastening the string which held his raincoat together, when he suddenly fell forward across the desk. I pulled him back upright and then gently laid him down on the floor. His breathing was shallow and rather fast. I felt for his pulse, but it was hardly palpable. Suddenly Arthur started to cough and a few drops of red-speckled phlegm appeared around his lips. The cough continued for a couple of minutes and the bloodstained phlegm increased in quantity.

Leaving the old tramp on the floor, I ran to the surgery door and called for Miss Williams.

'Ring for an ambulance, will you?' I asked her. 'Tell them to hurry.' Then I shut the surgery door again and went back to the old man. I knew that the ambulance would arrive too late, that Arthur had managed to avoid going into hospital and that he'd never know I'd been prepared to break my promise to him. He died while lying on the surgery floor.

When they'd taken him away in an ambulance, I wandered out of the surgery and into the street, anxious for a few breaths of fresh winter air to take the taste of death out of my mouth. Outside the surgery door a small mongrel dog was sitting. He looked a very friendly little fellow, and somehow he didn't frighten me at all. He was sitting perfectly still, staring into the distance. I was so intent on watching him that I didn't see the policeman approaching.

'Hello, Doctor,' said the constable, stopping beside me. 'Is this your little dog?'

'Er, pardon?' I said, slow to come out of my reverie.

'Your dog?' asked the policeman, sociably. He bent down to look at the mongrel.

I hadn't answered when the policeman stood up again. 'Of course it's not,' he said. 'It's Arthur's dog.'

'Arthur's?' I repeated

'An old tramp who comes through here from time to time,' said the policeman. 'We give him a night inside occasionally when it's wet.'

'You won't be troubled with him any more,' I told the policeman. I explained briefly what had happened.

'I'd better take the dog with me,' said the policeman, 'or he'll be here with you for ever more. They were devoted to each other.' He bent down and fondled the dog's head lovingly. 'When old Arthur was inside,' he remembered, 'Dick here would just sit on the steps until he came out. I don't suppose you have a piece of string I could have, do you, Doctor?' asked the policeman. 'I'll have to make a lead if I'm going to take the dog with me. He won't come otherwise.'

I took the policeman back into the surgery. I felt certain that there would be something in one of the drawers. Dr Oaks was a great hoarder, and all hoarders keep string.

'This will do, if you don't want it,' said the policeman, bending down and picking up a piece of parcel-string from the floor. It was the piece which had been around Arthur's raincoat.

'Use that,' I agreed. 'That's fine.'

As he left, something on the desk caught the policeman's eye. I followed the direction of his gaze. I'd forgotten about the pigeon on my blotter.

'Just a present,' I explained, 'from a grateful patient.'

forty-seven

'I think it's about time you had a week off, and about time I did some work,' said Dr Oaks. 'If I'm going to get back to work I'll have to get into the swing of things again soon.'

'You've been doing surgeries,' I pointed out. Since early autumn Dr Oaks had been doing a surgery every Monday morning.

'Only the odd few,' he said. 'There is a difference between doing surgeries every day and doing one a week.'

'Well, if you're sure,' I said.

'I'm sure,' said Dr Oaks. 'I want to see if I've still got the energy and the inclination to earn my living as a general practitioner.'

'Will you need me when I get back?' I asked.

'Yes,' he said. 'This isn't a polite way of telling you I don't need you any more.' He grinned at me. I'd got to like him a good deal in the months I'd been working for him.

'Where will you go?' asked Dr Oaks.

'Paris,' I said straightaway.

'Paris,' he repeated. 'Why Paris?'

'For one thing, I love it,' I said, 'and, for another thing, I'll be far enough away from telephones, postmen and door-bells there.'

After surgery that evening I telephoned Margaret. 'I'm going to Paris for a week next Friday,' I told her. 'Will you come?'

'To Paris?'

'To Paris.'

'Single rooms?'

'If you like.'

'I like.'

'Will you?'

'Yes.'

We travelled on the night sleeper from London, waking up in Paris at about seven-thirty and having hot *croissants* and large cups of steaming black coffee for breakfast. I'd booked rooms at a hotel I always go to, in a small street just off the rue St Honorê. We took the Métro from the station to the hotel, as it's both cheaper and quicker, and left our bags in the hotel lobby. The hotel porter grinned broadly when he saw me, and murmured pleasantries in the totally incomprehensible French I remembered.

While we waited for our rooms to be cleaned, we walked north to the Café de la Paix in the Place de l'Opéra, and we sat and watched Paris go by for an hour. In the afternoon we took the Métro up into Montmartre and sat on the steps of the imposing Sacré Cœur. While we were sitting there, three young men settled themselves down on one of the stone balconies and began to unpack their music cases. One musician had a trumpet, one a saxophone and a third a clarinet. They erected a music-stand, put a sheet of music on it and began to play.

They played quietly, choosing soothing, delicate jazz music which seemed to suit the setting and the cool December air. With the view, it gave the day an extra dimension. At the end of the group's first contribution, the crowd on the steps broke into a round of spontaneous applause. After their second piece of music a man in a uniform appeared at the top of the steps. He waved angrily at the musicians and shoued at them, ordering them to stop playing and move on somewhere else. The crowd around him murmured angrily, and several people told him to go away. He muttered again and started to move forward. He couldn't get through the crowd, and the trio began to play again. A young man with a bushy beard stood up and shouted, 'C'est la vie!'

We ate on our first evening at a café at the top of the Champs Élysées, the sparkling, glittering heart of Paris. Then we walked

250

slowly back down the Champs and through a small park near the American Embassy. An open-air exhibition of modern sculpture had been organized there and was well floodlit. The exhibits were strange, to say the least. There was a huge wooden pole with pieces of metal sticking out of it, there were several chunks of iron painted in bright colours, and there were numerous designs in plastic and steel. There was an old motor-car covered in green-painted polythene sheeting, and a heap of sand had been arranged in what looked a significant way.

I couldn't resist the temptation to make my own contribution to the exhibition. I found half a dozen metal chairs (the variety so common in the Tuileries Gardens) and arranged them carefully around a waste-basket. Then I found some pieces of wood which had been used to help pack some of the sculpture, and, with these, linked chairs and basket together. The result, we both agreed, was most pleasing.

As I worked, a woman, wandering through the exhibition, stopped to admire my creation. She smiled and nodded, and immediately set to work herself. She used a lamp-post as the basis for her creation, balancing around this several planks. We were putting the finishing touches to our sculptures when a well-dressed gentleman in a friendly mood offered support and encouragement. A few minutes later he was busy sticking small pieces of wood into an abandoned pile of sand. He smiled as he worked. When we had all finished we admired one another's exhibits, shook hands and then went on our way.

The following morning we again set off for the Café de la Paix. We walked up across the Place Vendôme and, as we walked, I noticed in front of me a young woman who looked unsteady. Suddenly her legs went from underneath her and she landed on her back. She was obviously having an epileptic fit. I rushed forward to try to help and managed to stuff a clean handkerchief into her mouth. After a minute or two she quietened down and, slowly, her eyes opened, and she looked around her. She seemed confused and embarrassed.

In halting French I told her not to worry, explained that I was a doctor and asked her if she had any pain. She looked at me without any understanding. I felt quite hurt, for, although my French is poor, I had practised those few phrases while waiting for her to come round. As I knelt beside her, two gendarmes came across towards us. The taller of them bent down and opened the woman's handbag. He removed her passport, and I saw that she was an Australian. She understood my English explanation and even smiled a little.

We spent the rest of the day mooching about, visiting museums, looking in shops, drinking endless cups of coffee in delightful small cafés and relaxing in Parisian winter warmth.

When we got back to the hotel there was a telegram waiting for me. I hate telegrams, and I opened it with shaking fingers. It was from Dr Oaks.

'AM RETIRING,' it read. 'PRACTICE YOURS IF YOU WANT IT. STAY THE WEEK.'

'What is it?' asked Margaret, seeing my face.

I showed her the telegram.

I thought how much I'd enjoyed our two days in Paris, how much I'd enjoyed our evenings out and how often our snatched hours together were interrupted by people collapsing around us. I thought how pleasant it would be to have Margaret to prepare breakfast for me, to come home to at four in the morning after a hard night's work and to look after me. But, more than that, I thought how much I'd missed her when I'd been on call and unable to meet her.

'Are you going to accept?' asked Margaret.

'On one condition,' I said.

'What's that?' she asked.

'That you marry me.'

I think the hotel porter guessed that something unusual was happening, for he clapped me on the back and insisted on claiming a kiss from Margaret when he'd finally managed prise us apart.

We had four days left in Paris.

Patricia Jordan
District Nurse 75p

Born and bred in Belfast, trained in the hard school of student
nursing, Patricia Jordan found her niche in a small Northern
England town as a district nurse. With all the style of a born
storyteller she tells of the patients and their case-histories – the
comedy, tragedy and heart-warming humanity of her daily round –
and of the doctors and nurses who work alongside her.

'First class ... admirable reading' OBSERVER

David Taylor
Zoovet 75p

The drowning hippopotamus and the arthritic giraffe ... The
pornographic parrot and the motorcycling chimp ... Just a few of
the patients that are all in a day's work for David Taylor, one of the
world's most unusual vets. *Zoovet* is his story of the hilarity and the
heartache of animal-doctoring by jetliner across the globe.

'Good humour and abounding energy on every page'
WASHINGTON POST

Carol Dix
Say I'm Sorry to Mother 75p

If you were young and a girl in the special-offer decade they called
The Sixties ... then you'll remember Dylan and The Stones and the
sleeping-bag stories that came up from St Ives. If you were like
Carol and Heather, Georgina and Polly ... you'll not have forgotten
all the first times – the passions and the Pill – and the going home
after with your high ideals broken ... You'll remember The Beatles
telling you it was getting better all the time – and you really believed
them, didn't you?

'A brave chronology of our times' FAY WELDON

James Herriot
If Only They Could Talk 75p

The genial misadventures of James Herriot, a young vet in the lovely
Yorkshire Dales are enough to make a cat laugh – let alone the
animals, if only they could talk.

It Shouldn't Happen to a Vet 75p

'Imagine a *Dr Finlay's Casebook* scripted by Richard Gordon and
Thurlow Craig and starring Ronnie Corbett and you will understand
why James Herriot is on to a winner ... a delightful new collection
of stories' SUNDAY EXPRESS

'His easy and at times excruciatingly funny case history narratives
must rate as country classics and he throws in a stumbling, awkward
courtship for good measure 'FARMERS WEEKLY

Let Sleeping Vets Lie 75p

The hilarious revelations of James Herriot, the now famous vet in the
Yorkshire Dales, continue his happy story of everyday tribulations
with unwilling animal patients and their richly diverse owners.

'He can tell a good story against himself, and his pleasure in the
beauty of the countryside in which he works is infectious'
DAILY TELEGRAPH

Vet in Harness 75p

With the fourth of this superb series, James Herriot again takes us on his varied and often hair-raising journeys to still more joyous adventures in the Yorkshire Dales.

'Animal magic . . . James Herriot provokes a chuckle or a lump in your throat in every chapter' DAILY MIRROR

Vets Might Fly 75p

A severe case of World War Two takes James Herriot away from his vet's life in the Dales and into a training camp somewhere in England . . .

'There are funny cases, sad cases, farm animals and pets, downright dialect-speaking farmers, ladies of retirement, hard-bitten NCO's and of course the immortal Siegfried and Tristan' SUNDAY TIMES

Vet in a Spin 80p

Strapped into the cockpit of a Tiger Moth trainer, James Herriot has swapped his wellingtons and breeches for sheepskin boots and baggy flying suit. The disappointments, triumphs and frustrations of his RAF carreer remind him repeatedly of incidents in his veterinary practice.

'Marks the emergence of Herriot as a mature writer, with a smooth flowing style, good dialogue and a clutch of new characters like Gertrude, the beer-swilling pig, and Roddy Travers, the travelling man who carried his huge lurcher dog in a pram' YORKSHIRE POST

James Herriot
All Creatures Great and Small £1.50

the first Herriot Omnibus Edition

Follow the career of the world's most famous vet from his arrival in the
Dales countryside to the completion of his courtship of his wife-to-be,
Helen. Meet the colourful Siegfried and Tristan and a host of
unforgettable characters, both human and very much otherwise ...

'Warm, joyous and often hilarious ... there is humour everywhere'
NEW YORK TIMES

All Things Bright and Beautiful £1.50

the second Herriot Omnibus Edition

This second omnibus takes up the story of the world's favourite vet
from the closing chapters of *All Creatures Great and Small*. James is
now married and living on the top floor of Skeldale House. He's a
partner in the practice and his day is well-filled with the life of a
country vet, bumping over the Dales in his little car en route to a host
of patients from farm-horses to budgerigars ...

'Absolutely irresistible ... told with warmth, charm and never-
flagging good humour' EVENING NEWS

You can buy these and other Pan Books from booksellers and
newsagents ; or direct from the following address :
Pan Books, Sales Office, Cavaye Place, London SW10 9PG
Send purchase price plus 20p for the first book and 10p for
each additional book, to allow for postage and packing
Prices quoted are applicable in the UK